Versatile

Versatile

Human Intelligence in an Artificial Age

Angela C. Meyers

Versatile: Human Intelligence in an Artificial Age

Cover design by Cassandra Kronstedt

Interior design by Exeter Premedia Services Private Ltd., Chennai, India

First published in 2026 by
Business Expert Press, LLC
222 East 46th Street, New York, NY 10017
www.businessexpertpress.com

ISBN-13: 978-1-63742-185-7 (paperback)
ISBN-13: 978-1-63742-186-4 (e-book)

Human Resource Management and Organizational Behavior Collection

First edition: 2026

10 9 8 7 6 5 4 3 2 1

EU SAFETY REPRESENTATIVE
Mare Nostrum Group B.V.
Doelen 72
4831 GR Breda
The Netherlands
gpsr@mare-nostrum.co.uk

This book is dedicated in grateful, loving memory to my superhero grandmother, Georgia Ann Meyers. "Mamaw," as most folks called her, was a beacon of self-directed, lifelong, and lifewide learning. She demonstrated, through her actions and wisdom, that there are no limits to what one can achieve with a curious mind and a compassionate heart. Mamaw taught me that the power of intelligence, when blended with unwavering love, is a force capable of mending the world's deepest wounds. Her lessons in resilience, kindness, and the relentless pursuit of knowledge have shaped me into who I am today. Because of her, I realized that it is through learning and loving that we hold the true power to transform the world. For her example and the life-changing gift of her boundless love, I will be forever grateful.

Description

Polymathic talent is the future. But without systems that understand and support them, even the brightest minds burn out. In *Versatile: Human Intelligence in an Artificial Age*, Dr. Angela C. Meyers presents a practical guidebook for the gatekeepers of talent—organizational leaders, HR professionals, coaches, business strategists, and career counselors.

Drawing on the emerging science of polymathy and her own groundbreaking doctoral research, Meyers offers an emotionally intelligent roadmap for recognizing, developing, and unleashing multidimensional brilliance in the workplace. As AI transforms every industry and individuals are asked to perform the work of entire teams, the need for *versatile generalists*—those with emotional depth, integrative thinking, and adaptive capacities—has never been greater.

More than a manifesto, *Versatile* is a toolkit for cultivating human range. With frameworks, training-ready chapters, and reflection prompts, it equips organizations to thrive amid accelerating change. This book is both a wake-up call and an invitation—to redesign how we develop and deploy human potential, and to build cultures where creativity, complexity, and compassion become competitive advantages.

Contents

Praise for the Book

"Angela Meyers' book is a major achievement in polymathy studies and a unique and compelling addition to the literature on fostering business innovation. In beautifully written, highly accessible and well-organized chapters, she lays out the connections between polymathy and creativity, why businesses need polymaths, how polymaths train themselves, what unique benefits they bring to the table, how best to employ their unusual mixtures of skills and knowledge, and how to foster their success—and by doing so, how to ensure the success of your business! I expect this book to become a best-selling classic!"—**Dr. Bob Root-Bernstein, coauthor of *Sparks of Genius: The Thirteen Thinking Tools of the World's Most Creative People* and polymathy studies scholar**

"It's rare to come across someone with the depth of intellect and sensitivity that Dr. Angela possesses. Her groundbreaking work in modern polymathy studies—particularly her dissertation, 'In Pursuit of Polymaths'—is a remarkable contribution to humanity. Her ability to perceive patterns and insights that others overlook is nothing short of extraordinary. As a futurist, Dr. Angela is not only expanding our understanding of multidisciplinary genius but applying her intellect where it truly matters. We need more minds like hers—visionary, compassionate, and fearlessly forward-thinking."—**Dr. Martine Rothblatt, Founder of SiriusXM and United Therapeutics**

"Dr. Angela Meyers is probably the only person I know who could write this book. First, she is thoroughly familiar with the research on polymathy, having conducted original research herself. Second, she has considerable practical experience working with organizations. In short, she has the versatility to write Versatile. *The product is not just impressive, but also useful."*—**Dr. Dean Keith Simonton, author of *The Genius Checklist* and editor of *The Wiley Handbook of Genius***

"Dr. Angela Cotellessa Meyers is a major voice in polymathy scholarship and practice. This book is describing foundational research on the nature of polymathy and makes it clear why polymathy matters in our fragmented world. An important read for human resource professionals and leaders challenging common notions of talent, especially in time of profound technological change."—**Dr. Zorana Ivcevic Pringle, Director, Creativity and Emotion Lab, Yale University and Author of *The Creativity Choice***

"A global metacrisis, exponential technologies and severely-fragmented knowledge specialization are catapulting us into an emerging Transformation Age without most of the epistemic and institutional resources society actually needs to thrive in the 21st century. Even worse, very few people see the big picture: these are all centered deeply in outdated models of talent and skill development. But Angela is one who does, and in this book she outlines why we urgently need the creative cross-boundary and cross-domain skills of our polymaths. Every institutional leader should be reading this book very carefully if they want to prepare their organizations for what's ahead."—**Robb Smith CEO, Institute of Applied Metatheory**

Why Did I Write This Book?

In 2018, I completed my doctoral dissertation, titled "In Pursuit of Polymaths: Understanding Renaissance Persons of the 21st Century." More than a simple "check the box" dissertation, I was extremely passionate about this topic. As a lifelong aspiring Renaissance woman, I believed that this group of capable, daring, self-expressive people was truly worthy of understanding. I researched the constructs of polymathy, self-directed learning, openness to experience, and creativity—found in the scholarly literature—and I also interviewed highly accomplished, modern polymaths. Hearing directly from polymaths about what their experiences have been like—and then identifying trends and themes among that group of people—really helped me understand this audience. In fact, at this point, given my passion for supporting these types of people, I consider myself a kind of spokesperson and a champion for them—like a mother hen for polymathy.

I have spent the last decade or so of my life, since 2015, dedicated to learning about modern-day polymaths, and polymathy as a human phenomenon worthy of understanding. I will probably spend the rest of my life dedicated to promoting polymathy as a path for individual and collective human thriving. Much of the information I have written about in this book is based not only on my doctoral-level research but also the continued learning and engagement I have had with polymaths over the years, particularly in the Polymaths Place community. As you read this text, keep in mind that my focus has been both on studying polymaths in a very rigorous, academic way, and in a real-world, practical way, through Polymaths Place and through connecting with myriad polymaths who find me based on my research, writings, talks, or social media content. Much of the information presented in this book is based on the knowledge I have gleaned in both of those arenas—inside and outside of academia.

I originally wrote this book in 2020–2021, but then had to set it aside to tend to personal and professional matters elsewhere. For several years, the manuscript sat mostly drafted—but still unfinished—as the world continued to change, and artificial intelligence arrived in the mainstream. In hindsight, I'm grateful for the delay. It gave me the opportunity to think more deeply about how polymathy intersects with this new reality. Human versatility, I now believe more than ever, is a defining competency of our time. In an age shaped by exponential technologies, the ability to adapt, integrate, and creatively collaborate with machines becomes essential. As someone who has followed Ray Kurzweil's technology predictions for years, I saw this moment coming—and this book is one response to it.

Why now? Because polymathic generalists are not only important—they are urgently needed at a time when AI takes over more and more highly specialized tasks.

Who Is This Book for?

This book is primarily intended for the gatekeepers of organizations: Human Resources (HR) professionals and business leaders. HR professionals are well positioned to attract, recruit, place, and retain polymathic professionals. Business leaders, in turn, are critical for nurturing and leveraging their full potential once they're inside the organization.

It is also written for the many professionals who work to shape organizations from the inside or guide them from the outside—including:

- Career counselors, who support individuals navigating nonlinear paths.
- Organizational development consultants, who help improve systems and culture.
- Business strategists, who design structures for agility and innovation.
- Industrial–organizational psychologists, who study how people thrive at work and what leadership and talent look like in evolving environments.
- Executive coaches, who support high-potential, complex thinkers as they grow into leadership.

- Workforce futurists, who track how jobs and skills are transforming.
- Learning and development professionals, who build cultures of continual growth.
- And, of course, this book may speak most deeply to polymathic professionals themselves—especially those who've felt unseen or underutilized in traditional work environments. If that's you, I hope these pages offer both validation and vision: a reminder that you are not the problem, and that your range is an asset—not a liability.

Whether you are designing hiring systems, running a company, advising a client, coaching a leader, or navigating your own polymathic path, may this book give you language, insight, and inspiration to see human potential more fully—and to build workplaces and teams where that potential can thrive.

In many ways, I consider this book to be a *magnum opus*—the most important synthesis of my work as a scholar, professional, and intellectual to date. It distills more than a decade of research, dialogue, lived experience, and hard-won insights. My deepest hope is that it helps shift the conversation in organizations—for good—for the betterment of humanity.

Angela C. Meyers
October 2025

Acknowledgments

I am deeply grateful to the individuals listed as follows for their invaluable support of this book and my broader work as a thinker, scholar, and advocate for polymathy. Your encouragement and belief in the importance of promoting polymathy as a profound human phenomenon have meant the world to me. In no particular order—though alphabetized for clarity—I extend my heartfelt thanks to:

Professional Acknowledgments

- **Waqas Ahmed**—I deeply appreciate the work you've done to advance the modern understanding of polymathy. Through your writing and thought leadership, you've helped expand how interdisciplinary thinking is understood and practiced today, and I'm grateful to be part of a shared effort to shape and advance this field alongside you.
- **Dr. Rami Amin**—Your thoughtful feedback, intellectual companionship, and enduring belief in me have helped refine both my ideas and my spirit. Your friendship is a gift.
- **Dr. Michael Araki**—My scholarly brother. Your sharp intellect, collaboration, and friendship have been an endless source of stimulation and insight. I am honored to walk alongside you in this emerging field.
- **David Epstein**—You are a rock star. I'm honored to know you and inspired by your clear-eyed thinking and advocacy for the power of range. Your work lights the way.
- **Chris Foltz**—I'm deeply grateful for your mentorship, friendship, and the example you set as a true applied polymath, using your gifts in service of others. Your belief in me and your invitation to join the Human Intelligence Movement expanded my thinking and strengthened my commitment to reimagining education in the Age of AI.

- **Sebastian Fuller**—For recognizing the promise of polymathy and for playing a vital role in the creation of the MBA in Polymathy and Transdisciplinary Studies. Your work is opening doors for future generations.
- **Dr. Karin Huebner**—At the University of Southern California's Academy for Polymathic Study, thank you for encouraging my efforts and affirming my vision.
- **Barry James**—For your encouragement, loyalty, and friendship. You've believed in my work and in me—and that support has made all the difference.
- **Dr. Scott Barry Kaufman**—For championing human potential and supporting my work with compassion and integrity. Your kindness has touched me deeply.
- **Yasuhiko Genku Kimura**—Yasuhiko passed away in 2025, shortly before publication of this book. His lessons on the authentic self-helped fuel my commitment to polymathy as a path to wholeness. His mentorship and friendship were a blessing in my life.
- **Dr. Michael Marquardt**—My dissertation chair and mentor. Your guidance during my doctoral journey was essential in shaping both this book and my scholarly voice.
- **Jeremy Pesner**—Thank you for the generosity and encouragement you've shown me from the very beginning. From opening doors to encouraging me to step into new intellectual arenas, your belief in me has helped me move forward with greater confidence and clarity.
- **Michéle Quesenberry**—Your teachings on Internal Family Systems helped me see that just as all our internal parts matter, so do the many expressions of ourselves in the world. You planted the seed that led me to study polymathy as a way to honor our full, multifaceted humanity. I'm so grateful for your wisdom, your example, and your steady presence in my life.
- **Dr. Michéle Root-Bernstein**—Your thoughtful scholarship and generous support have deeply enriched the field of polymathy studies—and my own thinking.
- **Dr. Robert Root-Bernstein**—My scholarly father. Thank you for laying the academic groundwork that made polymathy

studies possible. Your pioneering vision paved the way for scholars like me to follow. I am forever grateful for your trailblazing work.

- **Dr. Ron Sheffield**—Thank you for believing in me and encouraging me to write this book. Your steadfast support and inspiration sparked the journey that brought it to life. Without you, this book would not exist.
- **Dr. Dean Keith Simonton**—Your groundbreaking research into genius and polymathy has expanded our understanding of the extraordinary human mind. Thank you for your contributions to this field.
- **Dr. Florian Stummer**—For your tireless dedication to advancing polymathy research and your passion for the mission we share for polymathy. I'm grateful to be on this journey with you.
- **The Polymaths Place community**—You have been a wellspring of joy, insight, and camaraderie. Your thoughtful engagement throughout the writing process enriched this book more than you know. I'm honored to be your advocate and cheerleader.

Personal Acknowledgments

- **To my daughter, Lily**—My guiding light. You inspire me every day to build a world where you and others can grow into your fullest, bravest, most radiant selves. May you always know your infinite worth and possibility.
- **Tiffany Fox**—My best friend and safe space since childhood. Thank you for loving me through every chapter of life. I love you forever.
- **Jessica Johnson**—Our friendship has spanned decades, seasons, and versions of ourselves. Through it all, your warmth, honesty, and loyalty have remained constant. You feel like a sister to me—rooted, real, and right there when it matters most. I carry your support with me always.
- **Sara McConnell**—We first met in girlhood and your steady presence and unconditional love are the kind of rare gifts that

only come once in a lifetime. You are chosen family, a ray of sunshine, a compassionate supporter, a deep seer, and I'm so grateful we're still growing alongside each other.

- **To my big brother, Paul**—You've been both a trusted adviser and a steady source of strength. I'm endlessly grateful for your love, your guidance, and your friendship.

Finally, to you—the reader: Thank you for engaging with this book and the ideas within it. Your curiosity and openness to understanding how we can empower polymathic individuals—especially in the age of artificial intelligence—inspires me. My deepest hope is that this book encourages leaders of all kinds to recognize, support, and elevate polymathic generalists as powerful assets in shaping resilient, innovative, and humane organizations that make the world a better place for us all.

CHAPTER 1

Why Polymaths Should Matter to Businesses

> "In order to change an existing paradigm, you do not struggle to try and change the problematic model. You create a new model and make the old one obsolete."
>
> —Buckminster R. Fuller

Wendy is a 22-year-old recent college graduate with a bachelor's degree in math. She is intelligent, energetic, and hard-working. Her first job out of university is an arts management gig at a leading museum in New York City. In that role, she works with singers and artists, and her work touches areas such as contracts, operations, and logistics. Although Wendy functions in a business role for this museum, she also knows what it is like to be an artist; she has sung in operas, in fact. Wendy interacts well with creative people given that she identifies, in part, as an artist herself. In combination with her arts background, though, she has experience in coding, is a talented mathematician, and is naturally business savvy; she is a true Renaissance woman. In fact, she knows how the museum could use structured data to inform business choices, cut costs, be more efficient, and streamline processes through the strategic use of technology.

So, at the end of her first year in the job, she pitched an idea to her management about how to improve and streamline much of her work. Her idea is that she can automate parts of her job and then spend that time to undertake new projects and expand into areas where she can also add even more value within the organization. More specifically, her idea has to do with optimizing scheduling and logistics. So, Wendy writes a computer program spec—not the full computer program, but an overview of how the program could be constructed, which would automate or outsource roughly 80 percent of her job using computational thinking and leveraging artificial intelligence (AI). Afterall, as Wendy explained, having humans do this kind of work is inefficient and error prone—not to mention expensive. Given her skill sets with technology, mathematics, and business operations, she has just the right combination of skills to develop a solution for her organization that would help them improve efficiency and open the door for Wendy to spend more time adding unique human value, while letting tech do more of the grunt work.

To Wendy's surprise and dismay, her idea was met with complete resistance. The answer management gave to her proposal was an absolute "no." The answer was, "go do your job like you have always done it; go do what is written in your job description." So, Wendy, a bright and capable young woman, felt as if her employer did not want to actually use her talent; they wanted her to stay in a narrowly defined role, doing narrowly defined tasks in a very specific and narrow kind of way. They did not want automation, efficiency, or change. And even though Wendy loved the organization, their mission, and the actual work the business did, she knew she could not stay working there.

Wendy began making her exit plan that very same day. In describing her decision, she said, "I'm not willing to stay in a place that wants to put me in a box and only asks for that part of me." Someone like Wendy wants to work in a business organization that, of course, expects her to meet the requirements of her job. Specifically, in an ideal world, she would like to spend 75 or 80 percent of her time at work focusing on what is in her job description. But she wants to be allowed to leverage her other skills and interests with the remaining time available. She wants to feel fulfilled, like she is constantly growing and improving herself as well as the organization for which she works. So, Wendy quickly left the museum after the exchange described earlier.

Fast forward a decade or so later: Wendy is a successful business founder, start-up adviser, consultant, and public speaker. She has published several books, co-hosted a successful podcast, and has presented a TED talk. She's also a faculty member for Harvard University. In her free time, she sings in a community choir, runs, hikes, and volunteers in her community. In other words: Wendy is a huge professional success, a real mover and shaker, with many talents across different disciplines. Wendy is a *polymath*.

What can be learned from this example? Did Wendy select the wrong job or the wrong employer? Did the museum hire the wrong person? What this example shows is that the museum's management did not think strategically about how to leverage *polymathic talent.* Indeed, Wendy is an amazing person and employee; she brought energy and enthusiasm to her work and wanted to help make operations more efficient. What organizational leader would not want an employee like Wendy on their team? Sadly, the museum lost Wendy as an employee, though she was oozing energy and enthusiasm to contribute to the organization positively, because they did not realize that what they had in their midst was a polymath, and they had no idea how to leverage her polymathic skill sets.

Definition of the Word Polymath

Before delving deeper into the concept of polymathy, let's begin with the meaning of the term itself. The prefix *poly* means "many," and the Greek root *manthánein* means "to learn." Contrary to what it may sound like, *polymath* has nothing to do with mathematics—it literally means "many learnings." A polymath, then, is someone who engages in many learnings across various fields over time.[1]

The term *polymath* was first used in the English language in the 17th century, although the term itself dates back to Heraclitus in Ancient Greece.[2] But despite its long history, the concept has often remained misunderstood or undervalued—particularly in the modern era of specialization, where society has emphasized going deep in one area at the expense of cultivating breadth.

Polymaths are those who have chosen **both**—to develop depth *and* breadth in their approach to work, learning, and life. They pursue knowledge across fields, often integrating seemingly unrelated disciplines into a unified framework of understanding. While related terms such as

---

[1] Retrieved from www.dictionary.com/browse/polymath.

[2] Granger, H. 2004. Heraclitus' Quarrel with Polymathy and Historiê. *Transactions of the American Philological Association* 134, pp. 235–261.

Renaissance person, *polyhistor*, *multidisciplinary expert*, *generalist*, or *Homo Universalis* have been used, none fully capture the depth of engagement and integrative power implied by the term *polymath.*

Given the emerging nature of polymathy studies as a field, there is not yet a single universally accepted definition. These particularly influential scholars have offered valuable definitions that continue to shape the conversation:

Robert and Michèle Root-Bernstein define polymathy as:

> *Active engagement in multiple interests or endeavors, integrating vocations with avocations, simultaneously or serially, across the lifespan.*[3]

In their view, *active engagement* implies more than casual interest—it means making, building, or contributing through committed work or serious play. This activity may emerge in formal or informal contexts (vocation or avocation), and it may unfold either simultaneously or sequentially over time.

Dr. Michael Araki, another leading voice and someone I deeply respect, offers a complementary perspective:

> *Polymathy is the lifelong and lifewide approach to knowledge pursuit, its development and application, distinguished by the concomitance of breadth, depth, and integration.*

Dr. Araki aptly describes polymathy as a "life project," emphasizing that polymathic learning is not confined to traditional education or professional achievement—it includes learning from lived experiences, personal reflection, experimentation, and unconventional paths. This definition brilliantly positions polymathy as an evolving relationship with knowledge over the lifespan.

---

[3] Root-Bernstein, R., and M. Root-Bernstein. 2020. "Polymathy." In *Encyclopedia of Creativity*, eds. M. Runco and S. Pritzker, 375–380. Cambridge, MA: Academic press. doi: 10.1016/B978-0-12-809324-5.23671-7

Building on these excellent foundations—and in the spirit of scholarly expansion—I would like to propose an additional definition that reflects my own research, practice, and lived experience with polymaths:

> *Polymathy is a self-directed, lifelong, and lifewide learning practice fueled by curiosity. Polymaths continuously learn, unlearn, and relearn, refining their mental models to achieve a unified, consilient understanding of knowledge across disciplines. This approach empowers them to cultivate a holistic understanding of truth.*

At its heart, polymathy is about being so skilled at learning that this learning naturally extends across many domains—and deepens over time. It is the opposite of narrow specialization, yet far more substantive than dabbling. Even the term *generalist* falls short of capturing the level of inquiry, expertise, and integration that defines a truly polymathic orientation.

Once a person develops polymathic awareness, it unlocks a host of cognitive and creative benefits. A polymath's wide and deep base of knowledge enables them to:

- Integrate disparate concepts.
- See connections others miss.
- Zoom in to analyze details and zoom out to understand systems.
- Use analogical thinking to generate creative insights.
- Innovate by synthesizing inputs into something new and valuable.

This last point—synthesis—is worth particular emphasis. While integration is about blending and holding ideas together (like ingredients in a mixing bowl), synthesis is more alchemical. It's the melting pot from which novel frameworks, models, or creations emerge. This is where the *true power* of polymathy lies: not just in knowing many things, but in using that breadth and depth to synthesize new understanding—insights that would be inaccessible through any single discipline alone. In this way, breadth and depth are the prerequisites for polymathy. Integration is

The Polymathic Synthesis Model

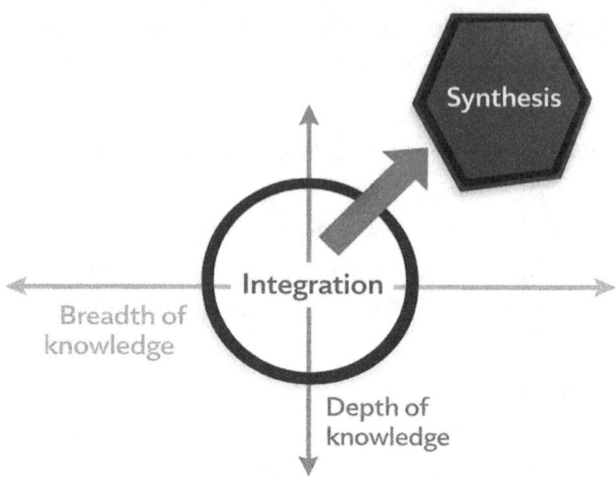

the bridge. And synthesis is where the real payoff is—where new knowledge is truly created.

In other words, breadth is about exploring broad information. Depth is about deepening understanding. Integration is about holding knowledge in a mental database, integrating it into memory. Synthesis is about creating entirely new paradigms based on your breadth, depth, and integration.

Polymathy is often described in terms of breadth across domains and depth within them, yet neither dimension alone accounts for the distinctive value polymathic thinkers bring to complex problem-solving. What differentiates polymathy at its most powerful is not simply the accumulation of diverse knowledge, but the capacity to hold breadth and depth together in a coherent integrative field from which something genuinely new can emerge. The "polymathic synthesis model" captures this process. It conceptualizes polymathy as a progression from breadth and depth, through integration, toward synthesis: a qualitative transformation in which novel frameworks, insights, or ways of seeing arise that would be inaccessible through any single discipline in isolation.

The color progression in this diagram reflects a value gradient in knowledge. For example, breadth is yellow, and depth is blue—and together, they make green integration. Further, synthesis is represented in purple to signal the creation of higher-order, novel frameworks. The dimensional shift in form underscores that synthesis is a qualitative transformation rather than a linear extension of breadth or depth.

Whereas integration mixes perspectives into a large database of knowledge, synthesis melds it into an entirely new creation, where the total becomes greater than the sum of the parts. Knowledge possession or internal integration matters; knowledge creation—through synthesis—is where the real payoff for polymathy lies. Just because someone is able to remember and connect, compare, or contrast ideas through an integrative approach does not guarantee creative problem solving. However, thinking which synthesizes perspectives, generates new knowledge, and is therefore critical for true innovation to occur.

In this way, polymathy is not merely an academic or professional trait. It is a way of being in the world—a deeply curious, self-authoring approach to learning, unlearning, and reimagining knowledge over the course of a life. And while it comes with many "side effects"—creative thinking, adaptability, critical thinking, brain plasticity, leadership, intercultural competence, and more—polymathy itself is not defined by those outcomes. It is, quite simply, the sustained practice of broad, deep, and dynamic learning in the pursuit of truth.

Cognitive Range vs. Cognitive Flexibility

In conversations about intelligence, learning, and talent, two related but distinct capacities are sometimes confused: cognitive range and cognitive flexibility. Cognitive range refers to breadth. It is the span of domains, concepts, disciplines, and ideas a person can access or discuss. Someone with high cognitive range may draw from history, psychology, economics, technology, literature, and science. They possess a wide mental library of many conceptual reference points. Cognitive flexibility refers to adaptability. It is the capacity to revise beliefs when warranted, shift perspectives, tolerate ambiguity, integrate conflicting information, and adjust one's own thinking in response to changing realities. It is less about what you know and more about how you use what you know.

A person may have significant cognitive range yet remain rigid. They may cite many fields while filtering all evidence through a fixed worldview. Breadth without flexibility can become intellectual ornamentation.

By contrast, cognitive flexibility allows knowledge to stay alive. It enables learning rather than mere accumulation. It supports collaboration across differences, better decision-making under uncertainty, and wiser responses to complexity.

Polymathic potential is strongest when these two capacities work together. Range supplies material while flexibility creates movement. One expands the map; the other allows navigation. In an era defined by rapid change, complexity, and artificial intelligence, organizations and societies need both. Yet flexibility may be the rarer advantage, because it requires humility, self-awareness, and the courage to update one's own mind.

Why Polymathy Matters for Business Organizations

Many people have never heard of the word polymath before, so why does it even matter for organizations? The reason why this should be on the radar of any Human Resources (HR) professional or organizational leader is because polymaths can be a very strategic addition for an organization to have in its arsenal—especially in modern times, when the workscape has become more complex than ever. Indeed, given how complicated operating a business in the modern world can be, it is often quite important for organizations to be able to flex, change, adapt, and grow; this requires an orientation toward learning. Organizational agility is critical. Stagnation, and just doing things tomorrow as they were done yesterday, can often be a poor strategy if organizational sustainability and long-term success is your goal. As the saying goes, "Adapt or die." So, what strategies can an organization implement in order to help bolster their chances of long-term success?

For organizations that seek not only sustainability but also innovation, which helps them stay competitive in the marketplace, polymathic people could be a perfect solution toward achieving that goal. Here is why: in the past, innovation could occur within single silos, when there was still so much to discover within individual disciplines. But over time, knowledge within those disciplinary silos has been mostly discovered. Nowadays, as the world becomes more complex, innovation in modern day frequently occurs at the *intersection* of disciplines. Creativity is often born out of unique combinations that had not been put together quite that way before.

Plus, now we exist in the age of AI. AI as a tool is polymathic, in the sense that it is not domain-limited. It is interdisciplinary by design. And so, users of AI tools should also think in interdisciplinary, holistic ways, to ensure that the solutions cocreated between humans and AI are as well-informed as possible. If a narrow specialist is working with an AI tool to try to identify solutions that are holistic, this could be a challenge, since the person working with the AI tool has limited, domain-specific knowledge. For that reason, because AI itself is polymathic, the superusers of AI tools, in my view, will be polymathic people.

This is not to say that narrow specialists, within their defined and narrow silos, cannot also be creative. But their creativity exists in a different kind of way, and many of those within-discipline innovations have already been exhausted. For example, polymaths are distinctly capable of doing analogical thinking. Analogical thinking is when we use information from one domain and apply it in another area to solve a problem. It is a powerful tool to solve difficult challenges creatively.

Polymaths are uniquely positioned to be able to help organizations develop creative solutions to difficult problems, because of their large toolkit of skills, knowledge, and experiences. They tend to be creative types. They live and therefore think outside the proverbial "box." They can creatively combine information in new ways to come up with novel solutions.

The bottom line here is that polymaths matter—or at least should matter—to business organizations who are seeking:

1. Innovation and creativity.
2. Organizational sustainability.
3. A competitive advantage to adapt quickly to environmental shifts.
4. Efficiency.
5. Staying on the cutting edge and at the forefront of their fields.
6. Creating new knowledge.
7. Employees who will contribute in new and different ways over time.
8. A culture where employees are encouraged to exist and think outside the box.
9. Organizations who want to hire people dedicated to continual improvement in themselves and want to help their business continually progress as well.

10. Companies that want employees to bring their full selves and capabilities to work.
11. Businesses that, as a whole, continue to grow and improve over time in strategic ways.
12. The ability to collaborate with AI using systems thinking so that solutions are holistic rather than fragmented.

What organizational business leader would not want to include these goals in their short- and long-term plans? These ideals should matter within all organizations, and for that reason, all organizations should learn how to leverage the power of polymathic talent in strategic ways. Polymathic people who think broadly, forging connections between disparate ideas to spawn new insights, are valuable to organizations that want to be leaders in their field, experience continuous organizational improvement, or want to obtain and sustain a competitive edge. But how are we to take advantage of this unique skillset in employees if we blindly believe the narrative that specialists are the best for all roles? How are we to support an organization reaching its fullest potential, if it is made up of individuals living in silos—in their own echo chambers? How are we to identify big-picture solutions in creative and innovative ways, if we depend only on disciplinary specialists—with their disciplinary blinders on—to find those solutions? We need a better way.

The Learning Organization

According to Peter Senge, in his book, *The Fifth Discipline: The Art and Practice of the Learning Organization*, learning organizations naturally—as the name implies—learn from their experiences, and continuously experiment to find better ways of working.[4] A learning organization is one that acquires knowledge and innovates quickly enough so that they can adapt to a changing landscape. They have cultures that encourage employees to continually learn, think critically, and take risks with new ideas. In fact, learning organizations encourage employee contributions, even if those

[4] Senge, P. 2006. *The Fifth Discipline: The Art & Practice of The Learning Organization.* New York, London, Toronto, Sydney, & Auckland: Doubleday.

contributions are imperfect or end up being "mistakes." Because a learning organization proactively makes efforts to educate their employees, the organization is better positioned to adapt to rapidly changing environments, such as changes with technology or the larger business landscape. Indeed, in a fast-paced and rapidly changing environment, a learning organization is able to acquire knowledge, develop skills, and innovate fast enough to survive and even thrive, while their counterparts who do not engage in these behaviors go out of business.

As you can see, there are parallels between a learning organization and polymaths. Polymaths are voracious learners at the individual level while learning organizations are a kind of learner too, just at the organizational level. Polymaths can be great assets in a learning organization to add value since they hold many of the same values and approaches to work. A business leader seeking to enhance their organization's capacity to be a learning organization should, therefore, select and develop employees who will continuously learn, be brave, take risks, and experiment for the sake of continuous organizational improvement.

VUCA Settings, Harsh Learning Environments, and Wicked Problems

Polymathic people are well-suited to work in demanding, ever-changing environments because of the broad set of skills they bring to help tackle those issues. They have more tools in their toolkits to help navigate challenging terrain. One way that this kind of environment is described is by the term "VUCA." VUCA stands for Volatile, Uncertain, Complex, and Ambiguous. In a VUCA setting, an organization needs to be able to adapt quickly and smartly. Another way of describing the habitat where polymaths are well-suited is in a "harsh learning environment." In a harsh learning environment, patterns are not predictable, compared to a kind learning environment where one improves performance through simple rote practice and predictable routine. Third, polymaths are uniquely positioned to add value in the context of "wicked problems." A wicked problem is one where it is extremely difficult or even impossible to solve—mostly because of its complex and interconnected nature. A wicked problem is the opposite of a "tame" problem. Wicked problems, or wicked domains, are ones in which the rules of the game are not always clear and may even change periodically. So, to even attempt to solve a wicked problem, a multidisciplinary understanding and plan of attack is required—exactly the kind of approach polymathic people bring by default.

Marcus Kirsch, in his book *The Wicked Company*, defines tame versus wicked problems this way:

> **Tame Problem:** A problem that does not change while you are working on it ... tame problems are solved by companies designed to solve those kinds of problems well—tame companies, if you will.
>
> **Wicked Problem:** A problem that changes after you started working on it ... wicked problems are solved by companies designed to address those kinds of problems well. Wicked companies, if you will.[5]

Marcus also makes a point that collaboration is no longer just about collaboration among people—it is really about breaking down silos to fully understand the problem at hand. Of course, organizational structure, approaches, and culture matter if you want to help break down those silos.

Although polymaths are uniquely positioned to be able to thrive in harsh, VUCA environments working on wicked problems, they can also contribute and do well in non-VUCA environments, not working on wicked problems. Perhaps a polymath working in a kind learning environment could help make operational improvements, as well, based on their exposure to different ways of working. They may have sparks of insight where they can imagine new and improved ways of doing the same old work. But overall, polymaths are most uniquely positioned to work well in harsh learning environments especially in comparison to their more specialized counterparts. However, polymathic people could also be leveraged in order to add efficiencies and make improvements working on other, not-so-wicked problems, too.

[5] Kirsch, M. 2019. *The Wicked Company*. Virginia Beach: Koehlerbooks.

Just as the world's problems are becoming more difficult to contend with, should our solution be to continue growing more and more narrowly focused—and for that to be the only approach? This approach will backfire. It will hurt us. Yes, we need those deep experts, but we also very much need others with broader perspectives.

The Age of Specialization

In earlier centuries, it was common for individuals to possess a broad array of skills and knowledge across multiple domains. However, with the rise of the Scientific Revolution, maintaining expertise in diverse areas became increasingly challenging. To manage the vast cognitive demands, knowledge was divided into distinct, manageable fields. This shift led us into the age of specialization, fostering the development of large organizations capable of remarkable achievements on a global scale. Yet, as a consequence, knowledge became increasingly fragmented, and individuals began to understand more deeply within narrower areas.

Consequently, while our society as a whole possesses greater knowledge, we lack individuals with broad skill sets who can view the larger picture. Can you see the risks of having a complex system without people dedicated to finding big-picture solutions? If individuals put on professional blinders so they can focus inside their respective silos, it may mean that they become very expert in their area of specialization, which sounds great on the surface. However, we still need people who can scan larger landscapes and come up with big-picture solutions. Like Henry Ford's assembly line, in the industrial era, we chose to create an intellectual division of labor even as we shifted into the knowledge economy. This is an old school approach that worked for us for a long time. But now, that approach limits us from reaching our collective potential as a species and also puts us at risk. And if we continue down a path where we encourage nearly everyone to specialize, it may cost us in terms of solutions we do not find, innovations we never realize, and individual potential that goes unlived.

Today, as technology takes on more of the routine "grunt" work, we have the opportunity to move beyond the assembly-line mindset and let tech shoulder part of our cognitive load. This shift enables humans to focus on what is uniquely ours: creativity, innovation, and envisioning big-picture solutions. In addition, we bring empathy, ethical reasoning, imaginative vision, adaptability, and the power of collaboration to our work. These qualities allow us not only to solve problems but also to infuse our solutions with depth, values, and a sense of humanity. Technology will help us realize our fuller potential by relieving us of the burden of lower-level tasks and empowering us to add value that is distinctly human.

But in the early 21st century, there are few incentives for professionals to try to become polymathic. We live in an age where specialization is the dominant narrative still and is seen as the necessary requirement for career success. Most organizations still seek out specialists for almost all jobs and encourage employees on their team to develop deeper and deeper expertise over time. When hiring, most organizations *discriminate against* polymathic people, because they believe in the lie that *everyone* must be narrow and specialized within their organizational teams. Is there a better and more strategic way in which organizations can select their individual contributors? The answer is a resounding "yes."

While specialization is valuable in certain contexts, it often lacks the breadth of thinking, experiences, and expertise needed for truly innovative solutions. To foster creativity and synthesis, we need people who can build bridges across disciplines and weave information in new ways. Achieving this requires individuals with broad exposure who can connect diverse ideas. For effective cross-pollination of ideas and meaningful connections, society—and organizations within it—must recognize the importance of teams that blend both specialists and generalist polymaths. Success lies in bringing the right people on board and positioning them where they can have the greatest impact.

Indeed, both approaches have value within organizations—but most organizations are very lopsided toward having specialists on their teams, almost exclusively, and few polymathic individuals. Polymaths versus specialists think and work differently—and both matter. But one, the polymath, is undervalued—and therefore this is a ripe area for opportunity if organizations can figure out where and how to leverage their different types of talent appropriately. If organizations can do this—if they can tap into the talent of polymathic people—it could possibly be a game changer for them to be able to adapt, innovate, and truly leverage the intelligence and skill sets on their team like never before.

Here's the bottom line: society, and more specifically, businesses, need a combination of specialists and nonspecialists. We need people who can dive deep into their areas of expertise, who work in routine and stable fields, and who can really master their areas of specialization. But we also need people who are not single-disciplinary, narrow specialists, who can see big-picture solutions in more novel and strategic ways. We need a mix of individuals who are exclusively dedicated to one field, and we need others who have intellectual dexterity and can speak multiple professional languages, and in the process, make novel, useful linkages that position organizations to make big leaps forward as a result. We need to exploit what we know, and we need to expand into what we do not know yet; that is why we need specialists and polymaths, both.

The Age of Specialization and the Rise of the Metacrisis

The age of specialization brought unprecedented advancements across various fields, enabling experts to delve deeply into specific domains and solve increasingly complex problems. Specialization allowed breakthroughs in medicine, technology, science, and economics, transforming society. However, this intense focus on narrow expertise also fostered a fragmented view of knowledge, where understanding became compartmentalized and cross-disciplinary insights were often overlooked. This fragmentation has given rise to a metacrisis—a convergence of interconnected crises—because today's most pressing global issues are multidimensional and cannot be adequately addressed within isolated domains.

One of the critical consequences of specialization is the siloed approach it encourages, often leaving experts without a shared language or framework to tackle problems that span disciplines. Climate change, economic inequality, social polarization, and health crises, for example, all interact in complex ways that transcend any single field. By focusing too narrowly, specialists risk overlooking broader systemic issues or interdependencies, leading to solutions that are either incomplete or inadvertently harmful.

As a result, we often see innovations that address one problem but exacerbate others, creating cascading effects that worsen the overall crisis.

Additionally, the age of specialization has diminished holistic or systems thinking among leaders, policymakers, and citizens alike. When individuals are trained to excel within narrow parameters, they may not cultivate the skills to integrate knowledge across fields or consider the wider implications of their work. This can lead to "solutionism"—the belief that each crisis can be tackled independently through technical fixes—when what's truly needed is a unified, interdisciplinary approach.

In this way, the age of specialization has contributed to our current metacrisis by prioritizing depth over breadth and isolating streams of knowledge. Now, we need a shift toward polymathic thinking, where knowledge across domains is woven together to address the complexity of modern challenges. By embracing a more integrated approach, we can work toward solutions that foster resilience and adaptability in the face of global crises, benefiting humanity as a whole.

The age of specialization didn't just enable industries to advance—it also encouraged them to operate in silos, often without consideration for the wider, irreversible impacts of their actions. By focusing solely on narrow goals and profit-driven metrics, entire sectors have overlooked the ripple effects of their decisions. For instance, the agricultural industry has specialized in high-yield monoculture farming to meet global food demand. Yet this has come at the cost of soil degradation, loss of biodiversity, and reliance on chemical inputs, with severe consequences for ecosystems and human health. Similarly, the pharmaceutical industry's focus on rapid drug development has, at times, overlooked long-term impacts, as seen in the opioid crisis, which emerged from short-term solutions to pain management without considering broader societal costs.

The technology sector, too, illustrates this pattern: while revolutionizing communication, connectivity, and information sharing, rapid specialization has led to issues such as data privacy erosion, social media addiction, and misinformation. By prioritizing user engagement and profit, technology companies have unintentionally created platforms that contribute to division, addiction, and loss of personal privacy, with far-reaching effects on democracy, mental health, and social cohesion.

This narrow focus on specialized, short-term goals, often at the expense of the larger picture, has set the stage for our current metacrisis. Prioritizing profit over society's well-being creates a cascade of interconnected crises that span environmental, social, and economic dimensions. To address today's complex challenges, we must adopt an interdisciplinary perspective that acknowledges the interdependence of global systems. Only then can we work toward sustainable solutions that promote the well-being of all, rather than a select few.

The Ambidextrous Organization

A business that has organizational ambidexterity is one that is able to use techniques for exploitation and exploration at the same time.[6] In other words, an ambidextrous organization can leverage their talent to master what they do best now, and also build capacity for what they can do in the future. This type of business is able to manage today's demands, while also preparing and being adaptable to flex as demands change over time. Just like an individual who is ambidextrous can use both the left and the right hand comfortably and with skill, organizational ambidexterity means that the organization is able to both exploit and explore skillfully. It is incumbent upon the leaders of organizations to instill this value and make strategic plans to build this sort of capacity, and building a team of adept specialists as well as creative, talented polymaths is one of the best ways to build this capability. Naturally, specialists will be well-suited to exploit whereas polymaths will be well-positioned to explore new avenues to organizational success.

Unblocking an Organizational Blind Spot

Polymathic people exist on a spectrum, and we already have many of them, to varying degrees, in our midst. We also have many people who have the *capability* of becoming contributing polymaths, but the way that organizations function—frequently with a focus on hiring only

[6] Zabiegalski, E. 2019. The Rise of the Ambidextrous Organization: The Secret Revolution Happening Right Under Your Nose. Business Research Consulting.

specialists and then once hired, organizing them according to specialized functions—means that there are many people who could become valuable polymaths, but whose talents go unrealized because organizations do not elicit that skill set from them. In fact, many organizations that focus on hiring narrow specialists may have polymathic people in those roles who try to craft resumes that tell a story of specialization. And those organizations therefore have polymaths on their teams but do not leverage their full talent because the business leaders are not even aware of those employees' full background and capabilities. Polymaths working in specialist roles are like square pegs trying to be put into round holes; they may be able to be squished into that spot, but it certainly is not the best fit.

Many polymathic people try their best to fit into society's mold for specialization. They charade as specialists when, by nature and practice, they really are not. They are simply pressured into presenting themselves that way. People are taught to modify their resumes to tell a story that matches a job advertisement's specific requirements. Experiences that seem irrelevant to the position are just deleted. Polymaths often grow frustrated that they are not able to use their full skill set on the job; they feel underutilized and unfulfilled. They get bored. In other words, it is entirely possible and even likely that organizations already have polymaths in their midst, but do not even know it. There are underleveraged resources and talent that have not been uncovered; this is a waste. Plus, the retention of polymathic people in specialist roles and in organizations that do not appreciate the full breadth of their talent can be quite poor. Individual polymaths often leave specialist roles after a period of time to find new intellectual stimulation. In fact, many polymathic people become entrepreneurs, because they want to be able to use their full skill set professionally and oftentimes starting their own professional endeavor is the only way to accomplish that goal. Some polymaths forge unique businesses that leverage their multiple talents in different fields.

The point here is that organizations are missing out. But what if there was a way for organizations to leverage the multiple talents of individual members of their team? There is. But first, organizations must acknowledge this possible blind spot and take steps to unearth the full capacities and talents of the staff that make up their business.

This can be done in a variety of ways. For example, through *exploratory interviews* with employees already in your organization, you can ask questions to help uncover skill sets, interests, and information about the employee's background that might be unrealized simply because this sort of conversation has not taken place before, to help uncover their full skill set. Organizations can also use *skills surveys* to help unearth the hidden talent within their teams. Once this information is in hand, managers can more strategically make decisions about how to more fully leverage the talent already within the organization. But if managers do not ask, and do not seek to find out what buried treasure exists within their organizations, then it will remain unfound.

Intrapersonal Diversity

Most modern leaders understand the importance of having diverse teams. When groups are made up of diverse members, it reduces the likelihood for groupthink, increases the likelihood of more well-rounded and thoughtful contributions within the team, and is simply more inclusive of people from different backgrounds—which, of course, is the right thing to do from an ethics perspective. Typically, when leaders think about diversity, they are looking at race, sex, gender identity, sexual orientation, religion, and disability status. These are important, of course, and it is vital that organizations be as inclusive as possible to build a strong culture where individual differences are appreciated, and all types of people feel welcomed and included. Logically, organizations should mirror the larger society—and given that the larger society is diverse, so should organizations be, to match.

However, when people think about diversity, they almost always think about it in group settings—either at the meso level, within organizations, or at the macro level, at a much larger scale (i.e., communities, countries, etc.). However, there is a level of analysis that is almost always missing when it comes to discussions around diversity: the individual level of analysis. Indeed, diversity can and does exist within individuals in varying degrees, and in different ways. Sadly, this is almost always overlooked and never discussed, though. Ironically, the concept of diversity needs to become more diversified itself.

Diversity within one person—also known as intrapersonal diversity—is tantamount to polymathy.[7] Given that the topic of diversity is at the forefront as an important organizational concern that leaders must be sensitive to, wouldn't it make sense for leaders to consider the importance of intrapersonal diversity, or polymathy, as well as the more traditional types of diversity? This allows for a more holistic understanding of diversity and its impact at all levels and allows for organizations to benefit from diversity on multiple fronts.

Diversity within a person is important, and distinctly different from diversity that you find within groups of people. More specifically, when you have a group of people who are trying to bring forth different perspectives in order to collaboratively work on a problem, the only way that information can be shared, from a group member to others in the group, is through language (whether spoken, written, etc.). However, language between people is actually a roadblock; if we were able to telepathically communicate information to one another, to simply deposit information from one human brain into another directly, it would allow for a more pure, seamless transfer of knowledge. Is it worth acnkowledging that tech-telepathy is under human trial with the Neuralink brain chip? Information that has to go through the language filter frequently gets lost in translation, misunderstood, or missed altogether. Humans are limited by the language we can speak and understand, or even the degree to which we are adept in any given language. Depending on which language(s) a person speaks, there may be words that represent certain concepts more richly—or not.

However, within an individual, insights and flashes of inspiration frequently occur at the preverbal level. These sparks of insight that are not dependent on language and that can happen within an individual mind do not happen in groups of people this way. In other words, groups of people must rely on language to convey information back and forth; it is

[7] Cotellessa, A.J. 2018. In Pursuit of Polymaths: Understanding Renaissance Persons of the 21st Century. Doctoral dissertation, The George Washington University, Washington, DC.

a bumbling and imperfect way to try to collaborate and solve problems. Polymaths who have knowledge in multiple fields are well positioned to innovate and are not necessarily dependent on language to do so. So, an additional strength of intrapersonal diversity is that it allows for insights, innovation, and epiphanies that are not necessarily dependent on the limited tool we call language, because these perceptions can occur within a single mind.

Bottom Line of This Chapter

- Polymathic talent is a powerful, often untapped asset for modern organizations. Business leaders and HR professionals should intentionally cultivate and place individuals with intrapersonal diversity where their unique combinations of skills can make the most impact.
- Polymaths bring innovation, adaptability, and integrative thinking—key ingredients for solving complex problems and navigating change.
- Leveraging polymathic talent leads to greater creativity, agility, and long-term resilience in a fast-evolving, AI-augmented world.
- Embracing polymathy elevates individuals and organizations alike—and positions both to thrive amid uncertainty and opportunity.

Chapter 1 Reflection Questions and Discussion Prompts

Polymathic Talent and Organizational Success

1. Think about the story of Wendy. Have you ever had a workplace experience where your full range of skills wasn't valued or utilized? How did that impact your engagement and motivation?
2. How do you think organizations can better identify and leverage polymathic employees rather than pushing them into rigid, specialized roles?
3. What are some practical ways your workplace could support polymathic employees in expanding their contributions while still fulfilling their core job responsibilities?

The Role of Polymaths in Innovation and Adaptation

1. How do you see the benefits of polymathy playing out in the modern business landscape, especially with AI and rapid technological changes?
2. Can you think of an example where an interdisciplinary approach led to an innovative or breakthrough idea in your industry? How was that idea received and implemented?
3. In what ways do businesses benefit from having employees who think analogically—applying knowledge from one domain to another?

The Challenges of Specialization Versus Polymathy in Business

1. Have you ever been told (explicitly or implicitly) to focus on one area and not explore beyond it? How did that affect your career choices and learning?
2. Do you think the modern workforce is too specialized? How might organizations strike a balance between hiring specialists and fostering polymathic thinking?

3. Are there areas in your own workplace where overspecialization has caused inefficiencies or blind spots? How might polymathic thinking help resolve those issues?

The Learning Organization and the Value of Curiosity

1. Does your organization encourage employees to learn beyond their immediate job roles? If not, how could it implement more of a learning organization model?
2. What small changes could be made in your workplace to create an environment where curiosity, exploration, and interdisciplinary thinking are encouraged?
3. Have you personally experienced the benefits of being a lifelong, self-directed learner? If so, how has it shaped your career or personal growth?

The Metacrisis and the Need for Systems Thinkers

1. What are some major challenges (in business or society) that you believe could benefit from more polymathic or interdisciplinary thinking?
2. How does the current era of hyperspecialization contribute to complex, interconnected crises? What might be the risks of not fostering broader, systems-level thinking?
3. How can businesses prepare their employees to be more adaptable in an unpredictable world? What role might polymathic employees play in that preparation?

Unblocking Organizational Blind Spots and Recognizing Hidden Talent

1. How well does your organization currently recognize the full range of talents among its employees?

2. Have you ever hidden or downplayed certain skills or interests because they didn't seem relevant to your job? If so, what was the reason, and how might that have impacted your work satisfaction?
3. How can leaders and HR teams better uncover and support polymathic talent that already exists within their workforce?

The Future of Work: Polymathy and AI

1. Given that AI is inherently polymathic in its ability to analyze data across multiple fields, do you think polymaths will have an advantage in the future workplace? Why or why not?
2. How do you see AI shifting the value of human skills in the workplace? What unique strengths do polymaths bring that AI cannot replace?

CHAPTER 2

Understanding Key Elements of Polymathy

> "I have no special talent. I am only passionately curious."
>
> —Albert Einstein

Have you ever wondered what drives people to become polymaths? What sparks their curiosity, fuels their growth, and shapes their ability to master multiple fields? What would it take for you—or someone you know—to tap into a similar kind of potential? The purpose of this chapter is to explore these questions and uncover the key elements that make polymathy possible, both for individuals and within organizations.

First, we'll dive into the personal journey: What motivates people to embrace a polymathic life? What experiences and traits help them thrive in our ever-changing world? This section will illuminate how polymaths come to be and what it feels like to navigate life as someone with a wide range of interests and abilities.

Next, we'll shift the focus to you, the reader, especially if you're a leader or part of an organization. What can you do to support polymathic potential in others? How can you foster an environment where employees are encouraged to explore their breadth, not just their depth? We'll discuss practical ways to unlock innovation and growth by embracing polymathy in the workplace.

Finally, we'll zoom out to explore polymathy as a spectrum. Have you ever considered that polymathy isn't an all-or-nothing quality? Instead, it's a dynamic range of skills, interests, and expressions. Together, we'll unpack the dimensions of this spectrum, helping you understand the many ways polymathy can manifest and how these variations make each polymath unique.

Through these questions and ideas, this chapter invites you to think differently about how people learn, grow, and contribute—not just as specialists, but as multifaceted individuals with boundless potential. Are you ready to dive in?

Other Neighboring Terms in the Lexicon

Before diving in further, let me provide some similar terms to the word "polymath." There are other words or phrases that people sometimes use to describe a similar concept to that of polymathy. Here are a few of those words or phrases, my impression of what they mean, and how they relate to the term "polymath."

- **Polyhistor:** This is probably the closest term to polymath—it essentially means someone gifted in multiple areas, who inquires in multiple areas. This word conveys that you witness something, similar to how *hist*ory is witnessed.
- **Renaissance Person (also Renaissance "man," "woman," "soul," etc.):** This term comes from the Renaissance period of history in Europe, when there was an explosion of human achievement across domains—for example, Leonardo da Vinci's contributions in art, science, and medicine. Leonardo da Vinci is the quintessential Renaissance man. Being a Renaissance person implies that you have many different talents.
- **Generalist:** A generalist is the opposite of a narrow specialist, obviously. It is someone who has capacities across fields, domains, and industries—someone with skill sets and knowledge in "general" areas. Fittingly, "generalist" is a very general term. A polymath is a type of generalist—though a highly accomplished one. Being a generalist does not imply any level of expertise or excellence, though, whereas the term "polymath" does imply some depth of expertise—just in multiple areas. A generalist and a polymath are not the same concept. Although a polymath is a type of generalist, not all generalists will be polymaths.
- **Multipotentialite:** This term implies having multiple potentials. A multipotentialite would be someone who

is curious about many things. The term does not imply any achievement or accomplishment in anything, however—it only implies multiple potentials—and so it is different than the term "polymath" since "polymath" tends to imply achievement or accomplishment, rather than just potential.

- **Jack of All Trades:** You have probably heard the phrase, "jack of all trades, master of none," but you might not have heard the rest of that colloquialism: "though oftentimes better than master of one." In the common vernacular, jack of all trades sometimes implies a lack of commitment; it can be derogatory in nature, especially because people tend to associate it with "master of none." So, this term is very different than the concept of a polymath, which, in contrast to a jack of all trades, implies mastery in multiple areas.
- **Scanner:** A neighboring concept to that of polymathy would be someone who is a scanner; however, a scanner implies people who have a lot of breadth, but very little depth. Polymath on the other hand, infers that someone has both breadth and depth—there is some level of excellence and commitment, just across several different fields. Polymath is a distinctly different concept than scanner.
- **Dilettante:** This is equivalent to a dabbler or an amateur. A dilettante is a person who might have many interests but is not committed or notably knowledgeable in any of them.
- **Multipassionate**: A multipassionate person is someone with a strong enthusiasm for and engagement in a wide variety of interests, pursuits, or activities. This term emphasizes passion and energy rather than a specific level of achievement or depth of knowledge in any given area. While a multipassionate individual may excel in some areas, the term primarily reflects their joy in exploring diverse fields and their desire to immerse themselves in multiple passions. Unlike a polymath, whose identity is tied to breadth and depth across multiple domains, or a generalist, who has versatile skills without necessarily emphasizing passion, a multipassionate person is driven by curiosity and a love for variety.

As you can see, there are several different terms that vary in terms of their similarity—or not—when compared to the word polymath. The term polymath implies that someone has notable achievement and expertise in multiple areas (even though polymaths themselves are not all the same and polymathy exists on a spectrum).

Geniuses Versus Generalists

The field of polymathy studies is made up of a handful of different scholars; in pop culture, there are some thinkers, influencers, and authors who also speak on the subject. Sometimes when people use the word "polymath," they only mean it as a term to describe eminent geniuses—the top echelon of mankind—those who have accomplished the most, in the most creative and groundbreaking ways. Those influencers typically do not talk about it existing on a spectrum. Yet other thinkers use polymath to denote someone with literally "many learnings" across disciplines—who may not be an eminent genius, but who has the hallmark traits of breadth and versatility in terms of their skills and knowledge. It is important to be aware of these different ways that people view the term "polymath." It does not mean the same thing to everybody.

Nature Versus Nurture

You may be wondering if polymathy is due more to nature or nurture. The answer is likely both. There is some evidence that polymaths come to be that way because of their environment. Robert Root-Bernstein, whom I consider a preeminent scholar in polymathy studies, has written extensively on this. For example, his analysis shows that there is very little correlation between creativity and being innately gifted or talented. On the contrary, there is evidence that creative people tend to be more broadly trained, have a higher number of hobbies, and generally just have increased abilities in the fields they're interested in, compared to the average person.[1] In sciences, technology, engineering, and mathe-

[1] Root-Bernstein, R. 2015. "Arts and Crafts as Adjuncts to STEM Education to Foster Creativity in Gifted and Talented Students." *Asia Pacific Education* 16, pp. 203–212.

matics (STEM) fields, the avocational (hobby) interests of the most successful professionals are highly correlated with skills in the fine arts, like painting or music, literary accomplishments, or skills in trades such as woodworking, metalworking, electronics, or mechanics. It seems probable that polymathy requires a mix of both nature and nurture to emerge, but it certainly can be fostered in individuals—rather than simply being an inborn trait that some people are blessed with while others are not.

Finances and the Emergence of Polymathy

You may think that only people who have plentiful financial resources would become polymaths, but that is not the case. Certainly, for some polymaths, having disposable income helped them explore their curiosity, perhaps through educational opportunities, travel, hobbies, the ability to purchase books, and so on. However, for some polymaths, the opposite is true: not having much in the way of finances "helped" them become polymathic. The reason is because without much disposable income, this forced those people to learn how to do certain tasks on their own; work could not be outsourced. In other words, regardless of whether someone has plentiful or little financial resources, either way, that person could become polymathic.[2]

Family Functionality and the Emergence of Polymathy

Similarly, you may assume that only individuals who have very supportive, nurturing childhoods would grow to become polymathic adults—or even to show this early aptitude still as children. That is true for some polymaths, but not all. On the contrary, some polymaths had very difficult childhoods—whether it was divorce, domestic abuse, drug use in the household, or various other dysfunctional influences. For those people, frequently the dysfunction in their environment provided a kind of inspiration to get out of a bad situation. Frequently, the way to "get out"

---

[2] Cotellessa, A.J. 2018. "In Pursuit of Polymaths: Understanding Renaissance Persons of the 21st Century." Doctoral dissertation, The George Washington University, Washington, DC.

would be through learning and achievement. For some, the desire for mental diversions from the harsh realities of their day-to-day lives led them to become voracious readers, a sort of escapism through books. The bottom line here is that whether someone came from a traditional, functional household, or had a more chaotic upbringing—either way, that person could theoretically become polymathic.

Polymathic Values

Based on my research on polymaths over the years, I would say that polymaths have a few common values that almost all of them hold dear. They are as follows:

1. **Freedom:** Polymaths do not want to feel as if they are boxed or caged in; frequently when they describe their experiences, they use the analogy of thinking of breaking "out of the box." They want to be the curators of their own full lives, rather than simply living according to society's expectations of how they should be. Having flexibility and freedom to make their own way is a key trademark of polymathy. This goes hand-in-hand with the freedom to be authentic as well.
2. **Continuous Learning:** The word polymath literally means "many learnings." So, of course, the phenomenon itself cannot be separated from learning. Learning is a core feature of being a polymath. Polymaths value very much the ability to continuously learn, particularly in self-directed ways. They are curious, and so what they learn about will likely change fairly frequently. The bottom line is that a polymath is a learner. Because of their broad set of learnings, they are well positioned to think critically as well.
3. **Variety:** The very nature of polymathy, "many learnings," is rooted in a desire to constantly expand what one knows and experiences; variety is important. Many polymaths tend to prefer change and newness over stability and routine, though not always. But what is consistent among polymaths is the desire for a broad variety of learning experiences. They have a compulsion to learn—and the more, the better.

4. **Self-Improvement:** Underlying the behaviors of polymaths is a desire to become their best selves. Of course, different polymaths feel this drive to different degrees, although for many, they really do feel a strong urge for self-improvement and even self-actualization. Just as many polymaths desire to master the subjects they learn about, they also tend to have a fundamental desire for self-mastery, more generally, as well. There is a striving for and commitment to excellence you see with many polymathic people.
5. **Courage:** There is a certain amount of courage that is necessary for someone to become a multidisciplinary polymath in a day and age that tells us we should all become professional specialists in a single area only. Polymaths are a bit rebellious in this way; they think for themselves. They are willing to think, work, and ultimately exist "outside the box." Plus, to become polymathic in the current day, most polymathic people must feel a certain level of comfort with holding somewhat contradictory elements in their personhood; for example, someone might be very logical or scientific on one hand, but very artistic and playful at the same time. On the surface, these sorts of combinations do not seem to go together, because we are not used to seeing them combined in one person in our siloed age of specialization. At the same time, it is natural for a person to experience and express all the parts of themselves. The bottom line here is that to be a polymath, particularly in a professional setting in this age of specialization, that person must be willing to diverge from society's expectations—and that requires courage.

A Note on Intelligence

Polymaths tend to be very intelligent people; if polymath means, "many learnings," then clearly, the ability to learn is, at its core, required to be a polymathic person. Obviously, the ability to learn is also related to intelligence quotient (IQ). However, no studies have been done to date comparing the IQs of polymathic people versus nonpolymaths, or narrow specialists. Even if we did have this data, there likely would not be a clear cut-off for a certain IQ someone *must* have to be considered polymathic. At least currently, someone identifying as a polymath is something individuals self-select. Or sometimes, people refer to other people as being polymaths, as well. But there currently is no robust test or measure to determine if someone is or is not a polymath. While some have speculated about the possibility of a future body to certify polymaths, such an idea is fraught with challenges, given the diverse and multifaceted nature of polymathy.

Although polymathy has historically been understood primarily as a self-identified orientation rather than a formally measured construct, early efforts to develop assessment tools have begun to emerge. Dr. Michael Araki developed the *Polymathic Orientation Scale*, and I developed the *Knower-Learner Assessment*, an instrument designed to measure cognitive preferences for routine, stable work versus unpredictable work involving variety and uncertain solutions, as well as orientations between those poles. Such tools represent early attempts to operationalize aspects of polymathic orientation and may help individuals better understand their strengths, assist organizations in identifying interdisciplinary thinkers, and support researchers studying polymathy as a developing field.

The key takeaway here is that while polymaths often exhibit high levels of intelligence, polymathy itself is a multifaceted construct that cannot be reduced to a single, standardized measure such as IQ. There is no universal benchmark or minimum score that determines whether someone can identify as a polymath, as the essence of polymathy lies in its diversity, breadth, and depth across various domains. Polymathy is better understood as a dynamic and individualized phenomenon that develops progressively across the lifespan, shaped by intellectual curiosity, interdisciplinary engagement, and lived experience, rather than being confined to any rigid definition or numerical threshold. Polymathy can also be developed over the lifespan; so someone may not be a strong polymath, but they can develop into one through choosing breadth and depth of their learning.

Polymathy on a Spectrum

Just like many elements of the human condition, polymathy exists on a spectrum. You do not have to be an eminent, creative genius like

Leonardo Da Vinci to be considered polymathic. The point here is that there is a range of how polymathic a person is at any given time, and some people will be more polymathic than others. What this also means is that we can adjust where we are on that spectrum, through our own efforts. Everybody can choose to expand their horizons and learn. Polymathy is not only for the elite or from the geniuses in our world; polymathic approaches and broad learning are available to anyone, should they so choose to follow that path. Now, to be a proper, eminent, creative, genius polymath is still possible, but that will only be the case for a small sample of the population of those with polymathic tendencies.

Because polymathic pursuits, and polymathy itself, exists on a spectrum, this means that almost anyone can become polymathic. It is not so much a question of "yes," or "no," it is more a matter of to what degree someone has pursued breadth and depth in their personhood, or not. There is a range—different degrees of how polymathic a person is. Anybody can decide to expose themselves to a variety of subjects, experiences, and people—and learn along the way. Some people do not even decide this at all, and yet happen upon this way of life, for a variety of reasons, simply due to chance encounters and going with the flow of life. Clearly, however, polymathy is a way to enrich oneself, and this is possible for anyone to do.

Polymath Identity

Much of what I learned through my doctoral studies has to do with polymath identity; a critical point to understand is that polymath identity can be difficult to explain to others—and this is part of what people experience on their polymath journeys. It can be lonely and difficult for this reason, and others. Many people do not even know the word polymath, which can make forming an identity as such even more challenging. Many polymathic people feel like if they share all the various facets of their identity with other people, they might not be believed—or even worse, they will be viewed as bragging. Because of this, many polymaths engage in self-censorship; or if they do share openly about themselves, perhaps they do it in relatively small doses over time.

Plus, most people—as a general rule—tend to form their identity by finding groups of similar people they can fit in with. However, for many polymaths, they realize their identity as a polymathic person, because of the fact that they cannot really feel fully satisfied in any one group; they realize they are different, and that's how they come to understand themselves as being polymathic. This is important to know if you want to understand how someone becomes a polymath and how they tend to find their identity as such.

Further, polymath identity is actually an umbrella concept, because the fact is that polymaths may have multiple subidentities. They embrace variety in their personhood. For many polymathic people, they do not want to label themselves; categorization can feel stifling and therefore uncomfortable. Many people who are quite polymathic by nature do not even feel comfortable labeling themselves as such, because they are so used to defying convention and not fitting in "a box." And applying a label like "polymath" can feel like a strange and uncomfortable "box" to be put into, especially for people used to existing outside of the cage of specialization.

Yet other polymaths may not feel comfortable identifying as such, because they feel like their level of accomplishment is never enough. If a person compares himself or herself to Leonardo Da Vinci, they may believe they will never become a polymath—that the term is far too great. For these reasons, polymath identity is quite a conundrum. It is a rich way of experiencing an individual human life, and potentially also contributing to a larger collective in innovative ways. Polymathy is a way to explore having the full human experience, in a way that feels authentic to each person. At the same time, it is something we rarely talk about and that is undervalued, yet such a natural way of being in the world—it is in our human nature. But because it can be difficult to navigate identity as a polymath in the early 21st century, it may remain in the shadows—unless we decide to talk about it and appreciate it more. I hope that this book serves as a call to action for you to help do just that.

Openness to Experience

Polymathy tends to be correlated with high levels of something called "openness to experience." Openness to experience has been studied extensively in academia. It is the "disposition to be imaginative, nonconforming, and unconventional."[3] Someone high in openness to experience tends to like exploring multiple options, challenging assumptions, looking to understand different perspectives, being able to combine differing viewpoints, and actively analyzing different options.[4] These types of people tend to be flexible and are able to readily understand multiple perspectives.[5] People high in openness to experience tend to be intellectually curious, imaginative, and in general, open to trying new things.[6] It is worth understanding the link between polymathy and openness to experience, since to be someone who explores a variety of subjects and who has broad experiences, being open to those things is a necessary preamble.

Just as IQ is important, a new kind of eXperience Quotient (XQ) is also critical. How much—and how broad is your experience? That matters because it impacts what you bring to work. And a person's XQ is influenced by their openness to experience as a necessary precursor to having those broad experiences.

The Role of Self-Directed, Lifelong Learning

Society does not encourage people to become polymaths. On the contrary, we have lived in an age of specialization where the dominant ideology pressures us to focus narrowly, professionally. So, for a person to become polymathic in the age of specialization, it is necessary for a person to really take ownership over his or her own learning journey; polymathic living is not the standard path that has been prepaved for people. In other words, society has not encouraged nor rewarded polymathic pursuits, at

---

[3] Judge, T., J. Bono, R. Ilies, and M. Gerhardt. 2002. "Personality and Leadership: A Qualitative and Quantitative Review." *Journal of Applied Psychology* 87, pp. 765–780.

[4] Shalley, C. and J. Perry-Smith. 2008. "The Emergence of Team Creative Cognition: The Role of Diverse Outside Ties, Sociocognitive Network Centrality, and Team Evolution." *Strategic Entrepreneurship Journal* 2, pp. 23–41.

[5] Zhao, H. and S. Seibert. 2006. "The Big Five Personality Dimensions and Entrepreneurial Status: A Meta-Analytical Review." *Journal of Applied Psychology* 91, pp. 259–271.

[6] Burke, L., and L. Witt. 2002. "Moderators of the Openness to Experience-Performance Relationship." *Journal of Managerial Psychology* 17, no. 8, pp. 712–721.

least in the first quarter of the 21st century. Beyond that, becoming polymathic is a very personal journey. It is rooted in curiosity, and that is a very personal thing.

That is why self-directed learning is a critical component of becoming a polymath. A good definition of self-directed learning is "a disposition to engage in learning activities where the individual takes personal responsibility for developing and carrying out learning endeavors autonomously without being prompted or guided by other people." This approach aligns closely with the principles of the Montessori method, which emphasizes active, self-initiated exploration and learning, rather than passive absorption of knowledge. That is not to say that a person aspiring to be self-directed in their learning can't learn from a teacher, tutor, mentor, parent, or other more knowledgeable people—certainly, they may seek out guidance and knowledge from others. However, the defining characteristic of self-directed learning is that the individual drives their own learning agenda; it is their curiosity and initiative, rather than external direction, that shapes their educational journey.

Each polymath becomes a unique combination of learning and experiences—a real author of his or her own unique story. Being a polymath is really about curating your own learning journey—and it is also something that takes place over an entire lifetime. Polymathy is a way of approaching life—wanting to soak it all in, while learning and experiencing as much as possible. It is important to understand that polymathy is rooted in self-directed, lifelong, lifewide learning that takes place in a very authentic and personal way to each person on their journey to polymathy.

Time Management for Polymaths

One of the real challenges of being a polymathic person with many interests and pursuits, is managing time. Although it is not necessary to have multiple interests or parallel careers at once to be considered polymathic, that is the route that many polymaths seem to take. (The primary alternative is having sequential polymathic pursuits, mostly one at a time, one after another.) It is very common for a polymath to wear multiple "hats" at once or to juggle many proverbial balls in the air simultaneously.

The more accomplished polymaths tend to be good at managing their time. For this reason, one of the main pathways to becoming a polymath is by learning how to manage time well. Efficiency and organization help in this regard. That is not to say that people who are not the best time managers cannot be great polymaths; however, their efforts may be more difficult, or simply slower, as they struggle to self-organize in order to make progress.

Some polymathic people may start projects that they never finish; this is another reality of having many interests and pursuits, and limited time in which to work on them. Some of them feel easily distracted, due to their deep curiosity and desire for variety in their day-to-day experiences. Just as they become excited about a certain topic, that interest may quickly shift as something else comes along, even more interesting. Sometimes polymaths are seen as flighty or distracted by others. For this reason, prioritization is a real key for polymaths wishing to really harness their potential, and complete projects. This requires some discipline, of course, and there are many polymathic people who are able to navigate life where they feel both very curious about many things, but are willing to hunker down and focus, sometimes, to help them reach their goals.

When considering the role that time management plays in polymathic pursuits, sleep is also something to address. Some polymaths do well with little sleep, and that may be part of their strategy for how to simultaneously juggle multiple interests and even parallel careers at the same time. Some polymaths function well this way, and others need plentiful rest to fuel all their divergent interests. Given that sleep takes up about one-third of our lives, thereby taking up a significant portion of our time, it is worth realizing that some people can consistently take time away from sleep to focus on polymathic endeavors without much disturbance to their ability to function, while others will not perform well if they were to deprive themselves of the precious sleep their bodies crave. Not everyone is created equal in this regard, as some people need more sleep than others, thus reducing the amount of time left for other pursuits. Additionally, not all commitments are negotiable—many polymaths, particularly women who are often primary caregivers, may find that their responsibilities to others take precedence over sacrificing sleep for personal learning or creative exploration. Balancing polymathic ambitions with the demands of caregiving, work, and personal well-being is a complex and deeply individual process.

Intentional Versus Incidental Learning

There are two main ways someone can develop their polymathy, in terms of how they learn, at a basic level:

1. Intentional Learning
2. Incidental Learning

Just like these terms imply, the first scenario is where an individual purposefully plans their learning (for polymaths, that would be broad learning across different topics). The idea here is that it is done on purpose, with some forethought. The other path, incidental learning, is that which is unplanned.[7] It happens through the course of just living life, chance opportunities, and it may be entirely unstructured, too. Even though incidental learning is unintentional, it is still valuable.

Indeed, both routes have value. The point here is that the learning that makes someone polymathic can happen both through intention or by happenstance. That said, most polymaths do not decide "I want to be a polymath when I grow up." There is a mix of following one's passions and purposefully seeking broad variety in terms of knowledge and experiences, while also learning along the way information and having learning experiences that were not preplanned. Chance encounters play a role in how one's polymathy develops, as well. So, for someone striving to become polymathic, it is probably best to use a mix of both intentional learning where a person plans out what they want to become exposed to, while also being open to the flow of what happens in his or her life, and taking advantage of opportunities that arise, even if they were unexpected.

---

[7] Cahoon, B. 1995. Computer skill learning in the workplace: a comparative case study. Dissertation Abstracts International, 56/05A, 1622 (UMI No. AAI9531174).

Intellectual Learning Versus Experiential Learning

Very frequently, people who think about polymathy think only of learning as a heady, intellectual pursuit. Perhaps this comes through reading books, attending classes, scholarship, or professional practice—learning from peers or through doing work on the job. This type of intellectual learning is very brain-based and information-focused. However, there is also something very powerful about learning through broad *experiences*. Skills can be just as important as knowledge. Broad exposure can come in the form of travel, adventures, sports, arts, social experiences, or hobbies, for instance. Both approaches, whether *intellectual* learning or *experiential* learning, have value. In fact, many times, an avocation can inform or inspire a new way of doing work in a vocational setting. So, it is important to remember that polymathy can be developed through a mix of more intellectual pursuits, as well as experiences, whether inside or outside of school or work.

The Role of Language

When we strive to innovate in a group of people, we must use language as a pathway to share ideas. Because humans are not telepathic with one another, we rely on a tool—language—to help us understand and share ideas. When you consider a group of people who are trying to solve a problem together, or create a valuable innovation in a professional setting, keep in mind that there is a roadblock constantly in the picture: language. Language is an imperfect tool, and sometimes the message one person sends is not the same message another receives. Sometimes information gets lost in translation. People may speak different professional languages, per se, which makes this problem even more challenging. This can create real disconnects between understanding.

In contrast, one of the great powers of individual polymathic insights and innovations is that they are not dependent on language, necessarily. Someone can have a spark of insight, a new realization, or a groundbreaking idea that did not require language to reach that epiphany. Perhaps it is a picture that just popped in their head suddenly, or a moment of deep understanding beyond the language process.

While collaboration in groups will always be important for humanity to reach its shared potential, there is also power in bypassing the hurdle of language, through individual, preverbal insights. Of course, narrow specialists are also entirely capable of having these sorts of preverbal ideas, but their ability to create innovative insights will likely be limited within their single discipline. Polymaths, on the other hand, are well positioned to innovate at the intersection of multiple disciplines, and by harnessing their preverbal capacities, this could lead to tremendous progress that would never have been possible among a group of people, or by a single disciplinary specialist. Polymaths who are able to innovate in a preverbal sort of way, informed by a broad base of knowledge and experiences, are uniquely positioned to add particular value in our society.

How to Support Polymathic Exploration in a Business Context

So far, this chapter has helped to explain how most polymaths came to be that way, and provided some basic elements of what the experience of being polymathic is typically like, generally speaking. This next section will provide a few suggestions for how organizations can help elicit polymathic contributions from their employees.

1. **Create a Culture Where Intrapersonal Diversity Is Appreciated:** Of course, if you want to have a team made up, in part, of polymathic individuals, then a basic first step is to make it clear that you appreciate that kind of person. Executives can accomplish this through the storytelling they do, within their organization. Make it clear that diversity – in its many different forms—is appreciated—even diversity of thought, perspectives, and experiences that can exist within a single person. Be explicit that a core value within your organization is harnessing the power of narrow specialists and broad, polymathic generalists together. If you do not make this clear, then you run the risk of not being able to truly harness the talents of the polymaths that you may already have on your team—because they will not feel the freedom and support to contribute in polymathic ways. Be clear on this and create a culture where polymathy is articulated as something the business will tap into to help reach its fullest potential.

2. **See Mistakes as an Opportunity for Learning:** Another thing that executives should make clear to their employees is that it is okay to occasionally be human—to be imperfect. Actually, it is in those times that we can actually learn the most. Rather than criticizing employees—especially publicly—about shortcomings, leverage them to your collective advantage. Given polymaths are driven to continually learn, grow, and improve, doing this will be particularly appreciated by the polymaths on your team. If you view mistakes as an opportunity for organizational improvement, then your employees—especially the polymaths on your team—will feel freer to explore all the ways that they can contribute, rather than limiting the value that they can add, in an attempt to stay careful and safe.
3. **Pose Thoughtful Questions and Listen to the Answers You Receive:** One of the most important skills a leader should develop is the power to ask really thoughtful, poignant questions, and then be open to the answers that come in return. Polymaths are well positioned to make keen observations that you might not have considered before. They tend to be quite creative, especially given the broad variety of information and experiences that help to inform their perspectives. Listen to your employees, whether in formal "listening parties" or through informal watercooler conversations. Appreciate the unique perspectives the polymaths—and the specialists alike—bring to bear in tackling the difficult challenges in your organization. Those challenges may be day-to-day difficulties, or larger, strategic problems; in either case, focus on asking the right questions, and then you can get the right answers, potentially. If you do not ask the right questions, then you are not going to elicit the solutions your organization needs to thrive. Tap into the knowledge of the employees on your team—especially the polymaths who are eager to contribute to cocreating thoughtful, new solutions.
4. **Give Polymathic Employees Problems to Solve:** Polymaths are eager to use their capabilities; they want to add value. They want to be appreciated for what they bring to the table, professionally and otherwise. So, challenge them; give them an opportunity to rise to a challenge. They tend to appreciate being given a problem to solve. Remember that it is okay—and also quite strategic—to tap into the human resources on your team to the greatest extent possible;

polymaths are a resource that you can tap into especially to solve difficult problems. Give them as many resources as you reasonably can, to support them tackling the problem at hand. It is important to give polymaths challenges so they can use their talents, feel appreciated, and to develop their skills even further.

5. **Support Analogical Thinking:** Analogical thinking, as the name implies, is a type of reasoning using analogy; it frequently involves taking approaches or tools from one context and applying them in a new setting. This is a way to elicit creativity on your teams, and find innovative solutions, too. Polymaths tend to be natural analogical thinkers, given their broad base of knowledge and experiences. Make it clear that you are open to taking tools or approaches from one area of business—or even from outside of your organization—and applying them in a new context, in order to innovate. So, if you want to help support polymathic exploration, approaches, and solutions on your team, make it clear to those employees that you want them to actively engage in analogical thinking to the extent practicable. You may be surprised at the solutions that arise from this—and it helps a great deal to be very clear that analogical thinking is an approach you want your employees to engage in, for the sake of creativity and innovation.
6. **Support Flexibility:** When dealing with particularly complex challenges, it is crucial to allow your employees to have some amount of flexibility in determining how they can add value in the flurry of complexity around them. This allows them to focus on using their strengths. Polymaths tend to have a lot of capabilities as well, so allowing them flexibility in terms of how they do their work, the skills they bring to any given project, or in general how they show up, will be particularly valuable; if you try to reign them in too narrowly, then you may miss out on their full talent. Trust them to know how they can add value, and empower them to do so, to the greatest extent possible. Polymaths do not like being micromanaged, and they greatly appreciate having freedom to explore and express all that they are capable of, especially in a professional context. So, grant them flexibility to the greatest extent possible. If you run into

problems with a polymath not following through or coming up with solutions, then address that head-on. However, the point here is that if you start off trying to keep a polymath focused very narrowly, then that is counterproductive given that the whole point of being a polymath is that you have a lot of capabilities. Let them express all they are capable of—and an important element of allowing that to come to fruition is by granting them flexibility in how they do so, wherever possible.

7. **Encourage Authenticity:** One of the elements of being a polymath is being a real original; having a combination of interests, skills, experiences, and backgrounds that make someone quite unique, in his or her own right. If you want to tap into the full capacities of the polymaths on your team, then it behooves you to appreciate their unique "onlyness." Make it okay for your employees to be quirky and weird—for them to truly express who they really are. Doing so will ensure that, first and foremost, they feel comfortable at work—which is important. When people feel comfortable with being who they really are—when they can truly be authentic—then they will be happier and more engaged, and therefore much more likely to contribute. Unhappy employees do not tend to add as much value as happy ones do. Let people be different—let people be themselves. You can make this clear by the storytelling you do, by the example you set, and by the culture you cocreate in your business. Build a culture where people feel safe to be themselves, even if by society's standards, they are "weird." Make divergence an asset, not a liability, by appreciating everybody's unique essence and style.

More largely, it is important to create opportunities to support polymaths. If you really want to promote polymathic exploration in a business context so you can reap the rewards of their broad skills, then create tangible opportunities where polymaths, or those with polymathic potential, can be supported in very specific ways to both leverage and expand that part of their personhood. Be proactive in forging an environment where polymaths can thrive and watch the magic that can happen in your organization as a result.

Types of Polymathy: A Typology and a Reframe

Polymathy is not a binary identity that one either possesses or lacks—it exists on a spectrum and can vary by degree, life stage, or context. While some people are highly visible, high-achieving polymaths, many others express polymathic tendencies in quieter, less recognized ways. Before we dive into the many dimensions that make up the polymathic spectrum, it's helpful to understand that there are also different types of polymaths—ways that polymathy can show up depending on timing, context, or personal orientation.

Cambridge historian Peter Burke, a foundational thinker in polymathy studies, proposed a four-part typology that remains helpful for understanding these variations. He identifies four primary types[8]:

1. **Passive Polymaths**
   These individuals have a wide range of interests and read broadly across many disciplines, but they have built their professional reputation within a single field. Their polymathy shows up more in their personal curiosity than in their professional output.
2. **Limited Polymaths**
   These people are active in a small cluster of neighboring disciplines—such as sociology, philosophy, and history. Their knowledge and impact are significant, though typically concentrated in fields that naturally overlap.
3. **Serial Polymaths**
   Serial polymaths shift their focus over time, developing expertise in multiple areas across the course of their lives. Their polymathic journey is not simultaneous but sequential, marked by deep engagement with one field and then another.
4. **Proper Polymaths**
   Burke's final category refers to individuals who work across multiple distinct domains *simultaneously*, and who make significant contributions to each of those fields in real time.

[8] Burke, P. 2010. "The Polymath: A Cultural and Social History of an Intellectual Species." In *Explorations in Cultural History: Essays for Peter Gabriel McCaffery*, eds. D.F. Smith and H. Philosoph. Aberdeen: University of Aberdeen.

While Burke's categories are useful, the term "proper polymath" can feel unnecessarily hierarchical or exclusionary—as though only this final category represents "true" polymathy. In today's context, that language may do more harm than good by discouraging those who identify with other expressions of polymathic life.

As a more inclusive and contemporary alternative, I propose the term "Comprehensive Polymath." This phrasing preserves the original intent—describing individuals who integrate breadth and depth across multiple fields at once—without implying superiority. "Comprehensive" suggests wholeness and expansiveness, while avoiding the elitist connotation of being the *real* polymath.

This typology reminds us that there's no single path to polymathy. Whether one explores deeply and narrowly, widely and sequentially, or all at once, polymathic expression can be fluid. People may move between these categories across the course of their lives. A passive polymath in their twenties may become a comprehensive polymath by midlife. Or someone who was once a limited polymath may shift into serial polymathy as they change careers or passions.

Recognizing this variety helps us embrace polymathy as more than just a rare achievement—it is a form of human potential that can evolve. It also helps us avoid idealizing only one expression of polymathy (e.g., the Da Vinci archetype), and instead make room for many shapes, timelines, and flavors of multidimensionality.

The Polymath Spectrum

To complement Burke's perspective, I propose an additional framework: The Polymath Spectrum. Rather than classifying individuals into fixed types, the Polymath Spectrum conceptualizes polymathy as a developmental orientation that unfolds across stages of learning, identity formation, integration, and leadership. It recognizes that polymathic capacity can deepen and expand over time, and that individuals may move fluidly along this spectrum depending on context, opportunity, and life circumstances. The spectrum is not hierarchy of worth, nor a rigid ladder of advancement. Instead, it is a map of how polymathic potential often develops as curiosity broadens into exploration, exploration into integration, and integration into broader forms of influence and stewardship.

The stages of the Polymath Spectrum include:

1. The Latent Polymath
   "I'm curious, but I don't yet have permission."
   This stage represents the beginning of polymathic potential. Individuals at this stage often display wide curiosity, diverse interests, and a natural enthusiasm for learning across topics. However, social expectations and institutional pressures frequently encourage narrowing and specialization before this breadth is fully explored. Capacity exists, but the language and identity to support it have not yet formed.
2. The Emerging Polymath
   "I'm exploring, but I'm still apologizing."
   Exploration becomes more active at this stage. Individuals begin testing different interests, studying multiple subjects, or experimenting with different roles and identities. While connections across domains begin to form, coherence may still feel elusive. External validation often remains important, and many emerging polymaths wrestle with the familiar question: Should I just pick one thing?
3. The Practicing Polymath
   "I'm allowed to be many things."
   This stage marks a turning point. Individuals begin to embrace their breadth rather than suppress it. Learning becomes increasingly self-directed and interdisciplinary, extending beyond formal institutions into a lifelong practice of curiosity and connection. Identity integrity begins to form—not around a single specialty, but around a way of engaging with knowledge and the world.
4. The Integrative Polymath
   "I translate, connect, and make sense."
   Integration becomes the defining capability. Integrative polymaths move fluently across domains, synthesizing insights and identifying relationships others may overlook. They often serve as interpreters, strategists, or sensemakers within organizations and communities, helping bridge disciplinary silos and illuminate complex systems.

5. The Polymathic Leader
   "I design conditions for collective intelligence."
   At this stage, polymathy extends beyond the individual toward shaping environments that enable others to think and collaborate more effectively. Polymathic leaders build cultures, teams, and institutions that support interdisciplinary thinking, long-term perspective, and ethical responsibility. Their work focuses less on personal expertise and more on orchestrating collective intelligence.
6. The Polymathic Architect
   "I reimagine, design, and shape the architecture of knowledge itself."
   Polymathic architects operate at the level of paradigm and field-building. Their contributions may include reframing disciplines, creating new conceptual frameworks, or developing models that influence how knowledge is organized and applied. Their impact often unfolds gradually over time, shaping conversations and possibilities beyond their immediate context.

   The Polymath Spectrum should not be interpreted as a rigid progression. Individuals may move back and forth across stages depending on context, opportunity, or life circumstances. The spectrum is best understood as a developmental map, helping individuals and organizations recognize how polymathic capacity can emerge, mature, and contribute to society.

THE POLYMATH SPECTRUM

Latent → Emerging → Practicing → Integrative → Leader → Architect

Latent	Emerging	Practicing	Integrative	Leader	Architect
Hidden Potential	Exploring Many Interests	Owning Breadth & Depth	Connecting Ideas Across Fields	Designing Collective Intelligence	Field-Shaping Contribution

Polymathy as a Spectrum of Spectrums

Of course, by now you understand that polymathy exists on a spectrum. But here is a more nuanced way to think about it: some people are strong polymaths, while others are perhaps simply "polymathic" (with relatively weaker polymathic traits or achievements). Therefore, the word "polymathic" would be more appropriate in their case, rather than calling them "a" polymath. "A polymath" should, in my opinion, be reserved for the strongest cases, the people most distinguished across domains. The adjective, "polymathic," shows a lesser degree of achievement whereas the noun, "polymath," is more of a designation—a sign of significant, multidisciplinary achievement.

In trying to understand how polymathy shows up in people, and the different ways it can be expressed, it is important to consider the most holistic approach possible. Here are some of the different ways that polymathy can be expressed. On the polymath spectrum, it is a spectrum of spectrums—each one of these dimensions being stronger or weaker, depending on the individual at hand.

- **Self-Aware versus Unaware Polymathy:** Some people are fully cognizant of their polymathy and even use the word itself in describing their personhood, while others do not have a label for it or even ownership over that part of their identity—even if objectively, someone from the outside would say that person is polymathic or "a" polymath. There are varying degrees of self-awareness in terms of one's own polymathy.
- **Repressed versus Expressed Polymathy:** Some people may naturally be polymathic, but they withhold that sort of expression, perhaps because of society or familial pressures to specialize, for example. Polymathy can be repressed or expressed in varying degrees, depending on the person. In this dimension, someone has an awareness of their polymathic tendencies, but they choose to withhold it (which can be for a variety of reasons).
- **Personality Disposition versus Polymathic Achievements:** Some people might be polymathic when considering their capacities, without actually expressing those capacities in significant ways—in terms of their accomplishments. They may have the *potential* to be a great polymath without actually pursuing that potential—in other words, there is a

lack of follow-through. In some circles, this is called being a "multipotentialite," denoting the potential to become "multi." This is different than repressed or expressed polymathy; in the former case, the person has an awareness of their own polymathic tendencies but chooses to repress it while in the latter, they simply lack the follow-through to implement their potential. The point here is that polymathy is, in a way, a disposition—a capacity; and that capacity *may* lead to polymathic achievement or *not*, regardless of a person's level of comfort expressing or not expressing their polymathy.

- **Ownership of One's Polymathy:** Some polymathic people also feel self-conscious to claim they are a polymath, so they avoid using the word to describe themselves. For example, they may feel it is too great a word to claim—that they would be somehow boasting if they were to claim their own polymathy to other people. In other words, there are varying degrees of ownership over polymathic identity, as such.
- **Internal versus External Validation through Polymathic Pursuits:** Some polymathic people use their polymathy—being excellent and pursuing many different vocations and avocations—as a way to gain acclaim and to be more "valid" in the eyes of others—to be "successful." Yet other polymathic people simply love learning and experiencing so much, that their polymathic pursuits have very little to do with external validation, and everything to do with internal enjoyment—wanting to be the best, most informed person they can be, for the sake and joy of learning itself. Many polymaths who prefer externally validated sources will seek out credentials and degrees through their polymathic learnings—the type of stuff they could put on their résumés—whereas others pursue learning even if it is not information that they would necessarily advertise in a professional context.
- **Breadth of Knowledge and Talents:** Some polymaths tend to focus their learning on fields of study that are clustered relatively close to one another, whereas others have interests or professions that are more dissimilar in nature. For example,

someone might be artistic through painting, music, and dance, and not have much exposure to the sciences. Or someone may have professional experience in accounting and procurement, which are relative neighbors, both related to finance. Although the people in these examples are technically polymathic because they have breadth in their pursuits, they are all relatively "close" in terms of their subject matters. In contrast, another polymathic person might be an expert in mathematics while also having expertise in psychology; these two fields are farther apart, and so the versatility of talents the person in this latter example has is greater. This does not mean that one is better than the other—it just means that when thinking of polymathic people, and looking at the knowledge and skills they possess, it is worth noting how "different" the subjects are, at their command, versus how similar they are in nature. Polymathy, of course, can show up in many different forms and combinations, including the level of *breadth* or *versatility* of a person's talents.

- **Degree of Depth:** Some polymaths strive to be truly excellent—to have notable depth in each of the multiple fields they pursue. Others may be very deep in one field, while more shallow in second and third fields. Other "polymathic" people might be more average in terms of the level of depth in any given field. Understanding that the level of expertise polymaths possess in any given area is another way of understanding their unique combination that makes up their polymathy.
- **Intellectual versus Experiential Polymathy:** Some polymaths prefer for their learning to come in intellectual forms—through reading, classes, cerebral conversations, and other cognitively driven pursuits. Others, however, gravitate toward more experiential learning—engaging in travel, adventure, sports, and hands-on activities. The former approach is more "head," while the latter is more "body," reflecting differences in how individuals absorb and engage with knowledge. These tendencies align with broader theories

of learning styles and preferences, where some people thrive in structured, abstract, or theoretical learning environments, while others learn best through direct experience, physical engagement, or immersion in real-world contexts. Many polymaths incorporate both approaches to varying degrees, blending intellectual and experiential learning in ways that suit their unique curiosities and life experiences.

- **Vocational versus Avocational Polymathy:** Another way of asking this: is the person's polymathy mostly expressed through work or hobbies? Some polymaths are highly focused on professional pursuits—and they want to concentrate their learning on subjects that pertain only to work or academic settings—where information being learned is productive, somehow. On the other hand, some polymaths are very enthusiastic about pursuing their polymathy through their hobbies—through having enriching experiences outside of work. This is another distinguishing factor when trying to understand the different ways that polymathy shows up in people.
- **Serial versus Concurrent Polymathic Pursuits:** Another way to understand how someone pursues their polymathy has to do with time: do they pursue multiple, different endeavors at the same or at different times? Although many polymaths tend to juggle many different types of learning and exploration at the same time, others may have "seasons" of polymathic exploration and expression rather than managing them concurrently.
- **Humility versus Pride in One's Polymathy:** Another differentiation you will see among various polymaths is: how proud are they, or not, of their polymathic capacities? Some polymaths are very proud—even condescending toward others. They are proud of their intellect and achievements, and in a sort of superior or snobbish way. Yet others are proud, but somehow manage not to be offensive to others even as they express the pride and confidence they have in their own knowledge and talents. Other polymaths are

quite humble, even though they may be extremely capable and accomplished. This is another "flavor" of polymathic expression to be considered.

- **Predictable versus Unexpected Combinations:** Another way that polymathic expression shows up is in regard to whether there is an element of surprise or not, in someone's combination. Are they multifaceted in ways that you might expect for them to be, or are there unforeseen elements of their personhood? For example, someone might not expect a person who has a PhD in physics and who is a professional physics researcher and professor, to also be a professional magician, covered in tattoos. Or you might not expect an author of adult education books to also ride motorcycles. On the other hand, you might *not* be surprised to find that someone who is a mathematician also enjoys baking and playing piano. Some combinations are more or less surprising than others, and this is another way of understanding polymathic expression in different people.
- **Introverted versus Extroverted Polymathy:** Some polymaths prefer very individual, introverted pursuits; for example, they like to read a book, watch videos, or do other forms of learning—or even work—in isolation. They find this more energizing than being in more social settings to learn or work. Other people may want to explore and express their polymathy through more social settings, in groups; they might want to learn in a class that includes discussion or exercises with other learners, or they might enjoy projects at work that are group-based, and find that process energizing. This is another dimension that creates different "flavors" of polymathic expression.
- **Argumentative versus Agreeable Polymathy:** Just like human beings who are not polymathic, of course, a person may tend toward agreeableness versus argumentativeness, overall. Although polymaths tend to be excellent critical thinkers, not all of them are argumentative and may tend to keep their opinions and observations to themselves, rather

than rocking the boat by disagreeing with the people around them. Others are high in contrarianism. Some polymaths enjoy debating or even arguing with others, whereas others prefer not to.

- **Inclusive versus Elitist Polymathy:** Some polymaths, especially ones who are very strong in their polymathy, may tend toward elitism—that is, wanting to keep polymathy relegated only to a very small fraction of humanity, making it off limits to anyone who does not "fit in" with their brand of polymathic expression. They essentially reject people who may be less polymathic, and do not embrace them as equals. Although relatively rare, it is important to understand that some people may try to feel "more than" others through their polymathic intelligence or accomplishments, whereas other polymaths may trend toward being more inclusive in this regard.
- **Level of Resiliency:** Although resiliency is not a capacity only expressed by polymathic people, it is something worth noting with polymaths in particular. In this age of specialization, polymaths are somewhat daring—they break the mold and forge their own paths in unique, bricolage ways. This takes some self-determination, self-authoring, bravery, and of course, resilience—to cope with the challenges involved with going against the grain, to some extent. Because of this, it is very uncommon to find a highly accomplished polymath who has a "victim mentality." Most polymaths feel empowered to learn and grow, even in the face of challenges. Polymaths tend to take risks, take responsibility, and take action; they are not victims of their circumstances, they are victors who rise to the occasion, even in the face of challenges. Of course, some polymaths may have more or less resiliency, in this regard—so this is another way that difference can show up among different polymaths.
- **Daring versus Cautious Exploration and Expression:** Another "flavor" of polymathy shows up in terms of how daring or cautious someone is in exploring and expressing

their polymathy. Polymathy itself involves learning and trying new things. While some people are very comfortable "going for it," or "breaking the mold," others are more self-conscious, and cautious, in doing so. Some polymaths may feel comfortable just "jumping into the deep end," so to speak, and "figuring things out as they go." Alternatively, others may prefer to "dip their toes in" first, have a "plan of attack," and just prepare as much as possible before embarking on a new venture or project, for example. Given polymaths, on the whole, tend to be brave—especially given that we are in the age of specialization and they are the opposite of specialists, thus in the minority—most polymaths tend toward being "daring." That said, not every polymathic person is going to be daring in their approach to living and learning, so it is worth noting that this is another differentiator among polymathic people. Some polymaths may be more careful and tempered in their approach to their polymathic learning and expression even if, on the whole, being polymathic in the age of specialization is, in and of itself, a daring act.

- **Degree of Autodidacticism:** An autodidact is someone who is self-taught. Some people are more skilled at teaching themselves information than others. Self-directed learning is a common theme among polymaths. Self-directed learning essentially means that a person sets the *agenda* for what they want to learn about—even if they end up learning information from a teacher, mentor, "more knowledgeable other," video, website, book, and so on. There are varying degrees to which someone can rely on an outside person or source of information to learn. However, since polymaths are good at learning—that is what they do—most tend to be both *self-directed* and *autodidactic* in their approach to learning.
- **Integrating Knowledge:** Polymaths, by definition, know many things, across subjects. Some polymaths, however, struggle to integrate their learnings, while others are, indeed,

able to apply lessons, tools, techniques, and approaches from one field to another (this is known as analogical thinking). This is where the power of polymathy can really pay off, by giving rise to creativity and through synthesis. Synthesis is not necessarily easy, though, so polymaths may vary in terms of their ability to exercise this particular superpower.

- **Degree of Openness to Experience:** A critical hallmark of polymathy is that a person, as a general rule, is fairly open to experiences. Openness to Experience is part of the "Big Five" personality traits and has been heavily studied in academia; it is also measurable. Of course, exactly how open to experiences a polymath is will vary from person to person. This human phenomenon exists on a spectrum, whereby some individuals are more open, and others are less open—naturally. It is worth clarifying, however, that openness to experience and polymathy are not equivalent constructs. Someone could be open to experiences, theoretically, and not actually follow-through to explore or develop their polymathic talents. However, openness to experience is a necessary precursor to becoming a polymath; it is very unlikely that an accomplished polymath would be low in openness to experience.
- **Degree of Imposter Syndrome:** Many polymaths sometimes feel "Imposter Syndrome." Especially when they compare themselves to narrow specialists in the age of specialization, they can feel "less than" in comparison, because perhaps they do not have quite the same degree of depth as their specialist counterparts do. Being aware of this is important when trying to understand polymaths—and it is also another distinguishing measure, when looking at any given polymath, compared to others. Some may have more "Imposter Syndrome" while others may have less.

The Bottom Line of This Chapter

This chapter provided an overview of how many people develop their polymathy—the factors that influence their polymathic development—and also explained what it is like to be a polymathic person, in general. Understanding the origins and experiences of polymaths is crucial to appreciating their unique contributions.

Key Takeaways Include

- **Nature and Nurture:** Polymathy results from a combination of innate curiosity and environmental influences. Both supportive and challenging environments can foster polymathic tendencies.
- **Financial Resources:** Both abundance and scarcity of financial resources can drive polymathic development, either by enabling diverse opportunities or necessitating self-reliance and resourcefulness.
- **Family Dynamics:** Both nurturing and dysfunctional family backgrounds can inspire polymathic growth through different motivational pathways.
- **Polymathic Values:** Common values among polymaths include a strong desire for freedom, continuous learning, variety, self-improvement, and bravery.
- **Intelligence and Learning:** While polymaths tend to be intelligent, their success is more about their commitment to lifelong, lifewide, self-directed learning, than just innate talent.
- **Spectrum of Polymathy:** Polymathy exists on a spectrum, with individuals exhibiting varying degrees and forms of polymathic expression. This includes different combinations of breadth and depth in knowledge and skills.
- **Types of Polymathy:** Different types include passive, limited, serial, and proper polymaths, each with distinct ways of integrating and applying their diverse knowledge.
- **Polymath Identity:** Forming a polymathic identity can be challenging in a specialized world, and polymaths often navigate feelings of being misunderstood or underappreciated.

- **Openness to Experience:** Polymaths are generally high in openness to experience, which drives their broad learning and curiosity.
- **Self-Directed Learning:** Polymaths take ownership of their learning journey, often engaging in both intentional and incidental learning.
- **Time Management:** Effective time management is crucial for polymaths to juggle their multiple interests and pursuits successfully.
- **Supporting Polymathy in Organizations:** Organizations can support polymaths by creating a culture that values intrapersonal diversity, viewing mistakes as learning opportunities, asking thoughtful questions, giving polymaths problems to solve, supporting analogical thinking, providing flexibility, and encouraging authenticity.

Understanding these elements of polymathy is essential for recognizing and leveraging the unique strengths that polymaths bring to both their personal lives and professional settings. By fostering an environment that appreciates and nurtures polymathic talent, organizations can tap into a powerful resource for innovation, creativity, and continuous improvement.

Chapter 2 Reflection Questions and Discussion Prompts

Exploring the Nature of Polymathy

1. How do you define polymathy? Do you see it as an identity, a skill set, or a way of thinking?
2. Have you ever felt drawn to multiple disciplines? If so, how have you navigated this in your life and career?
3. Do you think polymathy is an innate trait, or can it be cultivated over time?
4. What are some common misconceptions about polymathy that you have encountered?

Polymathy and the Spectrum of Learning

1. Polymathy exists on a spectrum, from general curiosity to mastery across multiple fields. Where do you see yourself on this spectrum?
2. How do you balance depth and breadth in your learning and professional development?
3. Have you ever experienced a shift in your learning approach, such as moving from a specialist mindset to a more polymathic one?
4. Do you think polymathy is becoming more or less valued in today's world? Why?

Polymath Identity and Self-Perception

1. Do you identify as a polymath or polymathic person? Why or why not?
2. How comfortable are you with the idea of being a generalist versus a specialist?
3. Have you ever hesitated to embrace your polymathic nature due to societal or professional pressures?
4. If you struggle with imposter syndrome, do you think it is linked to your polymathic tendencies?

Polymathy and the Role of Curiosity

1. What role has curiosity played in your learning journey?
2. How do you nurture and sustain your curiosity over time?
3. Have you ever suppressed your curiosity due to external pressures or expectations? How did that impact you?
4. In what ways does curiosity contribute to creativity and problem-solving in your personal or professional life?

The Influence of Environment on Polymathy

1. Reflecting on your upbringing, how did your family or educational background influence your learning style?
2. Do you think financial resources (or lack thereof) helped or hindered your ability to explore multiple disciplines?
3. Have you ever had a mentor or role model who encouraged polymathic thinking? How did they impact your growth?
4. What aspects of your environment (workplace, social circle, access to resources) support or challenge your polymathic nature?

Supporting Polymathy in the Workplace

1. Does your workplace encourage exploration beyond job descriptions? If not, how could it do so?
2. How can businesses benefit from employing polymathic individuals?
3. What challenges might polymaths face in a structured corporate setting? How can organizations better support them?
4. How can leaders create a company culture that values interdisciplinary skills and problem-solving?

Time Management and Productivity for Polymaths

1. Polymaths often struggle with juggling multiple interests. How do you prioritize your learning and professional pursuits?
2. Have you ever felt overwhelmed by your diverse interests? How do you manage this feeling?

3. What strategies have you found useful in maintaining focus while still honoring your polymathic tendencies?
4. How does your approach to time management influence your ability to pursue multiple fields or projects?

Polymathy and Personal Fulfillment

1. Do you pursue polymathy for external validation (e.g., degrees, career success) or for personal fulfillment?
2. How has having diverse interests enriched your personal life beyond work and education?
3. Have you ever felt isolated due to having a broad range of interests? How do you connect with like-minded people?
4. What advice would you give to someone who wants to embrace polymathy but feels hesitant or unsure how to start?

Polymathy and the Future

1. With the rise of AI and automation, do you think polymaths will become more valuable in the workforce? Why or why not?
2. How do you see polymathy evolving in the coming decades?
3. If polymathy were more widely recognized and encouraged, how do you think society would change?
4. What steps can you take today to more fully embrace your polymathic potential?

CHAPTER 3

Polymathy and the Family

"I don't want to get to the end of my life and find that I lived just the length of it. I want to have lived the width of it as well."

—David Ackerman

Although this book is intended for a business audience, and more specifically for professionals who want to understand polymathic talent so they can manage and leverage it strategically within their organizations, it is important to also understand how polymaths came to be that way as people first. So, the purpose of this chapter is to understand how families and upbringings impact polymaths as people—and therefore how they show up to work as professionals. Afterall, employees are human beings; you cannot separate who a person is, their background—their story—from the "professional" persona they express at work. We all bring our histories along with us, wherever we go—including to our jobs. As Chester Barnard said, "we hire people for their skills but the whole person shows up for work."[1]

If you are in business, and you want to truly understand your polymathic employees—how to keep them engaged, maintain high employee morale, minimize turnover, and maximize the use of your human capital—then it is critical that you care about your employees not just as tools, but as real people. You must view your employees as unique individuals who each have their own perspectives, feelings, and experiences that impact how they show up at work on a daily basis.

Even though each person is unique, and their life stories and upbringings were experienced through their own, singular lens, there do seem

[1] McDonald, B., and Hutcheson, D. 2017. *Don't Waste Your Talent: The 8 Critical Steps to Discovering What you do Best.* The Highlands Company.

to be trends in how different polymaths came to be polymathic people today. This chapter will review some of those themes that are consistent among different polymaths when it comes to their personal and family lives. Hopefully, this information will help you understand your polymathic employees as real people a bit more deeply.

There are some important questions to consider in this regard, to understand the trends that we see among polymaths as a group, when it comes to their family lives. For example, what in a polymath's upbringing impacted their development into a polymathic person? Indeed, there are some consistent motifs in the stories that polymaths tell in this regard. And how would those experiences in a polymath's upbringing impact how they show up professionally? For that reason, this chapter is dedicated to polymathy and the family. Because if you are an organizational leader, it is critical to understand the human element of your staff so that you can more fully and genuinely understand the polymathic professionals on your team as people first and engage with them as members of your team accordingly from that vantage point.

Family Influence on the Emergence of Polymathy

In my research on polymaths, one of the consistent storylines I heard from them is that their upbringing strongly impacted who they are today. This is probably true for anyone, not just polymaths. But one interesting facet of what I heard from real-life, accomplished, modern-day polymaths is that whether their upbringing was dysfunctional or functional, they could still become polymathic people as adults.

For instance, for the people who came from dysfunctional families, developing their own polymathy was almost always a way "out" of a difficult situation. By developing skills, knowledge, and capabilities, their own polymathy was something that helped them get a ticket out of tough circumstances; their polymathy gave them options. And so, for some people, a very difficult upbringing actually *helped* make them polymathic. Their difficult upbringing motivated them to create options for themselves, and the way to create those options was by having more tools in their toolkits, so to speak. Said differently, the way for these individuals to have options for a better future was to become polymathic. This is an important point to understand.

An added benefit of polymathic learning is that it often served as a mental escape for those whose environment on a day-to-day basis was challenging. Reading, of course, was a way to mentally go to a different "place" and in the process, learn, too. Many polymathic children in harsh environments frequently became avid readers, and this became a habit that usually stuck with them for life. Of course, readers are learners.

However, the opposite could also be true—that a pleasant environment could facilitate the development of a child's polymathy. For people who came from very healthy, "normal" households, many people reported that it was precisely this kind of supportive, nurturing environment that helped develop their polymathy. By having caregivers who lovingly supported the child to explore his or her interests, this could also *help* that child become polymathic.

The point here is that you cannot assume if you have a polymathic employee, that they must have had a traditional family constellation, wonderful parents, and an easy childhood. And alternatively, you cannot assume that a polymathic employee on your team had a difficult upbringing either. The fact is that polymaths can come from healthy, functional backgrounds, or from dysfunctional, difficult ones. That said, although you may never know all the facets of your employees' childhoods—since probably most employees do not divulge that kind of information in a professional setting, typically—it is important to keep in the back of your mind that regardless of whether or not that employee's upbringing was more positive or negative, on the whole, that the way they were raised definitely did impact who they became as adults. And their histories also influence how they show up professionally, too—even if they do not talk about it.

Financial Resources and Polymathy

Another interesting finding of my research is that financial resources also had a similar split pattern, just like the family influence discussed in the last section did. In other words, whether someone had little financial resources, or a lot of financial resources, they could still become polymathic people. Financial resources are closely tied to family experience, so this dimension warrants a brief additional discussion here.

For example, some polymaths explained that they grew up poor. And it was because they did not have money to outsource certain tasks to others to take care of, that they were forced to learn new skills to fix various problems that arose. For example, if someone needed car repairs, but could not afford to hire a mechanic, that might have forced that person to learn how to do the repair himself or herself. And because of that experience, the person developed a new skill set along their polymath journey. Or, as another example, a polymathic person might have wanted to learn about a certain topic, but not be able to afford a tutor or class to explore that subject more. So, as a result of the limited financial resources, that child might have explored reading books from the local library or researching the topic on the Internet (or through various other low-cost means), to teach themselves what they wanted to know. In other words, growing up with limited financial resources could actually help someone develop their own polymathy, and adopt polymathic behaviors such as self-directed learning.

But the opposite is also true: children whose families had a lot of financial resources could also become polymathic as a result of having money at their disposal; this allowed them to more easily pay for lessons, classes, tutors, travel, hobbies, sports, and so on. Indeed, having financial resources could make it easier, in some ways, for someone to explore their polymathy; having money readily available to spend on learning and exploring new skills would help that person become more polymathic.

And the reciprocal relationship between finances impacting polymathy was true as well: for people who are already polymathic, their polymathy influences their finances, too. On one hand, their polymathy could save them money, because it would mean that person can do more themselves, without having to pay others to take care of skill-based work for them. For instance, a polymath does not have to pay someone to do electrical or carpentry work at their house, because those are areas of competency for the person already. Alternatively, because a polymath has so many interests, they might easily spend a lot of money (rather than save it), because a particular hobby might require spending money to purchase supplies or experiences. For other polymathic people, not having resources could also limit their polymathic explorations if they could not figure out a way to learn or experience something due to a lack of financial backing to do so. Clearly, even for people who are polymathic, there is a strong, dyadic relationship between their polymathy and their finances.

Another thing to be aware of is that for adults who are polymathic, some do so out of need or even desperation. In other words, having a main job with side hustles, gigging one's way through life to make ends meet—is a kind of polymathic expression—even if out of desperation or survival needs. Although having multiple professional endeavors to make enough money to get by does not mean that someone is highly accomplished in any of those endeavors, necessarily, juggling multiple professional hats is polymathic in nature. And it is worth noting that sometimes those efforts are not by choice, or for the pure joy of those multiple endeavors—sometimes it is a way of navigating through life to reach your financial (or other) goals. Sometimes polymathic pursuits are stressful.

In sum, finances are something that can force, facilitate, or even limit polymathic exploration—it just depends on the situation at hand and the person involved. What is common among everyone interviewed, though, is that money definitely has a relationship with polymathy in one way or another; it is something that polymaths must consider as they journey through life.

How to Encourage Polymathic Behaviors in Someone Else

Given this chapter is focused on polymathy and the family, you may be wondering how parents might purposefully choose to instill polymathic attitudes and behaviors in their children. And interestingly, the fact is that some of those very approaches might also apply to professionals in the workplace, as well. As a business leader, you can encourage polymathic values in your employees, based on the "lessons learned" from how parents of successful polymaths fostered polymathic approaches in their children. There are two main ways polymaths reported that this could be done—how others could help support their developing polymathic skills.

The first practice is through purposefully facilitating ***exposure*** to a variety of different types of people, subjects, and experiences; variety is key. In fact, adult polymaths explained that, interestingly, almost all of them had parents who were very different from one another. Not a single polymath who was interviewed reported that their parents had a lot in common in terms of their capabilities and interests. For example, perhaps mom was a skilled artist and dad was an accomplished engineer. Or perhaps both parents were also polymathic—unique and perhaps unexpected combinations of skills and capabilities. Sometimes, it was even a sibling who helped a child learn. But the point here is that it appears that having relatives, especially parents, who are very different from one another supported a child becoming more polymathic. This makes perfect sense because what this means is that the child had a broader base of exposure by having a mom and dad who were ***not*** like one another. This just allowed more opportunities for the child to learn about a broader array of subjects. Alternatively, if someone's mom and dad were very alike, that would mean the possible exposure to varying sets of experience and knowledge would be more limited and narrower, thus making it harder for the child to be exposed to a variety of topics on a day-to-day basis in the home.

This observation could be applied to the workplace as well. If you would like to develop more team members with polymathic talents and approaches, then it is important to allow your employees to be exposed and have significant exchanges with people who come from a variety of backgrounds, departments, and roles within the organization (or even outside of the company). Through those exchanges, the employee will learn increasingly more about the perspectives and practices of different people seeing organizational issues through different lenses. That person can learn through osmosis, over time. But if the employee only engages with others doing similar work, in the same department, who might happen to see issues from the same perspective, then the chances of this learning through osmosis will be diminished. Being exposed to diversity of thoughts and perspectives is important so employees do not exist in echo chambers. So, the bottom line here is this: allow and even encourage employees to purposefully engage with team members from different departments so they can expand what they know, and possibly even cross-fertilize ideas. Actually, that very exposure could even lead to an added bonus, which is collaborative business innovations.

The second way that polymaths said their parents helped their polymathy emerge was through caretakers who encouraged the child to engage in *self-directed learning*, without too much advice or "management" of the child's interests. In other words, by not directing, but mostly just allowing a person to freely explore, this could help them develop their own polymathy. Certainly, a parent might interact and support a child learning about something, but the selection of *what* to learn about was chosen by the child. Self-directed learning basically means that the individual learner is at the forefront of their own learning as opposed to the onus being mostly on a teacher, tutor, mentor, or peers to guide their learning journey; the individual is more personally responsible for his or her own development. It is a concept that emphasizes human capacity, the ability to change one's own behavior, and self-evaluation as opposed to these facets coming from external sources.[2] This is not to say that the child would not learn from others, because self-directed learning may certainly involve seeking out more knowledgeable people from which to learn. But the differentiator is that the child set their own learning agenda—and that is critical.

In other words, by simply supporting the child to follow their curiosity, a child could naturally explore in a polymathic kind of way, over time. And in this way, the child would also learn about taking ownership over their own self-directed learning paths, rather than becoming dependent on others setting the agenda for what a child learns. Sadly, however, this is how most schools operate: memorize what a teacher tells you and learn what the instructor says, rather than supporting the child to follow and learn about what seems most interesting or useful to him or her (and as a result, probably much easier to absorb, remember, and apply).

---

[2] Danis, C. 1992. "Advances in Research and Practice in Self-Directed Learning." In *Guideposts to Self-Directed Learning: Expert Commentary on Essential Concepts,* eds. G.J. Confessore and S.U. Confessore, 160–174. King of Prussia, PA: Organization Design and Development.

So, supporting self-directed learning of a child is one way that polymaths reported that a caregiver could help the child to become polymathic.

The same rule could also be applied to business leaders. Rather than dictating the kind of training or stretch assignments an employee "should" take in any given role, or what they must learn alone to do well in your organization, what if managers supported the employee to also follow their curiosity instead, to drive their own development, even if those topic areas seemed, on the surface, unrelated to the professional role in the company? Connections between those subject areas might be drawn in unexpected ways that might make the business more innovative or competitive precisely because of allowing for this flexibility and freedom in the employee's developmental journey. And it would probably lead to the employee feeling much happier about their own professional development, given they had individual agency in determining what they learn about, rather than being driven to learn about something someone else decided that they should. These sorts of learning explorations might also lead someone to want to strike up a new avenue of work altogether—in which case, this would advance their polymathy even further. The bottom line here is that suggestions for what an employee should focus on, in terms of their learning, may be helpful, as managers can certainly recommend areas an employee might consider focusing on, to expand their knowledge base. But there is also something to be said for the value in letting a grown adult have a say in their own learning and development, too.

Behaviors That Diminish Polymathy in Others

Interestingly, some interviewees reported that family sometimes had a negative impact on their polymathy. In fact, several respondents shared that they had dysfunctional families. One interviewee said that in her youth, her parents encouraged her polymathic pursuits, wanting her to be a well-rounded youngster, but as an adult, they were her biggest "roadblock," as they wanted her to pick one field and stick to it with more dedication. "Felicity" said, "My parents are the biggest doubters of me. It is hard for them. … They never encouraged my photography. But I don't know if they actively discouraged it. The great thing about my parents is that they always encourage education … I would say they are my biggest roadblocks." In other words, Felicity's parents thought that her exploration was fine as a youngster, but as an adult, she needed to focus in one area—and they felt a focus in a STEM field was much more worthy than in the arts. Felicity went on to share, "They totally shaped who I am, and yet I as an adult need to be a very focused, career-oriented woman. … What they think I should be doing with my time is different from what I know that I need to do with my time to fulfill both sides. They only want to hear about the job and the good girl stuff."

Felicity's parents sound like most of today's modern employers, who want to see a story of narrow specialization and a consistent story on a résumé. In fact, most of the time, if someone's résumé does not appear to be very specialized for a certain kind of role, that person might not even get an interview. So, if you, as a business leader, hire and develop employees with the idea that they need to be "focused" very narrowly, then you may not reap the rewards that polymathy can bring. It may seem counterintuitive to hire people who have not only deeply specialized in one area alone. What is important to note is that if you have certain kinds of roles in your company that polymathic people are well-suited for, then allow them to be broad in their approach to learning and work. Encourage and foster this kind of exploration, so that that person may bloom into their fullest, most polymathic selves, and so your business can reap the rewards of their multidimensional knowledge.

Juggling Polymathy With Relationships and Parenthood

Interestingly, the majority of polymaths I interviewed did not have children. One explanation is, it may be easier for someone to explore their polymathy more fully if they do not also have to juggle the responsibilities of parenthood and committed romantic relationships. The interviewee called "Dianna" shared, "Privilege; like the fact that I can jump from job to job because I don't have a spouse or a partner, you know, a husband who needs me to have benefits, and I don't have kids that I have to do something for, I [don't] have to live in a certain area. There's a hefty amount of privilege involved in being able to bounce around as much as I do and try the things I'm trying." It may be the case that it is easier to become a polymath or maintain polymathy without children, though some polymaths certainly do successfully juggle parenthood and their multifaceted careers and interests. For others, the very act of being a parent is polymathic in nature, because it allows for an important part of the human experience itself to be had, and moms and dads can learn a lot throughout the adventures of parenthood.

As it relates, dating as a polymath—finding the right partner—seemed a challenge for several of the people who were interviewed. Although this was not something that was asked about in the interview protocol, several interviewees mentioned it on their own. Trinity said,

> It's hard to date … because normally you find someone who only fulfills one part of you or one aspect. It's hard … my experience has been: it's hard … [My polymathy] definitely impacted who I chose to marry. I was explicit with my husband that I am a polymath because I wanted to marry someone who could handle me making sharp turns in my career and my life to follow passions that might seem disparate … someone who would not get easily shaken off, someone who was thrilled by it rather than terrified of it.

Finding a partner as a polymath seems difficult due, in part, to the fact that a polymath who has multiple unique aspects to his or her lifestyle and personality would require a partner who could understand and support those interests even as they change over time; finding such a person was not easy to do for the participants who talked about their love lives. Despite the challenges of navigating romantic relationships as a polymath, several respondents did mention that they had found partners successfully and were able to maintain long-term relationships with them. Based on what participants shared, however, it seems the key is finding a partner who is understanding and can be flexible as the polymath's identity (or multiple identities) evolves through the years, is key.

Further, although family was frequently something that encouraged polymathy in interviewees as young adults, as discussed previously, family sometimes also became a factor for suppression of polymathy later in adulthood as respondents tried to juggle the responsibilities of family life with the time demands of their polymathic interests. Consider what "Sebastian" shared as an example of this:

> It is all the more complicated now that I'm a parent. I knew what success looked like … I have known what success looks like in varying valances in my career over time. That … and this is sort of trite and stereotypical, but it's true, your sense of self and your vision for yourself radically shift if and when you become a parent, even if you're a poor or an absent or a necessarily absent parent. The prioritization just shifts. … I can't travel as much. I can't consult as much. I can't go to work nearly as much. If I want to be the parent that I want to be, and potentially my children need me to be, I really need to say no a lot more. And as … let's just call me a professional polymath, that's really … hard. We talked about other valances, but that difficulty … My varying work brings in a lot of the money that pays a lot of our bills, so it is a financial and a psychic struggle to be the professional that I want to be while also being the parent that I want to be.

Certainly, juggling multiple polymathic interests or professional responsibilities could be challenging alone, but add in the demands of family life, and it can make navigating all of that at once a real challenge.

In addition to how difficult one's polymathy could be with the pressures of being a parent, there were also implications for how one's polymathic pursuits could affect one's marriage. In fact, one interviewee discussed how pursuing his polymathic interests was a strain on his marriage, since he would spend so much time on his individual interests, and not enough time with his wife. Eventually, his resolution to this problem was to reduce his solitary pursuits and find more interests to pursue with his wife, together. In retrospect, he described the time-consuming exploration of his interests in the past, which he did alone, as "selfish" in the context of being married. This might also apply to polymaths who might not be married, but who have significant relationships that require notable time commitments. Taken together, it appears that being polymathic in the context of family life seemed difficult to navigate, especially in adulthood.

So, for a business leader who may have polymathic employees who are also married or are parents, keep in mind that this kind of juggling is a regular part of their experience as well. They must constantly prioritize how they spend their time, whether at work, at home, or elsewhere. Of course, this is true for anybody, but this kind of time management is particularly relevant for people who juggle a lot at once, like polymaths often do. This is something that leadership in an organization should be cognizant of.

Change and Polymathy

An interesting comment several of my interviewees shared is that they moved frequently as children; this sort of change was a regular part of their experience growing up. Remarkably, they all attributed that aspect of their childhood as something that spurred on their polymathy more. For example, an interviewee with the pseudonym "Dianna" said:

> In third grade, though, we moved to Illinois from New Jersey, and my whole world was uprooted because my dad had to get transferred at his job. … And we were there maybe six months, then we moved to upstate New York for a year, two different locations up there, so I had to learn how to be adapting to new friends, new situations, and that built in a resilience in me. … I think the moving around in middle school fostered this resilience.

Since moving frequently as a child required them to spend more time in alone-play and exploration, participants reported developing a sense of resilience, because each move required making new friends. Similarly, "Kevin" said that moving around frequently made him more "independent."

There might be lessons here for business leaders as well. For instance, could it be that job rotations would naturally support someone not only developing a broader array of skill sets but also becoming more "resilient" and "independent" over time, too (much the way that moving as children could do that)? As you consider the kinds of competencies you want to see in your employees, also consider how you can strategically help create an environment that fosters those very aptitudes; regulating the pace and types of change in your organization can be one lever that you push and pull on that might have ramifications for the proficiencies your staff develop as a result.

The Bottom Line of This Chapter

This chapter has delved into the family life of polymaths, revealing the various factors that shape their development and how these insights can inform organizational leaders in supporting polymathic employees.

Key Points Include

- **Diverse Family Backgrounds:** Polymaths can emerge from both functional and dysfunctional families. Their upbringing significantly impacts who they become as adults, influencing their polymathic traits.
- **Financial Influence:** Whether growing up with limited or abundant financial resources, both scenarios can foster polymathy. Limited resources often necessitate self-reliance and the development of diverse skills, while abundant resources provide opportunities for varied learning experiences.
- **Exposure to Variety:** Polymaths often benefit from exposure to a wide range of learning opportunities, people, and experiences. This diversity helps them develop a broad base of knowledge and skills.
- **Self-Directed Learning:** Encouraging self-directed learning is crucial for the development of polymathic abilities. Allowing individuals to follow their curiosity and set their own learning agendas fosters their growth and engagement.
- **Avoiding Overspecialization:** Pressuring polymaths to specialize can diminish their unique strengths. Organizations should recognize and value the breadth of knowledge and skills that polymaths bring to the table.
- **Juggling Responsibilities:** Polymaths who have families or significant relationships often face challenges in balancing

their diverse interests with the demands of home life. Understanding this dynamic is important for supporting their overall well-being and productivity.

- **Embracing Change:** Experiences of change, such as frequent moves during childhood, can foster resilience and independence—valuable traits for polymaths. Organizations can leverage this by providing varied experiences and opportunities for growth.
- **Parallels for Business Leaders:** The insights from polymathic family backgrounds offer valuable lessons for organizational leaders. Creating environments that support exposure to diverse experiences, encouraging self-directed learning, and appreciating the value of broad skill sets can help harness the full potential of polymathic employees.

By understanding these elements, organizational leaders can more effectively support and leverage polymathic talent, fostering a culture of innovation, adaptability, and continuous improvement within their teams.

Chapter 3 Reflection Questions and Discussion Prompts

Understanding the Impact of Family on Polymathy

1. Reflect on your own upbringing—what aspects of your family life do you think influenced the way you learn, explore new interests, or approach challenges?
2. Did your family encourage curiosity and exploration, or was there an expectation to focus on one particular path? How has this shaped your career and personal development?
3. If you are a parent, educator, or mentor, how do you (or could you) foster polymathic tendencies in the next generation?

Polymathy and Financial Resources

1. How have financial constraints or privileges influenced your ability to develop diverse skills and interests?
2. Have you ever learned a skill out of necessity (e.g., fixing something at home, self-teaching a subject due to lack of formal instruction)? How did that experience shape your approach to learning?
3. In a business setting, how can organizations support polymathic employees who may not have had equal access to educational or developmental resources growing up?

Fostering Polymathy in the Workplace

1. How does your organization currently encourage or discourage polymathic learning and development? Are employees given opportunities to explore beyond their job descriptions?
2. In what ways can you introduce more cross-functional collaboration in your team or organization to promote polymathic thinking?
3. How can leaders balance the need for specialization with the advantages of having employees with broad skill sets?

Juggling Relationships, Parenthood, and Polymathy

1. If you are a polymath, how do you balance your diverse interests with your personal relationships? Have you faced any challenges in this regard?
2. If you are a leader, how can you support employees who are juggling polymathic interests alongside family responsibilities? What workplace policies or cultural shifts might help?
3. What strategies can polymaths use to ensure that their passion for learning and exploration does not come at the expense of important relationships?

Change, Adaptability, and Growth

1. Have significant life changes (such as moving frequently, changing careers, or encountering unexpected challenges) contributed to your adaptability and polymathic tendencies?
2. How can organizations create environments that foster resilience and adaptability without overwhelming employees?
3. What is one change you could implement in your personal or professional life to further embrace polymathic learning and exploration?

CHAPTER 4

Evidence for the Benefit of Polymathy in Organizations

"Do I contradict myself?
Very well then, I contradict myself;
I am large—I contain multitudes."

—Walt Whitman

The purpose of this chapter is to not only shed light on the arguments for why polymathy can be valuable, theoretically—which is what most of this book has done so far—but to also provide real *evidence* from actual studies for why it can be particularly beneficial in a business context. This chapter will focus more deeply on the evidence and arguments for why polymathy is so critical in a business context.

Intrapersonal Functional Diversity Defined

According to scholars Bunderson and Sutcliffe, someone who is functionally intrapersonally diverse has a wide "breadth of functional experiences."[1] It basically means that they have worked in multiple *functional* areas professionally and therefore is a similar construct to professional polymathy. Similarly, scholars Chiocchio, Kelloway, and Hobbs describe intrapersonal functional diversity as "the extent to which members' prior experiences are individually heterogeneous or homogeneous."[2] What

[1] Bunderson, J. and K. Sutcliffe. 2002. "Comparing Alternative Conceptualizations of Functional Diversity in Management Teams: Process and Performance Effects." *Academy of Management Journal* 45, no. 5, pp. 875–893.

[2] Chiocchio, F., E.K. Kelloway, and B. Hobbs. 2015. *The Psychology and Management of Project Teams*. Oxford, England: Oxford University Press.

does intrapersonal functional diversity actually mean, though, in terms of what it does for someone's capabilities on the job? The following are some noteworthy findings:

- **Intrapersonal Functional Diversity Reduces Bias in Decision Making**
  Burke and Steensma theorized that intrapersonal functional diversity causes people to think more broadly and, as a result, be less susceptible to bias when making decisions.[3] It makes sense that if you have worked in multiple functional areas professionally, that you will see things from multiple perspectives. You may have less built-in bias as a result. You can adopt multiple perspectives. When it comes to decision making, those decisions may be more well-informed as a result.
- **Intrapersonal Functional Diversity Promotes Creativity and Innovation**
  Shibayama found that individuals working in research groups who have higher experiential diversity were better at fostering radical and incremental innovation.[4] This also makes sense—that people who have had broader experience professionally will trend more toward innovation. In other words, researchers (as a sample population) who are more cognitively diverse are better positioned to innovate, precisely because of their broad experiences.

Yap, Chai, and Lemaire also found that intrapersonal functional diversity has a positive impact on organizational innovation.[5] Interest-

---

[3] Burke, L.A. and H.K. Steensma. 1998. "Toward a Model for Relating Executive Career Experiences and Firm Performance." *Journal of Managerial Issues* 10, pp. 86–102.

[4] Shibayama, S. 2008. "Effect of Knowledge Diversity on Technological Innovations in Scientific Research." *From a Conference Called Entrepreneurship and Innovation – Organizations, Institutions, Systems and Regions*, Copenhagen, Denmark, June 17–20, 2008.

[5] Yap, C., K. Chai, and P. Lemaire. 2005. "An Empirical Study on Functional Diversity and Innovation in SMEs." *Creativity and Innovation Management* 14, no. 2, pp. 176–190.

ingly, they found that this was truer for smaller organizations, and less so the case for bigger firms. This might be the case because the larger the firm, the more bureaucratic the organization tends to be—thus making innovation more difficult to achieve, in general.

In fact, not only can innovation improve at the individual level based on one's polymathic exposure, but it can also improve innovation at the collective level as well—if polymathic employees are involved. In fact, Melero and Palomeras argued that generalist inventors—people with broad knowledge sets—are particularly valuable to teams operating with high levels of uncertainty.[6] The presence of generalists on a team trying to innovate helps with "recombination of knowledge" and "attenuates the typical barriers affecting team-working processes." Interestingly, they also note that it is important to have specialists on teams of innovators, too. They say that "the lack of specialized contributions in such teams may hamper the process of adapting each recombined component to the search for an innovative solution." As a result, they say that teams that include generalists will perform better than otherwise comparable teams, especially when there is uncertainty, and the path to the best solutions is unclear—but in this case, the contributions of specialists "plays only a secondary role."

A leading scholar in polymathy studies, Robert Root-Bernstein and colleagues found that Nobel Prize laureates demonstrated creativity in several different domains when compared to their less eminent peers who tended to be more focused on specialization.[7] And outside of work, hobbies could have a positive impact on professional achievements, as well. "Significant correlations were found between the number of adult avocations each scientist participated in and their success, as well as between specific avocations and success. Scientists who painted and drew were significantly more likely to be among the Nobelists and National Academy members than those who did not. Those who wrote poetry, did

---

[6] Melero, E. and N. Palomeras. 2015. "The Renaissance Man is not Dead! The Role of Generalists in Teams of Inventors." *Research Policy* 44, no. 1, pp. 154–167.

[7] Root-Bernstein, R., L. Allen, and L. Beach, et al. 2008. "Arts Foster Scientific Success: Avocations of Nobel, National Academy, Royal Society and Sigma Xi Members." *Journal of Psychology and Science and Technology*, 1, no. 2, pp. 51–63.

photography, and participated in various technical crafts, and those who had the widest range of hobbies were also more likely than the average scientist to be recognized as influential by their peers." A later study done on 20th century scientists found that the most successful scientists, including four different Nobel laureates, tended to be engaged in the fine arts or an avocation around crafts when compared to their less successful counterparts.[8] Clearly, there can be great benefits from polymathic thinking and approaches, as these examples highlight.

The bottom line here, though, is that people with multifaceted professional backgrounds (and even people with hobbies that are distinctly different from their work) are, indeed, better at innovation, whether at the individual level or helping their teams be coinnovative together. Polymaths can pull from their broad, prior experiences to come up with new solutions in creative ways. People who have broad, varied experiences and exposure are able to ignite cognitive processes that increase creativity.[9] Multidisciplinarity also gives way for new linkages to emerge; indeed, knowledge in one discipline can often inspire or be applied to other disciplines in new ways.[10] Therefore, if you as a business person are seeking innovation on your teams, having polymathic people with broad prior professional experiences can be a smart way to achieve the innovation you desire.

- **Intrapersonal Functional Diversity Increases Environmental Scanning**
  Angriawan and Adebe found a positive relationship between how long CEOs had worked in an industry, their intrapersonal functional diversity, and how much they

[8] Root-Bernstein, R., M. Bernstein, and H. Garnier. 1995. "Correlations Between Avocations, Scientific Style, and Professional Impact of Thirty-Eight Scientists of the Eiduson Study." *Creativity Research Journal* 8, pp. 115–137.

[9] Ward, T. 1995. "What's Old about New Ideas?" In *The Creative Cognition Approach,* eds. S.M. Smith, T. Ward, and R. Finke, 57–178. Cambridge, MA: MIT Press.

[10] Terjesen, S. and D. Politis. 2015. "In Praise of Multidisciplinary Scholarship and the Polymath." *Academy of Management Learning and Education*, 14, no. 2, pp. 151–157.

scanned the environment.[11] Of course, environmental scanning has positive implications for strategic decision making. If a business CEO does not look at the larger landscape, review their competition, or continue learning, then their decision making may be handicapped. Polymathic professionals, especially polymathic leaders, need to be able to continually learn by looking up and out—not just down within their organization. Given polymathic people are continuous learners, polymathic CEOs who exemplify continuous learning, by engaging in environmental scanning, help lead their organizations to perform better.

- **Intrapersonal Functional Diversity Improves Strategic Decision Making**
  Hitt and Tyler found that executives with broad functional backgrounds are better at evaluating options to make sound strategic decisions, when compared to their counterparts with narrower functional backgrounds.[12] One of the arguments Hitt and Tyler make has to do with "cognitive complexity." They explain their theory: "individuals' cognitive abilities affected the manner in which they perceived that uncertainty in the environment affected their performance. Therefore, the effects of cognitive complexity relate to the processing of information. As a result, it affects the number and type (complex) of criteria and alternatives evaluated in the decision." Interestingly, they also say: "We found that most top executives are generalists with broad functional experience ... Furthermore, we found that the strategic decision models varied across executives with different combinations of experience." The big takeaway from their research, as it pertains to polymathy, though, is that having varied

[11] Angriawan A. and M. Adebe. 2001. "Chief Executive Background Characteristics and Environmental Scanning Emphasis: An Empirical Investigation." *Journal of Business Strategies*, 28, pp. 75–96.

[12] Hitt, M.A. and B.B. Tyler. 1991. "Strategic Decision Models: Integrating Different Perspectives." *Strategic Management Journal* 12, pp. 327–351.

functional experiences (in other words, being polymathic professionally) affects strategic choices, mostly because the criteria on which those decisions are made will be broader. The person simply has more perspectives to take when making strategic decisions, and therefore the decisions the person makes will be stronger, and more well thought through, when compared to someone with a narrower, more focused, more specialized background.

- **Intrapersonal Functional Diverse Employees Are More Likely to Get Promoted**
  Campion, Cheraskin, and Stevens found that people who have broad experiences in several different functional domains are more likely to get promoted, when compared to their narrower counterparts.[13] This may be because they simply have more options for how and where they could get promoted (as opposed to specialists—whose eggs are all in one basket, and therefore whose career options are obviously more domain-limited). Or it might be the case that people who are polymathic by nature do better work. Or it might be the case that polymathic people with diverse professional backgrounds show an aptitude for continual, broad learning—which bodes well for continual learning and strong performance on the job.
- **Forecasting the Future**
  Human beings have a deep desire to anticipate the future; we all do it, with varying degrees of skill. Authors Tetlock and Gardner, in their book, *Superforecasting: The Art and Science of Prediction,* say that generalists are better at forecasting what will happen in the future, compared to narrow specialists.[14]

---

[13] Campion, M.A., L. Cheraskin, and M.J. Stevens. 1994. "Career-Related Antecedents and Outcomes of Job Rotation." *Academy of Management Journal* 37, pp. 1518–1542.

[14] Tetlock, P. and D. Gardner. 2015. *Super Forecasting: The Art and Science of Prediction.* New York: Penguin Random House.

In a business context, anticipating the future is particularly useful, especially in the face of threats and competition. Having polymathic generalists on your teams, then, can help in anticipating what the future may bring—and preparing for it in advance.

Diverse Thought Is Important in Organizations

For businesses to stay relevant, to have sustainability, and to compete in the marketplace, it is important that they not become stale. In fact, William Pollard has been quoted as saying, "Learning and innovation go hand in hand. The arrogance of success is to think that what you did yesterday will be sufficient for tomorrow." We cannot simply keep with the stagnant, status quo if we wish for our businesses to thrive. Times change. Environments change. Customers' demands change. Technology changes. There are so many factors impacting the business landscape, and which require us to evolve in order to survive: we too must change. And part of what helps an organization do this is through the *diversity of thought* on their teams. That is how new ideas arise—through new and multiple perspectives. Otherwise, if everyone thinks the same—if groupthink is allowed to flourish—then the chances of having this sort of adaptability—to change with the ever-evolving environment—becomes weakened.

A key to organizations evolving and sustaining themselves over time, even under harsh conditions, is by having diverse teams, made up of members who have diverse thought processes and capabilities. Polymaths should necessarily be a part of those diverse teams—along with specialists. A polymath is themselves someone with internal, intrapersonal diversity—which should be even more valuable for organizations seeking broad, diverse perspectives. Rather than only tapping into multiple perspectives from a team, polymaths may be able to bring diversity of thought *themselves*, on the individual level. Indeed, even a polymathic person can bring valuable, multiple perspectives given their large toolkit and broad knowledge they have at their disposal. This is invaluable for business leaders seeking diversity of thought and who want to stay relevant and competitive in the marketplace.

Nonhomogenous Teams Are Better, More Resilient Teams

A body of research has shown an important benefit of workplace diversity, and that is that nonhomogenous teams are more effective than homogenous ones. There are a variety of reasons why this is the case. First, working with people who are notably different from yourself may help you see things from different perspectives and thereby sharpen your own performance as a result; you can learn from your colleagues, basically. And a team consisting of knowledgeable and ever-improving, continually learning team members is at an advantage, compared to teams consisting of very similar, and more stagnant workers. So, a diverse environment can help a polymath—someone who on the individual level is diverse—become better and even more effective, because it helps to expand their learning. And this makes the team that person is on perform more effectively. What better way to build nonhomogenous teams than to make sure they consist of some polymathic employees—who themselves bring diversity to the table, at the individual level, in unique ways?

In fact, Rulke found that MBA students perform better when they are on a team of functional generalists as opposed to functional specialists.[15] In Rulke's study, participants were put into management simulation exercises. Those who used functional generalist strategies performed better than those using functional specialist strategies. Perhaps this is the case because a team of functional generalists will be able to understand each other more—to link and integrate with one another's perspectives better. Or perhaps this is the case simply because functional generalists will take a more holistic approach to problem-solving when compared to narrow specialists.

[15] Rulke, D.L. 1996. "Member Selection Strategy and Team Performance: Cognitive Integration vs. Social Integration in Cross-Functional Teams." *Academy of Management Best Paper Proceedings*, pp. 424–428.

Polymaths Help Their Teams Be More Effective

Furthermore, polymaths tend to help their teams become more effective as well. For example, Bantel and Jackson's study found that teams with functional diversity among its members tended to be more innovative.[16] Further, heterogeneity of functional (work) experiences and education level were actually the strongest predictors of innovation on teams. Said differently: do you want innovation on your teams? Then forge diverse workgroups. Bantel and Jackson also concluded that functionally diverse teams are better at developing clear plans and strategies collaboratively. In sum, teams whose members have more functional diversity are able to think more innovatively and collaboratively.

Polymaths Help Avoid Groupthink

Most business leaders understand how dangerous groupthink is. As it relates, Levi found that teams made up of diverse members have less groupthink.[17] Further, there are also a few studies that address how individuals who are diverse *themselves* impact the teams they are on—specifically in the team's ability to think better, on the whole. For example, Cannella, Park, and Lee found that "Intrapersonal functional diversity enhances information sharing on top management teams, improves 'sense making,' and leads to better integration of available information. Within-member breadth of experience directly increases group-level information sharing, which leads to enhanced decision making." [18] Cannella, Park, and Lee also say that the effects of intrapersonal diversity become even more positive as environmental uncertainty grows.

---

[16] Bantel, K. and S. Jackson. 1989. "Top Management and Innovations in Banking: Does the Composition of the Top Team Make a Difference?" *Strategic Management Journal* 10 (Supplemental 1), pp. 107–124.

[17] Levi, D. 2001. *Group Dynamics for Teams*. Thousand Oaks: Sage Publications.

[18] Cannella, A., J. Park, and H. Lee. 2008. "Top Management Team Functional 253 Background Diversity and firm Performance: Examining the Roles of Team Member Colocation and Environmental Uncertainty." *Academy of Management Journal* 51, no. 4, pp. 768–784.

Polymathic Employees Are Better at Understanding Their Colleagues' Capabilities

Similarly, Park, Lim, and Birnbaum-More found evidence that teams consisting of "multiknowledge" employees (when a person understands multiple functional areas) are more likely to have members who understand the skills, strengths, and capabilities of *other* team members.[19] This is an important point, especially because a team must collaborate and engage together, not as distinct agents in separated swim lanes that do not intersect. Because of this increased awareness for the strengths and talents of colleagues, individual team members share information more easily with one another, and in the process, produce better information sharing among team members, as well as more enhanced shared understanding on the team. They work more effectively as a kind of hive mind. This research validated that the more multiknowledge individuals there are on a cross-functional team, the more innovations the team creates—essentially due to more information sharing based on an understanding of others' strengths.

Polymaths Can Help With Change Efforts

Huckman and Staats hypothesized that a team's level of intrapersonal diversity positively affects team's performance, especially when the situation demands that the group change.[20] Their rationale: "With more diverse individual experiences, team members might map current problems to past experiences more accurately or use different cognitive representations more effectively to define and solve problems in new ways." Huckman and Staats said that "when cognitive problem-solving demands are high, diverse experience may improve performance by enabling access to a wider base of knowledge and improved

[19] Park, M.H., J.W. Lim, and P. Birnbaum-More. 2009. "The Effect of Multi-Knowledge Individuals on Performance in Cross-Functional New Product Development Teams." *The Journal of Product Innovation Management* 26, pp. 86–96.

[20] Huckman, R. and B. Staats. 2011. "Fluid Tasks and Fluid Teams: The Impact of Diversity in Experience and Team Familiarity on Team Performance." *Manufacturing and Service Operations Management* 13, no. 3, pp. 310–328.

information processing." Given that many organizations are almost in constant states of change, having polymathic employees—who tend to be adept at change—could be a strategic approach to helping those change efforts to be successful.

Becoming a Strategic Collective

It is not uncommon for an individual to think about reaching his or her potential; but what about our collective potential? How can we as individuals as part of a larger collective, think and act strategically to help realize our shared potential? How can we help humanity catapult forward? I believe the answer is, in part, by harnessing our cognitive diversity in strategic ways, so that we can support reaching our collective possibilities in amazing ways. We need people who are specialists, and we need people who are big picture, polymathic connectors, too. Combined, this is a powerful approach, especially when compared to the old model where basically everyone was a narrow specialist. Plus, part of how I believe we can reach our collective potential is by, as individuals, stepping into the full breadth and depth of our distinct capacities—that way we bring our best selves to the larger group.

But we need systems in place—a sort of scaffolding—to create an environment where we can collaborate in ways like never before to harness our shared capacities for depth, breadth, and integrative innovation. Technology helps makes this possible. This book shares some ideas for how business leaders can create the kind of environment that would give rise to this sort of collaborative *noosphere*. The solution does not exist only at the individual level or at the organizational or societal level; we need to adjust and make strategic changes at all these levels, simultaneously. As we support more individual polymaths, then an organization itself can also become more polymathic as well.

There are some challenges to get there, though. For example, hegemony is the process by which the dominant culture keeps its dominant position, using institutions such as business organizations to do so. What I am suggesting is that you become revolutionary in your business; that together, we create a new hegemony where specialists and polymathic generalists are *both* appreciated. Help the culture shift. We live in a world that is our cocreation; why not construct an ideal place where intellectual and intrapersonal diversity is welcomed rather than shunned?

Further, Institutional Theory says that businesses tend to replicate one another; over time, this is known as *institutional isomorphism*. Organizations tend to look and operate alike to gain organizational legitimacy.[21] Instead of mimicking other businesses, let your organization be the one on the cutting edge, setting the pace of change and showing what is possible when we think both strategically and collectively.

Hambrick argued that the advantages of top management team functional diversity can only be realized if the team overcomes fragmentation; in other words, they must act like a "real" team.[22] In fact, "behaviorally integrated" teams are better at dealing with complexity. They can integrate diverging opinions that result in balanced, well-considered, strategic decisions.[23] This integration is important, whether at the individual level or at the group level. This kind of "behavioral integration" involves joint decision making, teams that are collaborative, and considers both the quality and quantity of information exchanged.

Polymathic Agents in a Decentralized System

Complexity Leadership Theory is a burgeoning perspective in the scholarly literature. It basically says that in a Complex Adaptive System, where there is a lot of complexity, that solutions to problems cannot be predicted.[24] Obviously, if the solution could be easily predicted, the situation

[21] DiMaggio, P. and W. Powell. 1983. "The Iron Cage Revisited: Institutional Isomorphism and Collective Rationality in Organizational Fields." *American Sociological Review* 48, pp. 147–60.
[22] Hambrick, D. 1994. "Top Management Groups: A Conceptual Integration and Reconsideration of the "Team" Label." *Research in Organizational Behavior* 17, pp. 171–213.
[23] Carmeli, A. and Meyrav Yitzack Halevi. 2009. "How Top Management Team Behavioral Integration and Behavioral Complexity Enable Organizational Ambidexterity: The Moderating Role of Contextual Ambidexterity." *Leadership Quarterly* 20, pp. 207–218.
[24] Uhl-Bien, M., R. Marion, and B. McKelvey. 2007. "Complexity Leadership Theory: Shifting Leadership from the Industrial Age to the Knowledge Era." *The Leadership Quarterly* 18, pp. 298–318.

would not be considered all that complex. Rather, solutions *emerge* over time in unpredictable ways as interdependent agents collaboratively work together to solve problems—kind of how a neural-like network would. In a very complex situation, no one person can know, do, or be "it all" anymore. You need a system to work together to fix problems; you have to trust in the "wisdom of crowds," as James Surowiecki argues in his book by the same title.[25]

This can create a sort of hive mind, much the way that ants or bees work collaboratively as a larger single "whole," made up of constituent parts. In a simple system, centralization makes sense; as things become more complex, however, decentralization is more effective because it allows agents in the system to self-organize, collaborate, build community, and accelerate innovation. I believe that polymathic people are critical operators in this sort of a system, because they allow for linkages to be made between constituents. Polymaths are well-suited to see the bigger picture and connect the dots; they can harness the power of many specialists by synthesizing those perspectives and capacities while also bringing them together to paint a larger picture. We need those polymathic bridge builders; otherwise, specialist approaches may become disjointed and isolated from one another.

Polymathy as a High-Performing Business Strategy

Although polymathy is clearly very important at the individual level, for the sake of having a well-lived life, it is also relevant in the business realm. For an organization to be high-performing and to self-actualize as a business, it should be made up of individuals who are achieving their potential and exercising their capacities. How else is an organization to reach its fullest potential, if not utilizing the full capacities of its employees? Plus, it is in the interest of any business to treat their employees well; this leads to better engagement, employee satisfaction, and retention. If employees feel like they can bring their fullest, truest selves to work, then certainly they will feel more committed to that employer (as opposed to trying to do good work for a business where one has to self-censor and hide one's

[25] Suroweicki, J. 2004. *The Wisdom of Crowds*. Anchor Books.

true self). Employees want to matter to their employers; they want to be seen and appreciated for who they really are. The right thing to do—and the strategic thing to do—is for businesses to allow for this sort of authenticity in the workplace. A way of doing that is by talking about polymaths more. Our world will get better one person at a time and one organization at a time; but people make up the organization. Business leaders should strive to welcome neurodiverse individuals like polymathic people onto their teams, not only because it is the right thing to do, but also because it's the strategic thing to do as well.

The Whole Is Greater Than the Sum of the Parts

Polymathy is more than simple diversity of thought; it is stronger than that. It allows for interconnections, bridge building, expanded networks based on human connection, rooted in common interests; polymathy empowers creativity. In other words, polymathy does not just allow for diversity of thought—it promotes creativity, too. For example, analogical thinking, where information, approaches, or ideas from one discipline can be applied in another—is the superpower that polymaths have. With more tools in their toolkit, polymaths can more easily transfer knowledge or approaches from one domain to another—and in the process, innovations occur. Most innovations that would have occurred within disciplines have already been exhausted anyway. Where the big payoffs come nowadays is at the intersection of multiple disciplines. So, the bottom line is this: if you are looking not only for diversity of thought, but to supercharge that diversity of thought so that real innovations can catapult your business forward, then get some polymaths on your team—and empower them to bring their best selves to work every day.

Embrace Divergence

Rather than looking to employees to fit in, business leaders should focus on how they can elicit unique contributions from each of its employees. Look at people's strengths. Focus on how they can uniquely contribute. Look for ways to draw out a variety of intellectual perspectives so that the best ideas can rise to the top. Create a culture where people are encouraged to bring their best and fullest selves to work. Put systems and programs into place so as to avoid groupthink, and encourage creative new, even divergent, ideas instead. There may be challenges along the way to creating a truly diverse organizational culture, but there is potentially a great payoff to enrich the intellectual capital made possible through this sort of intra- and interpersonal diversity on your team.

After all, diversity is a key driver of creativity and innovation. For any company seeking to stay competitive in the business landscape, knowledge creation and innovation are critical; on the contrary, stagnancy can be fatal. Sadly, a lot of the time, specialists may have "blinders" on and tend to see the world through the single lens of their chosen discipline. They can be threatened by new ways of doing things. One way to obtain the kinds of innovative solutions businesses desire is to have a diverse team—made up of, in part, intrapersonally diverse individuals. Allowing for people to pursue their polymathy is, in a way, allowing for those individuals to self-organize, at least in the form of having more agency over how they contribute—even if those methods change over time.

Cognitive Flexibility and Organizational Change Management

Polymathy involves being cognitively flexible, through continual learning. Given that organizations frequently go through change initiatives, there is logic in having people on your team who are themselves flexible, by nature—at least cognitively flexible. Trying to initiate and implement a change effort if your team is made up of more cognitively fixed individuals will be an uphill battle. Having cognitively flexible polymaths on your team can be a strategic move to help shift the spirit of your team to being open toward change, since polymaths themselves tend to be more comfortable with change, newness, and variety.

Polymathic Employees Good for the Financial Bottom Line

Most polymaths tend to be good at juggling large workloads; they trend toward efficiency. They enjoy change, variety, and newness—so switching between tasks, projects, and various work demands is totally natural to them. They are quick learners. They are highly capable people. They do not enjoy being underutilized; they are highly talented, and want to be able to bring their full skill sets to work. In this way, when you hire a polymathic employee, you are literally getting more "bang for your buck." When thinking about how to improve your financial bottom line, consider investing into highly capable polymathic people to join your team because they are very likely to help you succeed from a financial standpoint, given they are so highly capable in multiple areas.

In this model, an employee's ability to learn becomes a commodity for purchase. No longer are people hired simply for having degrees or prior experience; we need people who are good at learning. This should be one of the skills you hire people for especially in VUCA/wicked/harsh positions. Not everyone is equal in this regard; some are better at acquiring new knowledge and skills than others. Some companies are even going so far as to stop requiring college degrees for their employees. What is more useful and, in many ways, predictive of on-the-job success, is if a person is a continual, quick learner—or not. You want people on your teams who are good at learning, because this translates into successful performance—and that will impact your company's bottom line from a financial perspective. Learning leads to more effective performance (when compared to someone in the same role who is less adept at learning), which leads to a better likelihood of financial success. We need people on our teams who are good at learning; we need polymaths.

The Challenge of Workplace Diversity

Of course, it has been touted for many years how important workplace diversity is, and it is true: diversity makes us better. Diversity makes our organizations better.[26] [27] Diversity can also be difficult to manage,

---

[26] Cox, T.H. 1993. *Cultural Diversity in Organizations: Theory, Research and Practice*. Barrett-Koehler, San Francisco, CA.

[27] Jackson, S., K.E. May and K. Whitney. 1995. "Understanding the Dynamics of Diversity in Decisions Making Teams". In *Team Effectiveness and Decision Making in Organizations,* eds. R.A. Guzzo and E. Salas, 204–261. Jossey-Bass, San Francisco, CA.

though—it is not necessarily easy to engage with people who see the world differently. That is why building an organizational culture that supports and appreciates difference is so important (which is the focus of Chapter 5).

Although most studies on intrapersonal functional diversity point to how valuable and effective people with broad backgrounds can be, both individually as well as on teams, Knight, et al. said that teams consisting of individuals with broad functional diversity might be ripe for more conflict.[28] Because some members of the team have developed their niche (lacking intrapersonal diversity), understanding others who think differently may take some additional effort and patience. So whenever thinking about the benefits of diversity—especially among the members of a team—keep in mind that there are challenges involved in navigating that diversity, in addition to the plethora of benefits that come with it as well.

The Risks of the Status Quo

There are downsides and risks of sticking to the old model, where everybody should be a professional specialist in organizations. Particularly in VUCA environments where the conditions are dynamic, then how things were done yesterday (the specialist approach) can really put businesses in a precarious position, when the situation demands adaptation. When environmental conditions are harsh, then the ability to think outside the box is more important than ever. That is not the forte of specialists; that is the territory of the polymathic generalist, and yet another reason why business leaders should make certain to leverage polymathic talent.

The Bottom Line of This Chapter

This chapter has provided a comprehensive examination of the evidence supporting the benefits of polymathy in organizational contexts.

---

[28] Knight, D., C.L. Pearce, K.G. Smith, J.D. Olian, H.P. Sims, K.A. Smith, P. Flood. 1999. "Top Management Team Diversity, Group Process, and Strategic Consensus." *Strategic Management Journal* 20, pp. 445–465.

Key Points Include

- **Intrapersonal Functional Diversity:** Polymathic professionals, with their broad functional experiences, bring a unique set of capabilities to the workplace, reducing bias in decision making and promoting creativity and innovation.
- **Enhanced Creativity and Innovation:** Individuals with diverse professional backgrounds are better positioned to foster both radical and incremental innovation. This is true at both individual and team levels, especially in environments characterized by high uncertainty.
- **Improved Decision Making:** Executives with varied functional experiences are better equipped to evaluate options and make strategic decisions. Their broader perspectives lead to more well-rounded and informed choices.
- **Promotion and Career Advancement:** Employees with diverse functional backgrounds are more likely to get promoted. Their broad skill sets and continuous learning attitudes make them valuable assets in multiple domains within the organization.
- **Superior Forecasting Abilities:** Generalists, or polymathic professionals, are better at predicting future trends and preparing for potential challenges, which is crucial in maintaining a competitive edge.
- **Value of Diverse Thought:** Diversity of thought is essential for organizational sustainability and innovation. Polymathic employees contribute significantly to this diversity, offering multiple perspectives and innovative solutions.
- **Team Effectiveness:** Polymathic individuals enhance team performance by improving information sharing and understanding team members' capabilities. Their ability to integrate diverse knowledge leads to more innovative and effective team dynamics.
- **Adaptability and Change Management:** Polymathic employees are adept at navigating change, making them valuable in dynamic and complex environments. Their cognitive flexibility supports organizational change efforts.

- **Financial Benefits:** Polymathic employees tend to be efficient, quick learners, and capable of juggling multiple tasks. Their broad skill sets provide more value for the organization, potentially improving the financial bottom line.
- **Challenges of Diversity:** While diversity, including intrapersonal functional diversity, offers numerous benefits, it also presents challenges. Managing diverse teams requires a supportive culture that appreciates and leverages differences.
- **Risks of Specialization:** Relying solely on specialists can be risky, especially in VUCA environments. Polymathic generalists offer the adaptability and innovative thinking needed to navigate these conditions effectively.

In summary, this chapter highlighted the significant advantages of having polymathic professionals within organizations. Their broad experiences, innovative capabilities, and cognitive flexibility make them invaluable assets, both individually and as part of diverse teams. By embracing and leveraging polymathic talent, organizations can enhance their innovation, adaptability, and overall performance.

Chapter 4 Reflection Questions and Discussion Prompts

Understanding Intrapersonal Functional Diversity

1. How would you define intrapersonal functional diversity in your own words?
2. Have you worked in multiple functional areas throughout your career? If so, how has that shaped your decision making, creativity, and adaptability?
3. In what ways does having broad functional experience differ from having deep expertise?
4. Do you think organizations recognize and reward employees with broad experience as much as they do specialists? Why or why not?
5. How can companies better leverage employees who have a wide range of experiences across different functions?

Reducing Bias in Decision Making

1. How can working across multiple disciplines help reduce cognitive bias in decision making?
2. Have you ever been in a situation where having diverse experiences allowed you to make a more balanced or objective decision? If so, describe the scenario.
3. What are some potential downsides to having too narrow of a perspective in leadership decision making?
4. How can organizations encourage decision makers to adopt multiple perspectives when addressing challenges?
5. What steps can leaders take to minimize bias and foster broader thinking in high-stakes business decisions?

Fostering Creativity and Innovation

1. How does working in multiple functional areas enhance an individual's ability to be creative and innovative?
2. Have you noticed a connection between your hobbies or outside interests and your ability to be creative at work? If so, how?

3. How can organizations encourage employees to develop polymathic tendencies to improve innovation?
4. What are some barriers to innovation in larger firms that smaller organizations may not face?
5. How can leaders create an environment where both generalists and specialists contribute effectively to innovation?

Environmental Scanning and Strategic Decision Making

1. Why do you think polymathic leaders tend to scan their environments more effectively?
2. Have you worked for an organization where leadership was either highly attuned to external trends or completely unaware? What impact did this have?
3. How can organizations train executives and managers to improve their ability to scan their industries and anticipate future trends?
4. Do you agree with the idea that polymathic executives make better strategic decisions? Why or why not?
5. How can businesses ensure that they balance both broad strategic thinking and deep technical expertise in decision making?

Career Advancement and Promotion

1. The chapter suggests that individuals with diverse functional experiences are more likely to be promoted. Why do you think this is the case?
2. Have you observed in your workplace that people with broader experiences get promoted more frequently? Or do you see more promotions going to specialists?
3. How can individuals looking to advance their careers intentionally develop intrapersonal functional diversity?
4. Do you think organizations should formalize career paths that encourage employees to rotate through different functional areas? Why or why not?
5. What potential challenges might arise when promoting employees with broad experience rather than deep expertise in a single domain?

The Role of Polymaths in Teams

1. How can polymaths enhance the effectiveness of the teams they are part of?
2. The chapter discusses polymaths helping their teams avoid groupthink—have you seen this play out in your own professional experience?
3. What are the benefits of having functionally diverse teams, and what challenges might such teams face?
4. How can leaders foster an environment where specialists and polymaths complement each other instead of competing for influence?
5. Have you ever worked on a homogenous team (everyone had a similar background and mindset) and a diverse team? How did the experiences differ?

Polymaths and Organizational Change

1. Why might polymaths be better suited to help organizations navigate change?
2. What role does cognitive flexibility play in managing change and uncertainty?
3. Have you ever experienced resistance to change in an organization? If so, what approaches helped ease the transition?
4. How can businesses proactively identify and support employees who thrive in change-intensive environments?
5. What strategies can organizations implement to build more adaptable teams that are comfortable with uncertainty?

Financial Benefits of Hiring Polymaths

1. The chapter suggests that polymaths provide more value to organizations because they are quick learners and highly capable across multiple areas. Do you agree? Why or why not?
2. How might organizations financially benefit from hiring polymathic employees?
3. What are some practical ways HR departments can identify and attract polymathic talent?

4. Are there risks associated with relying too heavily on polymaths in an organization? What might those be?
5. How can businesses balance hiring specialists and polymaths to optimize efficiency and innovation?

Embracing Diversity of Thought in Organizations

1. How does the presence of polymaths contribute to greater diversity of thought within an organization?
2. Have you seen examples where lack of diversity of thought led to poor business outcomes?
3. How can organizations measure whether they have enough diversity of thought within their leadership and teams?
4. What cultural shifts are necessary for organizations to truly embrace diverse ways of thinking and problem-solving?
5. If you were in charge of building a high-performing team, how would you ensure a balance between specialists and polymaths?

Overcoming Challenges of Workplace Diversity

1. The chapter acknowledges that functionally diverse teams may experience more conflict. Have you seen this happen in your own experience?
2. What strategies can organizations use to manage potential conflicts in diverse teams while maintaining the benefits of cognitive diversity?
3. Do you think polymathic employees should receive special training to help them navigate workplace challenges? Why or why not?
4. What role does psychological safety play in fostering an environment where polymaths and specialists can collaborate effectively?
5. How can businesses measure the effectiveness of diversity initiatives, particularly in relation to cognitive diversity and polymathy?

The Risks of the Status Quo

1. The chapter warns that organizations that fail to adapt may struggle to remain competitive. Can you think of an example where this happened to a company or industry?

2. How can businesses proactively avoid stagnation and promote continuous learning?
3. What are some early warning signs that an organization is becoming too rigid in its approach?
4. How can leadership encourage a culture of lifelong and lifewide learning to stay ahead of industry shifts?
5. What is one strategic change your own organization could make to become more polymath-friendly?

CHAPTER 5

Creating and Sustaining a Culture That Supports Polymathy

> "Be supportive of others the way you would want them to be supportive of you."
>
> —Ken Poirot

The purpose of this chapter is to understand how leaders can create and sustain a culture that supports polymathic contributions for organizational success. But first it is critical to ask, what prevents innovation—something critical for organizational survival? The context and culture of an organization does this. Organizational culture, in a nutshell, is "the way we do things around here." Peter Drucker, a management consultant, educator, and author on organizational management, has famously said, "Culture eats strategy for breakfast." What this means is that regardless of how solid and well-planned your strategies are, the culture of your business is more influential on its success (or lack thereof) than your plans are. In other words, it matters very little if you have polymaths on your teams, or if you have intentions of supporting and leveraging their capacities, individually or collectively. What matters more is: do you have an organizational culture that encourages and supports polymaths to thrive—where they can feel safe experimenting with new and possibly better ways of doing their work? Does your organization have a culture where people are encouraged to bring their full selves, and all their talent, to work? Or do they need to exist within professional boxes and silos, where "outside the box" thinking is summarily dismissed?

This is important to consider for any organizational leader: culture can be vicious. And frankly, influencing culture is one of the most important roles of any business leader. Accordingly, the purpose of this chapter is to look at why it is important to influence your organizational culture to support polymathic employees, and some practical ways you as a leader can do just that.

The Old Culture of Deskilling in the Age of Specialization

Before diving into the reasons why a culture that supports polymaths is important in modern day, first let us look at the dominant culture that has existed in many organizations previously: that of specialization and deskilling. Think of the era of Henry Ford's assembly line; the goal was to maximize efficiency. In order to do that, he invented the division of labor approach. This involved deskilling labor so they would focus more narrowly on repetitive tasks in which they would become highly specialized.

In the 20th and 21st centuries, we have continued this approach even beyond physical labor to include division of intellectual labor. We have chosen to know more and more about less and less. Did this sort of deskilling also dehumanize us? It may have made us more efficient, but at what cost?

The fact is organizations—like Ford's factories or even modern-day businesses—as a general rule, do not always necessarily tend to care about what is best for the individual; but they should. First, it is the right thing to do, to treat people like human beings who matter, rather than simply being a means to a desired end. Second, it can also be quite strategic. If employees feel dissatisfied, treated like machinery or "resources"—which can be dehumanizing, or that their talent is going to waste, oftentimes they leave. They do not stay in organizations where they feel undervalued or underappreciated. And turnover can be costly to the organization. Therefore, it can be quite strategic and better for the financial bottom line to retain employees, even imperfect ones.

Luckily, we no longer live in the era of Ford's assembly line. Technology has taken over much of the automatable work and will continue to do so increasingly for the foreseeable future. In the first quarter of the 21st century, we have seen a shift in the labor force due largely to modern technology and the era of information computerization. As technology can do more and more, it is becoming not only increasingly possible but also increasingly necessary that human beings do distinctly human work; that they add value unique to their human capabilities. This will only become more and more the case as technology continues to advance.

For these reasons and more, it is time to revive the appreciation of the polymath; polymathy *is* our distinctly human capacity, which we need to step into and leverage more moving forward. Our unique brains, our ability to learn our way out of problems, is our distinctly human capacity. Further, polymathic thinking enables us to see bigger picture solutions, to apply creative solutions, to innovate, to synthesize, to apply analogical thinking, and to build bridges between domains; so far, technology does not do these things. Humans no longer need to be cogs in wheels, because AI and automation can and will do much of that for us now and into the future. Now what we need humans to be, more and more, is polymathic.

Elements of Organizational Culture

Understanding the elements that create an organizational culture are important for any leader who wants to shape their organization's culture consciously and purposefully. In fact, this may be one of the most important roles a leader in an organization plays, is helping to create a healthy, effective organizational culture. So first, a few observations about culture.

Organizations often contain what Edgar Schein labeled as "basic assumptions." [1] He said that organizations contain three main elements that make up culture:

- Level 1: Artifacts, which are visible and assume physical space in the environment.
- Level 2: Values, which include core beliefs and are testable within the environment.

---

[1] Schein, E. 1985. *Organizational Culture and Leadership*. San Francisco: Jossey-Bass.

- Level 3: Basic underlying assumptions, which are ideas within the culture that become taken-for-granted as reality within a cultural group.

Can you reflect upon the artifacts, values, and basic underlying assumptions that exist within your organization? Do they promote a culture of conformity, or of diversity?

Organizational Change Efforts: Loosening Tight Systems to Maximize Polymathic Contributions

Heraclitus said it well: "The only thing that is constant is change." And according to Burke, 70 percent of organizational change efforts fail.[2] This begs the question: what can organizational leaders do to help organizational change efforts be *successful*? One way of setting up the organization for success during change efforts is to consider loosening and tightening the system as needed.

More specifically, a "loosely coupled system," according to Weick, is one that includes a lack of coordination, an absence of regulations, and a highly connected network.[3] Alternatively, a tightly coupled system, according to Weick, has a set of rules that are enforced by an inspection and feedback system and tends to be very bureaucratic. For example, a university is an example of a loose system, where the hierarchy is flat and the main employees in the system—faculty—tend to ignore the chain of command. In comparison, the Army would be an example of a very tightly coupled organization, where the hierarchy is steep, centralized, and it is very clear who is in charge.

Neither system is better than the other; each has pros and cons. The point here is that, depending on the context and the needs of the organization, it may sometimes make sense to tighten a loose system, or loosen a tight system. However, in this section, I will focus mostly on loose

[2] Burke, W.W. 2011. "A Perspective on the Field of Organization Development and Change: The Zeigarnik Effect." *The Journal of Applied Behavioral Science* 47, no. 2, pp. 143–167.

[3] Weick, K.E. 1976. "Educational Organizations as Loosely Coupled Systems." *Administrative Science Quarterly* 21, pp. 1–19. doi:10.2307/2391875

systems, because polymathic employees may be particularly well-suited in a loose system, where the bureaucracy and guidelines are not strict, and there is room for their creativity and innovation to emerge.

At first glance, it may appear that a loose system is bad, because it means less coordination and communication, potentially, and we are often led to believe that coordination and communication are very good things. But, there can be great strengths to having a loosely coupled system, depending on the environment and the demands on the organization. In fact, Orton and Weick say that loosely coupled systems are not flawed at all; they can be a social and cognitive solution when there is constant environmental change.[4] They also say that a loosely coupled structure allows for more flexibility as the demands change; in other words, in VUCA/complex/harsh/wicked environments, supporting loosely coupled systems can be a great strategy. In comparison, a more rigid, fixed, tight system might not be adaptable enough in a sea of change. Further, a loosely coupled system allows for adaptations and creates conditions where creative solutions can more easily emerge. In this sort of an environment, actors can be more self-determined. Orton and Weick also have argued that loose coupling fosters self-determination and a sense of self-efficacy. Loosely coupled systems can even reduce conflict between the different system elements because in these situations, such elements are not necessarily required to agree or even interact with one another, which thereby leads to fewer occasions for conflict.

Polymathic individuals may tend to perform better in looser organizational systems, where they are freer to determine the ways in which they contribute. Here are some tips for how to loosen your organization, in case it may be too tight:

- March has argued that **ambiguity** causes loose coupling.[5] So if you are in a system that might be too tight, and you want to loosen it so that the polymaths on your teams can

[4] Orton, J.D., and K.E. Weick. 1990. "Loosely Coupled Systems: A Reconceptualization." *The Academy of Management Review* 15, no. 2, pp. 203–223. JSTOR, www.jstor.org/stable/258154. Accessed 23 May 2021.

[5] March, J.G. 1987. "Ambiguity and Accounting: The Elusive Link Between Information and Decision-Making." *Accounting, Organizations, & Society* 12, pp. 153–168.

contribute to the greatest extent possible, then allow for more ambiguity and let your employees figure out the best path forward, rather than directing their work too much. See what they come up with; it might be a wonderful solution that you never would have envisioned.

- Another strategy is to **decouple** the organization. Decoupling involves diminished emphasis on connectedness, responsiveness, and interdependence. Encourage independence of actors in the system, and modularity of those people within the organization.
- Another way to loosen the system is to provide **limited oversight**. Do less management and less monitoring. By allowing actors more discretion—both in behavioral and cognitive ways—the system will become looser. Of course, some management will still be important, for example, building on subordinates' ongoing behaviors, focusing on only the controllable and essential behaviors, and then providing freedom for those employees to adapt their behavior based on local needs. Loose coupling calls for subtle leadership, and is a great way to empower employees to add unique contributions particularly when there are significant challenges to face, where solutions are not easily predictable.

Historically, organizational leaders have been taught to provide a specific, clear vision, direct their employees, and give guidance; however, when the environment is chaotic and the solutions are unclear, allowing employees to determine their own roles in the system can be a strategic move from a leadership perspective. This way, employees see what is needed at their local level and use their talents to resolve the issues they see ahead of them, rather than relying on the direction of a leader who may not fully understand the day-to-day needs on the front line. In these situations, having multiskilled employees is particularly useful, so that they have a broader toolkit to pull from as they tackle unpredictable problems on the job. *Strategic ambiguity* can become a tool you use on purpose to encourage polymaths to identify new solutions, if they are given the autonomy and freedom to do so.

Of course, it is important to create a culture where everybody is valued, and where solutions are cocreated through cooperative, distributed problem-solving, rather than top-down directives. Doing so is a strategic way to minimize resistance to change efforts as well; this is an added bonus. If employees feel that they are part of creating and delivering solutions, they will be more likely to support those efforts. In contrast, if they feel forced and instructed to enact someone else's vision, they may resist it.

Interestingly, Piderit has argued that we should think of "resistance to change" in more multidimensional ways.[6] It is not as if someone is just resistant or not; rather, she argues that there are multiple dimensions on which someone might resist a change:

1. Emotional
2. Cognitive
3. Intentional (or behavioral)

For example, someone might be cognitively in support of a change initiative, but emotionally resistant to it. In this way, someone could potentially be both in support of a change while also being resistant to it.

Piderit also has written about ambivalence to change. And despite what you may initially think, ambivalence is not necessarily bad. It can be important for change to occur; in fact, some ambivalence to change among employees can be useful, because it means they might just go along with it, rather than resist it too much. However, too much ambivalence might mean they are too disengaged from the change and do not want to do the work to support it. So, when thinking about ambivalence, it is important that employees have the right balance on this front, for a change effort to be successful.

In addition to Piderit's views on ambivalence, I want to emphasize that a way to sidestep too much ambivalence, is to include the people implementing change efforts in the decision-making process. If they feel a sense of ownership and pride over the decision making to implement the

[6] Piderit, S. 2000. "Rethinking Resistance and Recognizing Ambivalence: A Multidimensional View of Attitudes Toward an Organizational Change." *Academy of Management Review* 25, no. 4, pp. 783–794.

changes, then logically, they would be much more likely to be supportive of the actual implementation as well.

The point here is that organizational change efforts often fail; there are several strategies, however, that organizational leaders can use to help them be successful. Furthermore, having an organizational culture that values polymathic talent is a wise move for any business leader to make particularly in the context of organizational change efforts. When there is a culture of valuing employees, including those with polymathic talents, then including them in decision making should automatically improve the success rate of change initiatives.

More generally, the idea here is to care about your employees; value them. Create a culture where it is clear to them that that is the case—that leadership values their intelligence, talent, perspectives, and their human potential—even, and including, their polymathic potential, capacities, and contributions.

Polymathy and Democracy

John Dewey, in his seminal book, *Democracy and Education: An Introduction to the Philosophy of Education*, wrote about the diversity of individual talent "and for the need for free development of individuality in all its variety."[7] This description sounds a bit like a polymath, especially given the word "variety." The reason Dewey felt that there was a link between broad, diverse individual development, education more largely, and representative democracy is because democracy only works when citizens are properly equipped to make informed, intelligent choices as voting members of that republic. Democracy necessarily requires an educated populace to be effective. In other words, democracy naturally requires active engagement of its citizens to work—and only is effective if the people voting and participating in that government are educated enough to make wise decisions in the way they behave in that democracy. That may include being informed enough to make educated votes to elect political leaders, voting on ballot proposals in elections, or otherwise getting involved in their communities through civic engagement.

---

[7] Dewey, J. 1916. *Democracy and Education*. New York: The Macmillan Company.

If it is true that an educated populace makes democracy more robust, as Dewey argues, then certainly citizenry with polymathic tendencies ("many learnings") is an important way to strengthen that democracy. It takes a certain amount of personal power to engage civically as well—and so there are not only links between polymathy and democracy but also polymathy and expressing one's own power. Although the purpose of this book is focused on polymaths in businesses, if you consider the fact that many organizations exist within democratic societies, then this point is worth considering as part of the larger context, and just another reason why polymathy is important for our society.

Zone of Proximal Development for Polymaths

Vygotsky talked about the "Zone of Proximal Development."[8] The Zone of Proximal Development basically represents a range of someone's capacity—where their learning is at right now, and where their potential learning ceiling is. Given that polymathic people tend to want to continue to learn, develop, and grow themselves into more capable, learned, powerful human beings, the Zone of Proximal Development is a good way of summarizing the range where someone's development can and should occur. The Zone of Proximal Development represents where someone can step further into their own personal power, by harnessing their capacities for additional development.

Create a culture where the Zone of Proximal Development is something you and others think about, and work to address whether individually or as a larger collective.

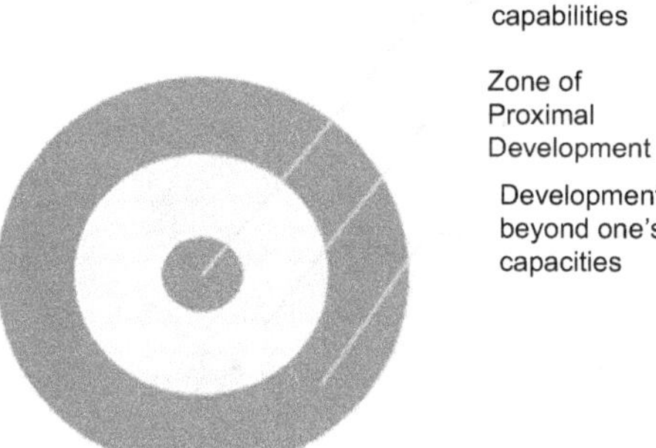

[8] Vygotsky, L. 1978. *Mind in Society*. Cambridge, Massachusetts & London, England: Harvard University Press.

Practical Methods to Create and Sustain a Culture Supportive of Polymaths

Here are some ideas of practical ways for how you can help create a culture where polymaths feel understood, valued, and supported—so that their talents can come to fruition:

- **Make it okay to fail.** Redefine failure as not trying or not learning. If failure in any given situation is likely, then encourage failing fast.
- Communicate that you know the **employees on your team are not just their jobs**; see them as real human beings with lives, interests, responsibilities, and stressors that exist outside of work.
- **Acknowledge the difficulties** employees face (whether in their polymath journeys as individuals or just as an employee with challenges to solve in the workplace).
- **Do sensemaking.** Explain where the organization is at, where you think you should be headed, and how you think you can get there. When difficulties occur, acknowledge them, and reframe them as opportunities, somehow.
- **Tell compelling stories** about the good work polymathic employees have done and are doing currently, alongside stories about how narrow specialists contribute to the team too; highlight both.

The Importance of Sensemaking and Storytelling

Organizational leaders play a critical role in creating effective business cultures, and one way that they impact and steer the organizational culture is through sensemaking and storytelling, in particular. These are powerful tools that leaders should learn how to wield to reach organizational goals. Here are some tips for how you, as an organizational leader and influencer, can effectively "make sense" and engage in effective storytelling:

- **Recognize and Harness Human Emotion:** As you engage in sensemaking, make sure to acknowledge the difficult or even positive emotions your employees may be feeling, at any given time. This way, they feel understood. Harness their emotions by telling stories that include emotional appeals. Emotions can fuel us to action, so use them wisely—and purposefully.

- **Talk About Values:** What is the ethos of your company? Have you identified and labeled them? What do you as a leader value, and what does the organization prize? Make sure to tell stories about the values you hold dear both individually as a leader, and collectively as an organization. Doing so ensures that people can "get on board" with your efforts, because they will understand the reasoning underpinning your business. The value-laden messaging you provide on this front can help people understand the "why" behind what you do as an organization. Tell a compelling "why," and you can impact the organizational culture positively.
- **Explain Your Organizational Purpose:** Many people want to be a part of making the world a better place, somehow. It feels good to be a part of helping other people, the environment, or other important causes. Make sure your company has a compelling purpose and drive that message home so people understand the importance of the work you do together.
- **Be Personal:** Share stories about who you are—even outside of work. Be human. Employees are much more likely to get onboard with your vision, to help you reach your targets, if they empathize with your experiences and if they trust you. One great way of building trust is by being yourself, authentically; people pick up on disingenuous behavior, so make sure you "keep it real," otherwise it may result in unfortunate results, like employees who do not support your efforts because they do not like your "style," or do not trust you to be real with them.
- **Display Artifacts of Achievement:** Make sure that the "sensemaking" you engage in is not just through words—use artifacts, too. Whether it is awards, certificates, trophies, framed letters from your customers, employee of the month awards, or other physical manifestations of success, make sure to prominently display those elements. And if you work in a mostly virtual environment, where such a physical display

is not possible, figure out ways to show off those markers of success as well, even if it is through pictures or visual storytelling, online.

Fostering a Culture for Polymaths

An organizational culture that involves upskilling, lifelong and lifewide learning, and problem solving is one that will appeal to polymathic employees. Here are a few reasons why, and some suggestions for how business leaders can help cocreate a culture conducive to these sorts of behaviors:

- ***Upskilling*** essentially means learning new skills. Who wouldn't want to lead an organization consisting of employees dedicated to improving their capabilities over time? This begs the question, then: how can a business leader help create a culture where employees feel motivated to continually expand their capabilities—to continually learn?
    - A practical way to help your employees "upskill," is through finding out what *they* want to learn about next. Be supportive in their endeavors to improve their knowledge, skills, and abilities.
    - At a basic level, try to understand the actual talent you have onboard. Understanding your workforce is critical if you want to empower it to its fullest potential.
    - Make sure to reward employees who are dedicated to continual improvement—in themselves and their work products. Give awards out; laud them publicly. Make sure everyone on your team understands that self-improvement is appreciated and rewarded in your organization.
- There is something to be said for ***lifelong learning***—which entails how a person continues to gain new knowledge throughout the years, *over time*; however, there is also an important place for ***lifewide learning***—which pertains to the *breadth* of learning a person engages in. This is important not just for employees on the front lines to do but also for

organizational leaders—you too should engage in continual learning, so that you may be as effective as possible in your role, too.

- A practical way to increase lifelong, lifewide learning is to find out what percentage of skills an employee is using in their current job; then figure out how to increase that percentage. This can be done through surveys, formal interviews, or plain old curious conversations. Make it your goal to ensure that your employees are using their skills to the maximum extent possible, rather than letting their talent go to waste.

- Organizations must ***solve problems*** to adapt and thrive. Polymaths are learners, and creativity is their superpower; so naturally, they tend to make good problem solvers. In order to tap into the problem-solving capacities of polymathic employees, it is critical that they understand that leadership actually values problem-solving—that they want it. In other words, going with the status quo, or just dealing with festering problems without tackling them head on, is not something that the organizational leaders want to see; it is important that polymathic people know that this is true for them to feel safe enough to share their problem-solving ideas and to implement them. If employees feel like every time they propose or implement a new solution, it is downplayed, minimized, or dismissed, they will quickly stop trying to help problem-solve and innovate.
    - A practical way to do this, in a real-world setting, is by encouraging ideation and implementation from the ground up. Enable your staff to come up with ideas and create solutions they own, not ones that leadership mandates.
    - Although individual polymaths tend to be excellent problem solvers, given their broad toolkit with which to resolve issues, it is also powerful for teams of people to collaboratively solve problems, of course. Of course, a single leader cannot know it all and do it all—especially

in complex systems with VUCA environments. It is important that any given leader understands the value—and the wisdom—of tapping into the power and knowledge of the network. Enable distributed decision making rather than top-down dictates so that the best, most thought-out solutions will rise to the surface.

- Create downtime—let people converse and dabble, then see what they come up with. Foster a culture where it is safe, and even encouraged, to have exploratory conversations and think outside the box. Some very creative solutions may emerge that could help solve problems in new and effective ways, through this kind of mental meandering.

Organizational Culture and Organizational Sustainability

Many times, when we hear the word "sustainability," we automatically think of environmental sustainability (which is, of course, an important topic and goal). However, sustainability, in a business context, literally means the ability to maintain the business—that the business can sustain itself. Said differently, sustainability means not going out of business; it means staying afloat. There are various critical factors that allow an organization to stay in business, at a high level; the following are a few of those critical elements:

- **Financial Performance:** Of course, for any business to stay alive, it has to perform well financially; financial health is critical to sustainability. Naturally, return on investment is critical. If a business sustains financial losses for many years on end, it will likely go out of business. It is important to have the right strategy in place that allows an organization to thrive, fiscally.
- **Employee Engagement and Retention:** Businesses conduct their work through their employees. Talent is critical, then, to stay in business; with no employees, there is no organization

(even in those businesses that rely heavily on technology and automation, people are still needed). An organization that is constantly losing its human capital will struggle to reach its goals. Turnover is costly and can be debilitating. So, when thinking about how a business can stay afloat and succeed, it is important to consider how keeping employees engaged—and in place—helps the business, well, stay in business. As it relates, much of this book is aimed at helping you, as an organizational leader, learn how to keep polymathic talent, in particular, engaged and for you to understand what it takes to retain top polymathic talent.

- **Relevancy:** Businesses exist to meet needs and solve problems; they need to offer relevant solutions. This means not only being customer-focused to actually meet a need that your audience actually has—even as those needs may shift—but it also means staying relevant in comparison to your competition.
- **Preparedness and Security:** In order to stay in business, the organization (including its people and its assets) need to be secure—both physically secure, and secure from an information technology standpoint. It is important to be prepared for as many possible eventualities—and to come from a posture of preparedness, rather than reactivity. So, make sure, as a leader, you pay attention to the ways in which you can be prepared for challenges that lie ahead. Polymathic people can be particularly useful in imagining what threats may be on the horizon, so make sure to loop them into any Continuity of Operations Planning (COOP) that your organization gets involved with—in addition to those specialist experts' perspectives. By bringing both types of outlooks together, you can build the most robust COOP plan to help your organization stay in business, even as challenges and threats arise.

All these elements, listed previously, are impacted by organizational culture. So, as an organizational leader attempts to impact and sway the organizational culture, keep in mind that any efforts should, of course, include attention to financial performance, employee engagement and retention, staying relevant and competitive, as well as sensitivity to being prepared for problems and possible threats. Polymathic employees are uniquely situated to be able to cocreate an effective culture in these areas, so be sure to include them in your plans related to these elements. Be sure to invest, whether it is investing attention, energy, resources, or money, into these areas to ensure that your business can thrive for many years to come; let your polymathic employees help you build robust plans to ensure your shared success and sustainability.

The Power Paradox: Creating a Culture of Distributed Decision Making

Much of this book focuses on how leaders can empower polymathic employees to contribute to the greatest extent possible; it is a call to action for leaders to create a culture where that is possible. Fostering an effective culture that invites polymathic contribution involves sharing power with those employees. Polymaths do not want to be told what to do; they want to be invited to solve problems creatively and thoughtfully—to unleash their talent in polymathic ways. Polymaths want to use their intelligence.

In the modern era, where problems tend to be complex in nature, it is, indeed, critical that leaders in formal positions of authority tap into the knowledge and skills that the workforce has (polymaths and specialists alike), rather than trying to "know it all" or "do it all" himself or herself. A leader depending on himself or herself alone to make decisions that impact the organization is a sure path toward choices that may only be considered from a limited vantage point, rather than robustly strategized by a larger collective; in other words, it is risky.

The irony is, that even a leader in a formal position of authority, if he or she wants to ensure the business succeeds, should lean into, more and more, sharing power with others; create a culture of shared decision making and distributed power to the extent that makes sense in your particular case. Modern leadership transcends any one person, just as decision making—especially for those most important judgments—should be based on the wisdom of a group, rather than a lone leader. Although leaders in formal positions of authority do have responsibilities to ensure the business succeeds, and that level of responsibility is distinctly different than the responsibilities that employees on the front lines grapple with, make sure to include others, even those who are not in formal positions of authority, on the path toward your shared goals. This helps ensure that decisions are well-informed. By sharing your power, and empowering others, you make your organization—and your own performance as a leader—more effective.

Beyond Organizational Culture: Society's Impact on Polymathy

No human being exists in isolation; we are all part of a larger culture, including cultures we exist in beyond the workplace. There are larger hegemonic forces at play, besides just our individual identities, which impact how our lives turn out—polymathic or not. The larger context interplays with individual volition to impact how a person's experience comes to be. No man or woman is an island unto him or herself; we are embedded in a larger system from which we cannot detach. We impact culture, and culture impacts us—in symbiotic ways.

Of course, culture exists at multiple levels: within individuals, on teams, within whole organizations, and of course, in regions and countries. And of course, as individuals develop their polymathy, that has an impact on the other levels of culture a person engages with—whether within their teams, organizations, or society more largely. So, there is a natural link between polymathy, and the culture polymaths themselves influence as they interact and cocreate realities with the people around them. Of course, the inverse is also true: culture also impacts the polymaths in return.

Specialist Versus Polymathic Cultures

What would a group of polymaths have as their culture? If there was a "culture" of what polymathy is, it would be a culture of learning since learning is fundamental—a necessary ingredient—to the development of polymathy within individuals. In fact, a group of polymaths would likely be distinctly different from the culture you would find in a group of narrow specialists. In the age of specialization, specialists value conformity, while polymaths value individuality. As a general rule, specialists look for information to be passed down to them from other experts, whereas many polymaths tend to embrace critical thinking for themselves and they prize innovation. Specialists tend to "know" while polymaths tend to "learn" (though of course, specialists also learn and polymaths also know).

Polymathic people, in the age of specialization, also must express bravery—particularly in organizational contexts that tend to want to give them "swim lanes" and "boxes" in which to exist, professionally. Polymaths engage in deviance from the norm. They are more individualistic than collectivist. They value broad learning rather than singular, deep learning. And so, if you were to compare a culture made up of polymaths, to a culture made up of specialists, those two groups would have distinctly different cultures.

Frankly, some cultures, more largely, may be more conducive to developing polymathic talent than others. For example, in socialist, egalitarian, communal groups, it may be that there is value in everyone being "the same" rather than standing out. In more individualist societies, there may be an ethos of—to each his own, live outside the box, make your own way. As a result, some countries—depending on their orientation in this regard—may develop more polymaths than others. More studies need to be conducted to explore this more formally—but the general idea here is that depending on the environmental factors, someone's polymathy may be more likely to emerge—or not. (Of course, genetics or "nature" matters, too, in addition to this particular kind of "nurture.")

A Look Into the Future: Polymaths as a Part of Human Evolution

In his seminal book, *The Phenomenon of Man*, Pierre Teilhard de Chardin argues that the evolutionary process involves two main trends:

1. The trend toward increased individuation, and
2. The trend toward increased cooperation.[9]

[9] De Chardin, P. 1955. *The Phenomenon of Man*. New York: Harper Perennial.

In other words, regardless of the species you look at, if you study them long enough, you will see a trend toward both individuation and increased cooperation across members of that species. Increased individuation means that members of a species become more unique—more differentiated—from others. Rather than being similar copies of one another, they become true individual members of that species. The species contains more variety between individual members; in this way, each member can contribute in new and distinctly different ways based on their uniqueness, which strengthens the larger whole. It also adds more variety to the gene pool, which is beneficial for the survival of that species. If all the members are very similar, then all the proverbial eggs are in one basket—in one type—and if the environment shifts and that feature is no longer advantageous, the whole species could go extinct. So, increased individuation is a sign of a more advanced species. Cooperation means that even though the different members of a species are distinct in their own ways, that they cooperate more collaboratively and holistically—thus making the group more robust. This way, the whole becomes greater than simply the sum of the parts.

Both these elements of evolutions describe, exactly, polymaths. Polymaths explore and express their onlyness. By becoming unique combinations of skills, knowledge, and experiences, they become more and more highly individuated. And one of the great advantages of being polymathic, is that it creates more options for them to connect with others—to find common ground and understanding. This is because the polymath has a broad base of experiences and tools with which to connect to others (as opposed to the narrow specialist, who might struggle to find connection with others unless those other people are also narrowly specialized in similar ways). These linkages allow for more connectivity, and for the whole to collaborate more holistically as one.

So, while each one (on the individual level) becomes more differentiated, it almost ironically allows for one (at the group level) to behave more like a single organism, made up of a collective operating in cooperative, strategic ways based on its rich, varied membership. Of course, there is something to be said for being able to connect with others who are different, but the natural human tendency is to bond and connect and collaborate with others whom you feel a connection to, based on some sort of mutual interest, in-group, or shared experience.

Given all of this, if you agree with this logic, that as species evolve, members of that species become more individuated while also becoming more cooperative with other even different members of the larger whole—then it makes logical sense, then, that polymaths could actually be part of the evolutionary urge for us human beings. In fact, it could be argued that without polymaths, we will not evolve; and that until and unless we promote this way of expressing our humanity, that we will remain stuck at a particular point in our evolution. Human polymathy expressed *is* evolution in action.

If you want to be a part of evolving our society and our culture more largely, support polymathy. Consider its long-term implications. As individuals become more individuated, through polymathic expression, they are also better able to integrate and collaborate with the larger whole. Look at humanity as if it were a single organism: individuation and cooperation of the component parts in that organism helps the whole evolve and adapt more intelligently.

As a business leader, of course, it is up to you to recognize that what we do in our work lives impacts our overall lives; we cannot completely separate our existence at work from our overall human existence. Therefore, with this logic, it is incumbent upon business leaders to help our species evolve—and one way of doing that is by supporting polymathic expression of your employees so they can reach their fullest potential even at work, and also help the collective evolve as well. But step one is to create a culture where polymathy is acknowledged and appreciated; hopefully, this chapter helped give you a glimpse into the ways in which you can make that happen in your business, and why doing so is so important.

The Bottom Line of This Chapter

This chapter focused on the critical role of organizational culture in supporting polymathic expression and contributions. Here are the key takeaways:

- **Influence of Organizational Culture:** The culture of an organization significantly impacts its ability to innovate and support polymathic employees. A culture that values diversity and encourages employees to bring their full selves to work is essential for leveraging polymathic talent.

- **Historical Context of Specialization:** Traditionally, organizations have valued specialization and deskilling to maximize efficiency. However, this approach can dehumanize employees and stifle their potential. Modern organizations need to shift toward appreciating and leveraging polymathic abilities.
- **Elements of Organizational Culture:** Edgar Schein's model identifies three elements of culture: artifacts, values, and basic underlying assumptions. Leaders should assess and influence these elements to create a supportive environment for polymaths.
- **Loosening Tight Systems:** Polymathic employees thrive in loosely coupled systems that allow for flexibility, creativity, and self-determination. Leaders can foster such environments by embracing ambiguity, decoupling organizational units, and providing limited oversight.
- **Value of Polymathy in Democracy:** Polymathy supports an educated and engaged populace, which is essential for a robust democracy. Encouraging polymathic development aligns with democratic values and promotes civic engagement.
- **Zone of Proximal Development:** Creating a culture that supports continuous learning and development is crucial for polymathic employees. Leaders should encourage lifelong and lifewide learning to help employees reach their full potential.
- **Practical Methods for Fostering a Supportive Culture:** Leaders can create a supportive culture by redefining failure, acknowledging employee challenges, engaging in sensemaking, and celebrating both specialist and polymathic contributions.
- **Importance of Sensemaking and Storytelling:** Effective leaders use sensemaking and storytelling to build trust, convey organizational values, and motivate employees. This helps create a cohesive and supportive culture.
- **Fostering Lifelong and Lifewide Learning:** Leaders should encourage upskilling and continuous learning, ensuring

that employees use their full range of skills. This promotes engagement and innovation.

- **Organizational Sustainability:** A supportive culture impacts financial performance, employee engagement, relevancy, and preparedness. Polymathic employees can play a vital role in these areas, contributing to long-term organizational sustainability
- **Distributed Decision Making:** Sharing power and decision-making authority with employees can enhance organizational effectiveness. Leaders should create a culture of shared decision making to leverage the collective intelligence of their teams.
- **Society's Impact on Polymathy:** The larger cultural context influences individual polymathy. Organizational leaders should consider these broader cultural forces and create environments that support polymathic development.
- **Specialist versus Polymathic Cultures:** Polymathic cultures value individuality, critical thinking, and innovation, while specialist cultures often emphasize conformity. Leaders should strive to create environments that support polymathic expression.
- **Polymathy and Human Evolution:** Supporting polymathy can be seen as part of human evolution toward greater individuation and cooperation. Leaders have a role in fostering this evolutionary process by creating supportive organizational cultures.

By embracing and supporting polymathic employees, leaders can enhance their organizations' innovation, adaptability, and overall performance. This chapter provided insights and practical methods for creating cultures that nurture and leverage polymathic talent.

Chapter 5 Reflection Questions and Discussion Prompts

Understanding Organizational Culture

1. How would you describe the culture of your current or past organization in terms of supporting polymathic expression?
2. What visible artifacts, values, or assumptions can you identify that reflect how polymathy is either encouraged or suppressed?
3. Have you ever experienced a mismatch between your own polymathic tendencies and the culture of the organization you worked in? What was the result?

Rethinking Specialization and Deskilling

1. In what ways have traditional models of specialization helped or hindered innovation in your experience?
2. Do you believe that organizations are ready to move beyond the "assembly line" mentality? Why or why not?
3. What would it look like for your organization to rehumanize work and value polymathic potential?

Loosening Systems for Innovation

1. Have you worked in a tightly or loosely coupled system? How did that structure impact creativity and autonomy?
2. What strategies can leaders use to create more flexible systems without losing accountability or cohesion?
3. When has ambiguity in your role or team led to innovation or positive change?

Change Management and Ambivalence

1. How have you experienced resistance to change—cognitively, emotionally, or behaviorally—in yourself or others?
2. What are some practical ways to include employees in the decision-making process during change initiatives?
3. Can you think of a time when ambivalence to change actually helped move something forward?

Storytelling, Sensemaking, and Leadership

1. Why is storytelling a powerful tool for building organizational culture?
2. Have you ever been inspired by a leader's personal story or values? What made it resonate with you?
3. How can sensemaking help during times of uncertainty or organizational transformation?

Supporting Lifelong and Lifewide Learning

1. What are some skills or knowledge areas you've developed outside of work that enhance your contributions professionally?
2. How might organizations identify and support polymathic learning paths among their employees?
3. What structures (e.g., learning stipends, mentorships, and sabbaticals) could help promote lifelong and lifewide learning?

Distributed Decision Making and Empowerment

1. What does shared power look like in a healthy organizational context?
2. Have you ever experienced a leader giving up control to empower others? How did that affect performance and morale?
3. What risks and benefits come with creating a culture of distributed decision making?

Polymathy, Democracy, and Society

1. How does supporting polymathy within organizations reflect democratic values?
2. What role do you think businesses play in the broader evolutionary movement toward greater individuation and cooperation?
3. How might your organization influence or be influenced by the cultural context it operates within?

Culture of Specialists Versus Culture of Polymaths

1. What are some cultural traits you notice in organizations that are predominantly specialist-driven?

2. How might a "culture of polymathy" change the way success, risk, or leadership are defined?
3. What small shifts could your organization make to move toward a culture that values individuality and broad learning?

Evolution and the Future of Work

1. Do you agree that polymathy may represent an evolutionary step in human development? Why or why not?
2. What future roles might polymathic employees play as technology continues to automate narrow tasks?
3. How can your organization prepare now to be a place where polymathic talent thrives in the decades to come?

CHAPTER 6

Polymathy and Leadership

"Leadership and learning are indispensable to each other."
—John F. Kennedy

The purpose of this chapter is to examine the relationship between polymathy and leadership, in an organizational context. First, this chapter will propose a definition for polymathic leadership. This chapter will also address leadership fundamentally being about influence, which is bolstered by polymathic thinking. Polymaths as leaders—and where their talent makes the most sense when formally leading teams—will be addressed. This chapter will explain why polymathic leaders are particularly well suited, for example, in leading a diverse team—even a team made up of specialists from different departments. This chapter also provides some evidence from academia with regard to why polymaths can be particularly well suited to leadership roles.

Polymathic Leadership Defined

Fellow polymathy scholar, Dr. Michael Araki, has defined polymathic leadership as "a pattern of *leader behaviors* that *encourages and inspires followers* to advance to higher levels of *depth, breadth and connectedness* of ideas, knowledge and competence."[1] In his definition, polymathic leadership is about how to influence polymathic behaviors *in others*. This is an important and noteworthy consideration for what polymathic leadership does: it empowers others to act, with a systems-thinking approach in

---

[1] Araki, M. 2015. *Polymathic Leadership: Theoretical Foundation and Construct Development* [Master's degree thesis]. Pontifícia Universidade Católica, Rio de Janeiro, Brazil.

mind—and it considers the importance of breadth, depth, and integration when identifying solutions.

Another way of looking at polymathic leadership is to consider the traits and behaviors of the leader himself or herself. For that reason, I propose this definition of polymathic leadership that adds this additional focus:

> *Polymathic leadership* is a process of influence wherein a leader actively models polymathic thinking and behavior—demonstrating breadth, depth, and integrative capacity—while also empowering others to explore diverse knowledge, cultivate multidimensional skills, and collaborate across domains to achieve shared goals.

In this second definition, the focus is on how the leader uses polymathic approaches to influence the team to action—while also encouraging the team to polymathic tactics as well; the focus is both on the leader himself or herself, and how they use polymathic approaches, which impact the team to arrive at effective solutions that are comprehensive by design, too.

Though the focus of these two definitions differ slightly—Dr. Araki's focus being on team behaviors involving breadth, depth, and integration, and my proposed definition involving polymathic thinking and behaviors coming from the leader himself or herself, to encourage the team to polymathic solutions, both essentially use a *polymathic mindset* to get at an important commonality: that polymathic leadership involves polymathic approaches, either by the leader himself or herself (focusing on the leader), and by the followers (focusing on the followers).

Polymathic Mindset

Previously, I referenced the concept of a "polymathic mindset," so I would like to take a moment now to describe what I mean by that term. Someone with a polymathic mindset is a person who is a continual learner, aspiring to think comprehensively. There is an inherent openness involved in this mindset—a focus on learning, expanding, growing, including rather than excluding. A polymathic thinker naturally considers multiple perspectives in a systems-thinking sort of way. They seek to make linkages among elements in a system, while keeping the bigger picture in mind. It involves being not only strategic but also creative.

Importantly, a polymathic mindset is not innate or fixed. It can be cultivated over time through deliberate exposure to diverse disciplines, reflective practices, and an intentional commitment to curiosity. By encouraging flexible thinking, broad reading, interdisciplinary exploration, and comfort with ambiguity, individuals can develop and strengthen their polymathic mindset—regardless of their background or profession. As you can imagine, a polymathic mindset is also foundational to polymathic leadership. There can be no polymathic leadership unless there is a polymathic mindset first.

Practices That Promote a Polymathic Mindset

While some people may naturally lean toward polymathic thinking, this mindset is **highly cultivable**. It flourishes not from innate genius but from consistent habits that prioritize curiosity, integration, and openness over certainty and specialization. Here are some practical strategies for nurturing a polymathic mindset in yourself or others:

1. **Follow Your Curiosity**
   Let curiosity—not just utility—guide your learning journey. Read beyond your professional field. Explore unusual questions. Give yourself permission to learn for the sake of wonder.
2. **Engage in Lifewide Learning**
   Learn not only in formal settings but also through hobbies, travel, conversations, artistic pursuits, and lived experiences. A polymathic mindset thrives on exposure to different ways of knowing.
3. **Connect the Dots Across Domains**
   Practice drawing analogies between disparate fields. Ask yourself: *What does this remind me of in another discipline? How could this idea be applied elsewhere?*
4. **Balance Breadth with Depth**
   Explore widely, but take time to go deep in select areas. Polymathy is not about surface-level dabbling—it's about deep curiosity expressed across multiple domains.

5. **Seek Out Diverse Perspectives**
   Polymathic thinkers actively seek out different worldviews, disciplines, cultures, and cognitive styles. Engage with people who don't think like you. Let their lenses challenge your assumptions.
6. **Practice Reflective Integration**
   Make time to reflect on your learning. Journaling, sketching conceptual maps, or even talking through ideas aloud can help you synthesize knowledge from across domains into coherent insights.
7. **Cultivate Comfort with Ambiguity**
   A polymathic mindset resists simplistic answers, remaining comfortable with complexity and capable of holding multiple, sometimes competing, truths at once. Practice staying open and curious even when clarity isn't immediate.
8. **Value Play and Experimentation**
   Serious play—trying new things, tinkering, experimenting—is essential for polymathic growth. This includes creative expression, side projects, and the freedom to explore without outcome pressure.
9. **Invest in Self-Directed Learning**
   Design your own learning journeys. Set goals, choose resources, and track your evolution over time. The more agency you have in shaping your education, the more polymathic your mindset becomes.
10. **Celebrate Multiplicity in Yourself and Others**
    Normalize complexity. Recognize that having many interests or identities is a strength, not a liability. Help others embrace their multidimensionality as well.

When practiced consistently, these habits create the fertile ground where polymathic thinking can flourish—not just in individuals, but across teams, classrooms, and organizations.

Polymathic Leadership Behaviors

A polymathic leader, when faced with a problem, would naturally seek to do the following:

1. ***Apply prior learnings*** he or she knows to solve the problem at hand. The more prior learnings that can be used to solve the problem, the better.

2. ***Learn more information*** to solve the problem. Where is information needed? How can that information be gleaned? How can that information be applied? A polymathic leader will always strive to ensure that solutions are the most well-informed possible—and having a lot of information to solve the problem will be helpful in this regard.
3. ***Leverage other people's knowledge, skills, insights, and experiences*** to help solve the problem.
4. ***Learn from the experience.*** How can this experience help future problems (which may or may not seem directly relevant)?

The key trademark, I would argue, of polymathic leadership involves *learning while leading.* This type of leader applies a polymathic mindset, where learning is central. Especially given problems are ripe opportunities for learning to take place, a polymathic leader would always be seeking to *apply learning to problems*, while also *using the problems to learn more.* This is an important point.

Leadership as Influence

Leadership is about influence; to influence others effectively requires having an arsenal of information, a solid strategy, and the ability to both understand, then tailor your messaging based on the audience at hand—to convince them of something, or perhaps even inspire them to take action. Because polymathic people are learners—they have a broad array of information in their heads and at their fingertips, they tend to be good strategic thinkers. And because of their varied experiences, they also tend to be good at connecting, engaging, and understanding other people, or at least seeing multiple perspectives. In other words, polymathic people tend to be natural influencers. Their multifaceted backgrounds put them in a position to be able to influence effectively. So, if leadership is about influence, polymathic people are well positioned to do just that—even if they are not in formal positions of authority. And if a polymath is in a formal position of leadership authority, their polymathy may help them be more effective, because they can influence others from a polymathic perspective; they can wear multiple different hats, and appeal to different audience members based on their position and background.

Example of a Polymath Leader

In 1962, at a White House dinner honoring the Nobel Prize winners from the Western Hemisphere, President at the time, John F. Kennedy, gave a toast, and said the following: "I want to tell you how welcome you are to the White House. I think this is the most extraordinary collection of talent, of human knowledge, that has ever been gathered together at the White House, with the possible exception of when Thomas Jefferson dined alone."[2] Thomas Jefferson is considered one of the greatest Presidents, and perhaps one of the greatest minds, in recorded history.

Thomas Jefferson lived from 1743 to 1826. He had multiple careers and many different hobbies, which he excelled at. For example, he, of course, worked in politics. He was Governor of Virginia, Ambassador to France, Secretary of State, Vice President, and President of the United States. Plus, he was the main author of the Declaration of Independence. And he cofounded the Democratic party, which still exists today. He was a busy man. But politics was not his only focus.

Jefferson also founded the prestigious University of Virginia, was an avid agriculturalist, anthropologist, architect, astronomer, bibliophile, ethnologist, farmer, geographer, horseman, botanist, horticulturist, inventor, lawyer, linguist, mathematician, meteorologist, naturalist, paleontologist, political philosopher, scientist, violinist, and writer—to name a few. He was also a polyglot, speaking fluent Greek, Latin, French, Spanish, Italian, German, and of course, English.

Some noteworthy accomplishments he made as America's third president include allowing the Alien and Sedition Acts to expire, completing the Louisiana purchase from France, which doubled the size of the United States at the time and removed a possible rival from our borders, and he also authorized the Lewis and Clark Expedition. For these reasons and more, he is considered by many to be one of the greatest American presidents.

Was he great because he was a polymath? There are other presidents who were not polymathic who were also great. But the bottom line is that Jefferson was not just an amazing founding father and president but

---

[2] Johnstone, R.M., Jr. 1978. *Jefferson and the Presidency, Leadership in the Young Republic.* Ithaca, NY: Cornell University Press.

also an impressive human being—a true Renaissance man. His achievements spanned so many fields—plus he made connections across fields, as strong polymaths often do. He was creative and successful, and his polymathy helped him to express those capacities. Indeed, like Jefferson, many of the great leaders in history were also polymathic. Societies have been shaped by many polymathic leaders over the millennia. That said, not all polymaths will be good leaders; but if you look at those individuals who are the strongest leaders, and who have also impacted history, chances are high that they are also polymathic.

Leaders Must Be Adaptable

Charles Darwin said that it is not the strongest of the species that survive—rather, it is the most adaptable to change. Of course, rigidity does not make a good leader, and neither does inflexibility or close-mindedness. Rigidity speaks of death whereas flexibility indicates life. Plus, given that change is the one constant we can count on in life, leaders, to successfully influence and aspire their teams to achieve great things, must themselves be adaptable. This is true more now than ever before, given the complexity of our world, and the fast-paced nature of change. Polymaths tend to be very good at being flexible—obviously, the fact that they have many different facets to their personhood—notably more so than the average person—indicates their desire to have variety, and therefore adaptability, in their lives.

Good leaders must adjust their strategy depending on how the game plays out; polymathic people, as a general rule, enjoy change, variety, and newness. Because they are used to having many different, sometimes even parallel, careers, hobbies, and experiences, more generally, they naturally "switch" between them. They tend to be efficient at this "switching." But the larger point here is that in the world we live in today, adaptability is paramount—whether that adaptability is for employees, leaders, or whole organizations. And polymathic talent is adaptable. Their "many learnings" give them the ability to switch focus, draw out different skills, or think from different perspectives. And these are all qualities that are particularly useful for people in formal positions of authority—for leaders—because the ability to adapt helps them succeed, especially when the storms of change come—as they inevitably will.

Where Polymathic Leadership Makes Sense in Organizations

If a leader oversees a group of people working in multiple functions, then a leader who is diverse, who has broad exposure and can speak multiple professional languages is well positioned to function as that group's head—even if that team is made up of a variety of different narrow specialists. This is not to say that all polymaths will make great leaders; because indeed, some polymaths want to explore their curiosity, learn, grow, and contribute—but not in a leadership role. However, other polymaths are very well suited to leadership positions.

Polymathic skills can be a great asset to someone functioning in a formal leadership role. Polymathic leaders who have worked in a variety of functions, across different domains, have a kind of intellectual ambidexterity. They can understand the functions under their purview more fully given they have worked in multiple fields. This contrasts with a leader who has been very specialized over the course of his or her career. They may prefer to discuss and oversee only the department in which they have had a lot of experience, rather than being multipronged and knowledgeable in multiple domains, even if they are charged with leading those different functions.

Another word of caution: narrow specialist leaders will tend to gravitate toward what they know, and what comes easier to them—which, given their background—would be a single functional area. This sort of bias could even lead a business astray if a leader preferentially invests resources into a function they know, while diminishing the importance of functions with which they are not as familiar. In contrast, polymaths who have had exposure across more areas are well suited to manage teams whose work is in multiple functional areas; putting a specialist in charge of a team whose work they may struggle to understand or relate to could be problematic.

Naturally, polymaths come in various shapes and sizes; not all are destined to be great leaders in an organizational context. In fact, some polymaths tend to avoid roles where they would have to manage other people because they simply do not enjoy that kind of work. In other cases, polymaths naturally gravitate toward positions involving leadership, management, and more generally, influence. It depends on the person at hand, regarding if they are suited to a leadership position or not.

For those polymaths who are, in fact, comfortable leading or managing a group of people, their polymathic backgrounds can be particularly useful. For example, for a person managing a diverse team, the polymath leader may be able to speak multiple professional "languages," which helps them better manage that diverse team. Further, polymaths may tend to have larger professional networks from a wider array of domains—and so for a leader, wanting to support a diverse team—that network may prove beneficial to help advance team efforts.

Like a hub in a network, the polymath leader can make more connections to different types of employees, given their broad base of experience and exposure in different disciplines. This is valuable for organizational executives to be aware of: that polymaths who are also effective leaders can play a pivotal role in managing *diverse* teams, given the breadth of their own prior experiences, which helps them to understand the various roles on a team better. If you put a specialist in charge of a diverse team, that specialist leader may have trouble connecting with and understanding individual contributors who come from different functional backgrounds. Polymaths can make excellent project managers and, if it suits them, excellent team leads—especially when they are leading groups of people with a wide variety of professional experiences across fields. In his book, *The Polymath: Unlocking the Power of Human Versatility*, Waqas Ahmed explained that one of the world's leading futurists, Ray Kurzweil, believes that a leader on any project should be polymathic: "Experts in highly specialized fields can be part of a team, but the team leader needs to bridge multiple disciplines."[3] That said, on the contrary, specialist leaders may be more appropriate when leading a group of narrow specialists on their team, naturally.

[3] Ahmed, W. 2018. *The Polymath: Unlocking the Power of Human Versatility.* Wiley.

The Evidence for Polymathic Leadership

A number of different researchers have conducted studies that provide evidence that polymaths can actually be quite effective in leading certain types of teams. Of course, not all polymaths are suited to leadership positions. But for individuals who do have the temperament, desire, and background, which would make them appropriate for leadership roles, they can be quite effective in leading teams. Here are a few highlights of what the academic literature tells us about polymathic leadership.

Researchers Day and Dragoni said that someone with higher levels of intrapersonal diversity will have better leadership capacity.[4] In other words, organizational teams who have an intrapersonally diverse polymath in a formal leadership role may fare better than teams who have leaders with less intrapersonal diversity. And this is true regardless of whether those experiences a leader has had were pleasant or challenging, or whether or not they were professional experiences or from a nonwork setting—all of these types of experiences can enhance leadership performance. Variety is key here.

Further, Bunderson and Sutcliffe found that intrapersonal functional diversity—that is, the breadth of functional experiences professionally that someone has had—"has significant and positive implications for team processes and performance."[5] They posited that a team leader who is intrapersonally functionally diverse can help their teams perform better. Logically, then, organizations can considerably benefit if they purposefully seek out and develop management teams made up of individuals who are functionally broad rather than just narrowly specialized in a single functional area. Importantly, Bunderson and Sutcliffe also said that intrapersonal diversity is most powerful for project team performance in difficult, volatile, uncertain environments, more so than stable ones. It could backfire to put a polymath into a position of leadership over a team

---

[4] Day, D., and L. Dragoni. 2015. "Leadership Development: An Outcome-Oriented Review based on Time and Level of Analysis." *Annual Review of Organizational Psychology and Organizational Behavior* 2, pp. 133–156.

[5] Bunderson, J., and K. Sutcliffe. 2002. "Comparing Alternative Conceptualizations of Functional Diversity in Management Teams: Process and Performance Effects." *Academy of Management Journal* 45, no. 5, pp. 875–893.

with very stable, routine, rote tasks to accomplish. Polymaths thrive in more challenging situations, so it is best to put them in positions where they can face challenges, step up, and lean in to address them. Bunderson and Sutcliffe also noted that "organizations can benefit considerably by seeking and developing management teams composed of individuals who are functionally broad and not just narrowly specialized in a single functional area."

Angriawan and Adebe found a positive relationship between the length of industry tenure for chief executive officers, the level of their intrapersonal functional diversity, and the extent to which they scan the environment.[6] This sort of external awareness has positive implications for strategic decision making, of course. No doubt, executives should have great external awareness, facilitated through environmental scanning, as they guide their organizations.

Similarly, Hitt and Tyler found that executives who have broad functional backgrounds are more effective when evaluating options and making strategic decisions when compared to their counterparts who have narrower, more domain-limited functional backgrounds.[7] This makes sense. By having more varied, broad experiences, polymathic executives may be better positioned to make sense of various options in front of them, which would help when making strategic judgment calls on behalf of their business.

Lastly, Yap, Chai, and Lemaire stated that intrapersonal functional diversity can foster innovation.[8] Given how important it is for organizational leaders to foster innovation, then it may be beneficial to have leadership that is polymathic within organizational teams. After all, polymaths themselves tend to be highly creative, so it makes sense that they would promote and support creative innovation among their own team

[6] Angriawan A., and M. Adebe. 2001. "Chief Executive Background Characteristics and Environmental Scanning Emphasis: An Empirical Investigation." *Journal of Business Strategies* 28, pp. 75–96.

[7] Hitt, M.A., and B.B. Tyler. 1991. "Strategic Decision Models: Integrating Different Perspectives." *Strategic Management Journal* 12, pp. 327–351.

[8] Yap, C., K. Chai, and P. Lemaire. 2005. "An Empirical Study on Functional Diversity and Innovation in SMEs." *Creativity and Innovation Management* 14, no. 2, pp. 176–190.

members. This also relates to organizational change initiatives because creativity is fundamentally related to change: imagining change demands creative thought processes, and then actually implementing change efforts requires changes in behavior—perhaps even creative behavior in order to achieve the desired results.

What these studies tell us is that individual thinking as well as leadership performance tend to improve when those very leaders have more functional intrapersonal diversity—in other words, when they are more polymathic.

Openness to Experience and Leadership

Polymaths, by nature, tend to be high in "openness to experience," which is a measurable trait considered part of the "Big Five" personality traits. (The other four are extraversion, agreeableness, conscientiousness, and neuroticism.) Because polymathy involves constantly learning new things, of course someone has to be very open to new experiences to facilitate that very learning. Interestingly, Kickul and Newman found that those high in openness to experience are more likely to become leaders in a group.[9] The reason is because those high in openness are more likely to initiate new ideas, ask questions, and freely share their opinions—essentially, to engage in behaviors considered typical of leaders.

If you believe that leadership is a skill that can be learned, then polymathic people—individuals who have an insatiable desire to learn—may also be those who tend to gravitate toward positions of leadership. In fact, Oakes, Ferris, Martocchio, Buckley, and Broach said that openness to experience is critical for skill acquisition—in gaining new skills.[10] Given polymaths are high in openness to experience, which leads to new learning

---

[9] Kickul, J., and G. Neuman. 2000. "Emergent Leadership Behaviors: The Function of 258 Personality and Cognitive Ability in Determining Teamwork Performance and KSAs." *Journal of Business and Psychology* 15, no. 1, pp. 27–51.

[10] Oakes, D.W., G.R. Ferris, J.J. Martocchio, M.R. Buckley, and D. Broach. 2001. "Cognitive Ability and Personality Predictors of Training Program Skill Acquisition and Job Performance." *Journal of Business and Psychology* 15, no. 4, pp. 523–548.

and skills, then it would make sense that polymaths could be great candidates to learn and grow into leadership positions within organizations. One caveat however; not all polymaths will be suited to leadership roles—it depends on their specific background, professional desires, temperament, interpersonal skills, and so on.

Organizational Development Agenda Setting

Leaders are often in charge of setting the agenda, in terms of where there are gaps or holes in the organization. Where is improvement needed? Where are the pain points? What needs attention or fixing? Organizational development is a way of improving an organization, whether those kinds of interventions involve employee training, organizational restructuring, obtaining feedback from customers or employees, team building exercises, and so on. But how is a leader supposed to figure out the best, most strategic areas to make these kinds of investments? Particularly if a leader has been a narrow specialist, making these sorts of judgment calls could be quite difficult. How can someone be an accurate diagnostician if they have been narrowly exposed through professional specialization? How can someone accurately prescribe a cure if they have not had adequate exposure to the problem? Given that an important responsibility of an organizational leader is setting the agenda in terms of the types of investments to make for organizational development, leaders who have broad experience and exposure—like polymaths do—are well positioned to be able to make these sorts of judgment calls adeptly. Their prior experiences—which are more varied—helps put them in a place to better understand the challenges and chart the best path forward from there.

Complexity Leadership Theory

We live in a complex world; an important perspective from the scholarly literature to consider given the complexity in which we exist, is Complexity Leadership Theory (CLT). CLT says that in a complex adaptive system, where problems are not easily solved, we need collaborative *networks* that can solve problems together.[11] Further, CLT says that the more complex the problem, the more complex the solution will need to be. According to CLT, the solutions to very challenging problems cannot be predicted in advance—they emerge over time, through the work of a collaborative, self-organizing, adaptive network trying to find solutions together.

If you imagine a neural network, where individual neurons work together to tackle problems, where do you think the most value is added in that system: by simple, one-dimensional neurons, or those that have multiple dimensions, capacities, and can have several linkages at once? Single disciplinary experts are like individual neurons that may be strong, but only have simple connections to the other neighboring neurons. Polymathic people are like hubs in the network because they are able to form multiple connections based on their multiple capacities. They have more influence in that network because of the additional connections they can make across ideas and with a larger number of other "neurons" in that network.

Indeed, within a team where complexity exists, where there are unknown unknowns, polymathic people who are multisided make great hubs of information. They are translators and bridge builders. They can connect the dots, ideas, and people because of their expanded and more diverse exposure. In this sort of model, in a complex adaptive system, leadership becomes decentralized. It is more about what the network can do, rather than any one individual—even those in formal leadership roles.

Managing Change

Another important role of any leader is managing change. Beyond just determining (albeit hopefully with input from other stakeholders) the change agenda, leaders are often responsible for ensuring that change efforts get put into practice—that the plan becomes reality. Change can

[11] Uhl-Bien, M., R. Marion, and B. McKelvey. 2007. "Complexity Leadership Theory: Shifting Leadership from the Industrial Age to the Knowledge Era." *The Leadership Quarterly* 18, p. 298–318.

be difficult, though. People often resist change. What can help make change initiatives easier, or support them to be successful—so that they actually come to fruition?

One answer is *foresight* to avoid roadblocks—this is an important role of the leader; helping the team overcome obstacles and elements that could derail the change efforts. Given that many change efforts fail, *avoiding failure* is an important consideration here. Ideation and scenario planning can help in this regard. Brainstorming is important. To the extent possible, preparing for the unknown, and expecting the unexpected obviously would help. These types of mental tasks are all the types of intellectual labor that polymathic talent is particularly well suited to do. They can zoom in and out between fine-grain details and bigger picture viewpoints. Because they exist "outside the box" professionally, this positions them well to also think "outside the box." And when dealing with change—trying to adapt to challenges, even ones that are unexpected—thinking about resolutions in new and creative ways is particularly advantageous.

Managing Talent as Leadership Imperative

A key tenet of this book is that effective organizational leaders and HR professionals should consider how to include and leverage polymathic talent strategically. Peter Drucker, who is a respected management consultant, educator, and author once opined that "success in the Knowledge Economy comes to those who do two things: identify and articulate their talents, and place themselves in positions to use them."[12] If you extend this logic, then success in the Knowledge Economy for HR professionals and business leaders would necessarily involve two things: identifying and articulating the full talents of employees, and putting those employees in positions to effectively use those skills, knowledge, and abilities. Therefore, the role of a leader is not simply to leverage their own skill sets—which of course, is important—but to ensure that the talent of other people on their teams does not go to waste. If leadership

[12] McDonald, B., and D. Hutcheson. 2017. *Don't Waste Your Talent: The 8 Critical Steps to Discovering What You do Best.* The Highlands Company.

is about influence, then a significant way of influencing the organization as a whole is to empower each individual to add the maximum contribution possible—and the best way to do that is to ensure that people are actually using their skills to the fullest extent possible (and this includes leveraging their polymathic talent).

Leaders Supporting Polymathic Talent on Their Teams

The role of a strategic, thoughtful organizational leader—especially in the context of reading this book—is figuring out ways in which a leader can empower *others* to embrace their polymathy. So, an important way in which leadership and polymathy interconnect is precisely in this way: that good organizational leaders should be figuring out how to support polymathic talent within the organization (in addition to supporting narrow specialist talent, where that approach makes sense).

Frequently, when organizations inadvertently push away high-performing, high-value polymathic talent, it is precisely because the polymath is frustrated that they cannot use their actual skills on the job—that they are being squished into a professional box that they do not want to be in. Therefore, a strategic move for an organizational leader is to actually understand how to attract, place, develop, and retain polymathic talent. If a leader can do just that, it could be a very advantageous business strategy to help improve the work taking place in the organization.

Polymathic Traits Related to Effective Leadership Behaviors

Would you rather have a leader who is polymathic—who can speak knowledgeably about many different things, based on their broad exposure and experiences—or would you rather have a leader who is a monomath, very highly expert in a single, niche area? My guess is that most people would prefer the polymathic leader. Plus, many of the traits typically associated with polymaths—curiosity, bravery, continual learning, the ability to connect over myriad subjects and find common ground with other people, an appreciation for seeing issues from multiple perspectives, a commitment to continued personal growth and learning—these are also the traits that make a strong and effective leader. Indeed, polymathic professionals can be truly excellent leaders—especially if that is the type of role they aspire to be in at work. Not all polymaths want to be in formal leadership roles, however, so it is important to consider that fact as well. The point here, though, is that the traits of highly effective leaders also overlap with the traits you tend to find in polymaths—and that is worthy of noting.

Leadership and Learning

An important role of any organizational leader, in a formal position of authority, is to be a continual learner themselves. This helps them as they make decisions, forge strategies, and fend off problems in the business. A leader who is not good at learning is likely to struggle and perhaps as a result, might sway the organization into unfavorable directions. Said differently, learning is critical to be effective as a leader. And that's exactly what polymaths are: learners. Polymathy and leadership mesh together in this way and feed off each other in a continual, symbiotic loop: one's polymathy should improve leadership performance, and a high-performing leader would naturally want to learn broadly, as polymaths do, which in turn helps them improve leadership performance even more. But learning is not just important for formal leaders—it is important for members of the team as well. The question is, how can leaders help support employees to be continual learners?

In the book called *Human Work in the Age of Smart Machines*, author Jamie Merisotis says it in this simple yet profound statement: "We prepare people for work through learning." Therefore, another important—truly critical role—of any organizational leader, is to encourage, convince, and incentivize their employees to look for learning opportunities wherever possible—to create a culture where learning is highly valued. (See Chapter 5 for more information on organizational culture.) Look for opportunities to layer learning—realizing that different people may learn in different ways. Look for opportunities to engage in traditional learning formats or approaches, as well as nontraditional ones. Look for opportunities to be creative. Be committed to learning yourself, and help others learn as well to truly supercharge your organizational performance.

Polymaths and Self-Leadership

A polymath, by definition, is someone with "many learnings." Chances are that nobody else instructed a polymath on what exactly they should learn, in the totality of his or her learning journey; polymaths are *self-directed* learners. They sometimes even rebel against authority, regularly employ sharp critical thinking skills, and strive to be the self-authors of their own life stories. Polymaths are in a way renegades, in the context of a specialist society, refusing to conform to the pressures society places on them to be narrow specialists, only. In other words, they live by their own rules, to some extent.

Given all these factors, it becomes clear that, by nature, polymathic behavior is a form of *self-leadership*. Self-leadership refers to a process through which individuals influence and regulate themselves to achieve the self-direction and self-motivation necessary to perform.[13] It is a form of self-authorship, or self-curation. I would be remiss if I did not acknowledge this in a chapter focused on leadership and polymathy. In other words, polymaths are often excellent at self-leadership—and that is important to know for anyone aiming to understand this particular segment of our society. Leadership is not just about influencing others; it is also about managing oneself. Polymaths are prime examples of people expressing self-leadership as they go against the grain and curate their own lives thoughtfully.

The Bottom Line of This Chapter

This chapter focused on the critical role of organizational culture in supporting polymathic expression and contributions. Here are the key takeaways:

- **Influence of Organizational Culture:** The culture of an organization significantly impacts its ability to innovate and support polymathic employees. A culture that values diversity

[13] Neck, C.P. and J.D. Houghton. 2006. Two decades of self-leadership theory and research: Past developments, present trends, and future possibilities. Journal of Managerial Psychology 21 (4): 270-295.

and encourages employees to bring their full selves to work is essential for leveraging polymathic talent.

- **Historical Context of Specialization:** Traditionally, organizations have valued specialization and deskilling to maximize efficiency. However, this approach can dehumanize employees and stifle their potential. Modern organizations need to shift toward appreciating and leveraging polymathic abilities.
- **Elements of Organizational Culture:** Edgar Schein's model identifies three elements of culture: artifacts, values, and basic underlying assumptions. Leaders should assess and influence these elements to create a supportive environment for polymaths.
- **Loosening Tight Systems:** Polymathic employees thrive in loosely coupled systems that allow for flexibility, creativity, and self-determination. Leaders can foster such environments by embracing ambiguity, decoupling organizational units, and providing limited oversight.
- **Value of Polymathy in Democracy:** Polymathy supports an educated and engaged populace, which is essential for a robust democracy. Encouraging polymathic development aligns with democratic values and promotes civic engagement.
- **Zone of Proximal Development:** Creating a culture that supports continuous learning and development is crucial for polymathic employees. Leaders should encourage lifelong and lifewide learning to help employees reach their full potential.
- **Practical Methods for Fostering a Supportive Culture:** Leaders can create a supportive culture by redefining failure, acknowledging employee challenges, engaging in sensemaking, and celebrating both specialist and polymathic contributions.
- **Importance of Sensemaking and Storytelling:** Effective leaders use sensemaking and storytelling to build trust, convey organizational values, and motivate employees. This helps create a cohesive and supportive culture.

- **Fostering Lifelong and Lifewide Learning:** Leaders should encourage upskilling and continuous learning, ensuring that employees use their full range of skills. This promotes engagement and innovation.
- **Organizational Sustainability:** A supportive culture impacts financial performance, employee engagement, relevancy, and preparedness. Polymathic employees can play a vital role in these areas, contributing to long-term organizational sustainability.
- **Distributed Decision Making:** Sharing power and decision-making authority with polymathic employees can enhance organizational effectiveness. Leaders should create a culture of shared decision making to leverage the collective intelligence of their teams.
- **Society's Impact on Polymathy:** The larger cultural context influences individual polymathy. Organizational leaders should consider these broader cultural forces and create environments that support polymathic development.
- **Specialist versus Polymathic Cultures:** Polymathic cultures value individuality, critical thinking, and innovation, while specialist cultures often emphasize conformity. Leaders should strive to create environments that support polymathic expression.
- **Polymathy and Human Evolution:** Supporting polymathy can be seen as part of human evolution toward greater individuation and cooperation. Leaders have a role in fostering this evolutionary process by creating supportive organizational cultures.

By embracing and supporting polymathic employees, leaders can enhance their organizations' innovation, adaptability, and overall performance. This chapter provided insights and practical methods for creating cultures that nurture and leverage polymathic talent.

Chapter 6 Reflection Questions & Discussion Prompts

Understanding Organizational Culture

1. How would you describe the culture of your current or past organization in terms of supporting polymathic expression?
2. What visible artifacts, values, or assumptions can you identify that reflect how polymathy is either encouraged or suppressed?
3. Have you ever experienced a mismatch between your own polymathic tendencies and the culture of the organization you worked in? What was the result?

Rethinking Specialization and Deskilling

1. In what ways have traditional models of specialization helped or hindered innovation in your experience?
2. Do you believe that organizations are ready to move beyond the "assembly line" mentality? Why or why not?
3. What would it look like for your organization to rehumanize work and value polymathic potential?

Loosening Systems for Innovation

1. Have you worked in a tightly or loosely coupled system? How did that structure impact creativity and autonomy?
2. What strategies can leaders use to create more flexible systems without losing accountability or cohesion?
3. When has ambiguity in your role or team led to innovation or positive change?

Change Management and Ambivalence

1. How have you experienced resistance to change—cognitively, emotionally, or behaviorally—in yourself or others?
2. What are some practical ways to include employees in the decision-making process during change initiatives?
3. Can you think of a time when ambivalence to change actually helped move something forward?

Storytelling, Sensemaking, and Leadership

1. Why is storytelling a powerful tool for building organizational culture?
2. Have you ever been inspired by a leader's personal story or values? What made it resonate with you?
3. How can sensemaking help during times of uncertainty or organizational transformation?

Supporting Lifelong and Lifewide Learning

1. What are some skills or knowledge areas you've developed outside of work that enhance your contributions professionally?
2. How might organizations identify and support polymathic learning paths among their employees?
3. What structures (e.g., learning stipends, mentorships, and sabbaticals) could help promote lifelong and lifewide learning?

Distributed Decision Making and Empowerment

1. What does shared power look like in a healthy organizational context?
2. Have you ever experienced a leader giving up control to empower others? How did that affect performance and morale?
3. What risks and benefits come with creating a culture of distributed decision making?

Polymathy, Democracy, and Society

1. How does supporting polymathy within organizations reflect democratic values?
2. What role do you think businesses play in the broader societal movement toward greater individuation and cooperation?
3. How might your organization influence or be influenced by the cultural context it operates within?

Culture of Specialists versus Culture of Polymaths

1. What are some cultural traits you notice in organizations that are predominantly specialist-driven?
2. How might a "culture of polymathy" change the way success, risk, or leadership are defined?
3. What small shifts could your organization make to move toward a culture that values individuality and broad learning?

Evolution and the Future of Work

1. Do you agree that polymathy may represent an evolutionary step in human development? Why or why not?
2. What future roles might polymathic employees play as technology continues to automate narrow tasks?
3. How can your organization prepare now to be a place where polymathic talent thrives in the decades to come?

CHAPTER 7

Human Resources and the Polymath

"It doesn't make sense to hire smart people and then tell them what to do; we hire smart people so they can tell us what to do."

—Steve Jobs

The purpose of this chapter is to discuss how organizational leadership can strategically leverage a combination of specialists and polymathic generalists on your teams, in concert. Of course, this has to do with the HR function—issues such as hiring, development, training, and so on will be discussed herein. But first, before diving into the action steps you may take to help leverage the power of polymathic people, I would like to first address what I believe your role as an organizational leader really is, at a high level. In other words, before focusing on the front-line workers, let's first examine what creates a solid base from which those employees can thrive. I believe that in your role as an organizational leader and influencer, that you play a critical role within the business, in the following ways:

1. **Unleash Human Potential:** First and foremost, as a business leader or HR professional, you should see your role as one of unleashing human potential. How can you support the people on your team—literally, the *human resources* at the organization's disposal—so that those resources are fully tapped and leveraged? Otherwise, what you have are resources that go wasted—which is not very strategic or advantageous at all. Further, how can you assemble a team that will cooperatively work together, in strategic ways, to harness the collective intelligence of a group? Unleashing human potential at

the individual level is critical—but so is putting systems in place so that the larger group can express their collective human intelligence as well. Doing so will be good for them, but also good for your business's bottom line. Further, it is important to see your employees as more than just a "human resource"—but as real people with perspectives that matter. Plus, when a leader helps their employees thrive, that lends itself to executive accomplishment and organizational success, as well.

2. **Support a Networked Collective:** Your role is also one of orchestrating and supporting the full power of a networked collective. Because what an organization is, is a collection of people, ideas, and resources. And if you are not using all the organization's resources to the greatest extent possible, then there is an opportunity there to further bolster and support the power of the collective. A leader can think of themselves as a hub of a neural-like network; we need the whole network to function cooperatively, and it is up to leadership to support that collective so it can do its best work, together.
3. **Strategize:** Of course, a leader's role is also to identify strategy—both short and long-term strategies that are thought out well, with both your staff and your customers in mind. Such plans should also be well-informed by a variety of players within your organization, rather than solely identified from your single vantage point. Of course, your particular viewpoint is very important and valuable, but it is also limited because it is just one perspective. There is power in considering multiple perspectives, especially when it comes to a matter as important as an organization's strategy.
4. **Be a Storyteller and Share a Vision:** Your role is also to identify the vision for your organization—the long-term end state. This is not to say that you come up with this vision on your own; it should be informed by the knowledge and wisdom of the larger group. But you are a sort of purveyor of these ideas, and in the end, organizational leaders need to be able to tell a story about where you are today, where you think the organization should be headed (based on input from many stakeholders), and why people on the team should get onboard with whatever change efforts are required to get from here to there. If you skip this step, then the people you are relying on to

implement your vision may resist, because they do not understand and agree with it. Invest time into sharing your vision by telling compelling stories; if you do so, you will reap a good return in the form of your staff on the front lines putting energy and enthusiasm into making the dream a reality because that vision is shared and understood, rather than simply imposed upon them.

5. **Navigate Complexity by Supporting Emergence:** Your role is also to support *emergence*. Oftentimes, in complex environments, it may not be exactly clear how we get from point A to point B. Sometimes, the details of how to enact strategy are not crystal clear, and the solutions *emerge* over time, in unpredictable ways. Solutions cannot be neatly predicted ahead of time in this context. Particularly in complex environments, the path forward may also be complex. In fact, the more complex the problem, the more complex the solutions are likely to be. Therefore, it is important to allow for this process of emergence—even emergent innovation—to occur. The best way to do this is to empower people on the front lines and really, at all levels of the organization, to wrestle with problems, experiment with ideas, and see which answers the collective believes to be best. The right solutions will rise to the top. However, this approach requires leadership to be open to the ideas and perspectives of staff at all levels within the organization, and requires getting comfortable, to some extent, with uncertainty.
6. **Influence Organizational Culture:** A leader's role is also to create a positive, healthy organizational culture where all these concepts can flourish. You do this in part through your storytelling—through communicating values that support the concepts described previously. Treat your employees well, and they will treat the business well in return. Value their perspectives—not just as an act, but as a real, genuine appreciation for multiple perspectives. Invite disagreement. Encourage people to challenge the status quo, or to play devil's advocate. Create an environment of psychological safety, where people feel comfortable having opposing viewpoints and even being vulnerable. Instead of criticizing failures, freely show appreciation for them because it shows that a person, or a team, was trying something new; further, those experiences are opportunities for learning

> and improving. Redefine failure as not trying. Lastly, see your staff as people; they are not machines. Allow them to enjoy work–life balance. Encourage them to bring their real, full selves to work. Listen to them. Your people are your most important asset—so treat them as such.

These foundational leadership qualities and approaches should underpin any specific actions you take to support and leverage the power of polymathic people on your team; these six values should be the basis of your approach, first and foremost.

Dishonesty as the Status Quo

We have lived in an age of specialization, where the dominant ideology has said that *everybody* should specialize in one field—not two or three. Further, we are taught that when we apply for jobs, we should look at the job advertisement, and tailor our résumés to mirror the ad—to tell a story of niche specialization to match that position as much as possible. We are told that doing so will increase our chances of landing an interview and perhaps even getting the job. In other words, we are fed a narrative that it is okay to bend the truth, and that we should hide who we really are when trying to land a new job. What kind of way is this to start off a relationship with a potential employer—by telling a fib, and hiding your full self?

Further, the trouble with this model is also that the person applying for, and potentially landing a job within a company, is not really encouraged or even able to bring their whole self to work. They are not able to express themselves authentically. Beyond the dishonesty this brings, that can also feel stifling. Frequently, what this also means is that the job is so narrowly defined that someone may be only using a small portion of their talent on the job—and so much additional potential capacity goes wasted. This can be very frustrating, too, for someone who is highly capable, intelligent, and creative—because those types of people want to be able to contribute their talent fully at work. It feels good to excel at what you do—but how is a person to truly thrive if they can only do so with a portion of their capabilities?

Polymaths tend to be highly intelligent and capable, and these highly competent people want to make a positive difference. But because we have lived in an age of specialization, where hiring managers frequently do not fully grasp the "two types" of professionals described earlier (mono-specialists and polymathic generalists), then that means that the polymaths must pretend to be specialists; that's the unfortunate status quo. For businesses that desire a more modern and strategic way of operating, though, this outdated approach to hiring should be abandoned. Rather than dishonesty being the status quo, honesty and transparency should be the new modus operandi. Further, organizations should strive to allow their employees to bring their fullest—and best—selves to work, rather than employees feeling pressured to compartmentalize and censor their full talents and interests.

Specialists Versus Polymaths: The Two Types Framework

I believe that the best teams are those made up of a combination of specialists thinkers and polymaths. This allows for a kind of organizational ambidexterity and flexibility. At a basic level, of course, you can think of a specialist as someone with deep expertise in a single discipline; a polymath, in contrast, is someone whose expertise may not be quite as deep, but this is someone who has multiple types of expertise (sometimes even in unique or unexpected combinations). Think of the specialist as one who has a very niche tool that they have singularly mastered, while the polymathic person has a broader array of different kinds of tools at their disposal. The specialist is a hammer, while the polymath is a Swiss Army knife.

Further, a specialist can be thought of as the shape of the letter "I" representing a single area of deep expertise, and a polymath could be thought of as the letter "H" since it depicts someone with multiple types of deep knowledge, and a connector between the two areas (symbolizing the ability of polymathic people to frequently connect the dots, innovate, and synthesize ideas from multiple fields). Some other thinkers have proposed that polymaths be considered a T-shaped employee, but I disagree. The shape of the T shows some shallow breadth and depth in only one area; H represents multiexpertise in at least two areas, with connections between them; and so I believe that H is a more representative shape for real polymaths than the letter T.

What is clear is that organizations need both types of people to flourish. As a leader, simply becoming aware of these two "types" is an important "take away" I hope you get from this chapter and more largely, from this book. Once you realize that there are two fundamental types of professionals that you may have on your team, then you can begin to look at what types of people make sense in certain kinds of roles, how you can support them differently, how you can leverage their talent in unique ways, and so on.

Each type is important, but for different reasons. We need specialists because of the deep command they have over their fields. And we need polymathic generalists because of the unique talent they bring to deal with uncertainty, ambiguity, to innovate, and to see new solutions where narrow specialists may not be able to. Imagine the specialist within a silo, looking deep down within their field. In contrast, the polymath looks down multiple silos but also looks up and around, to see the larger picture and the larger landscape. Polymaths are better at environmental scanning—which is important in business. While a specialist may literally have "blinders" on so they may focus on their chosen area of expertise, the polymath does not have the same kind of approach. Whereas a specialist can see deeply, a polymath can see broadly; organizations need both approaches in order to be high performing.

Of course, how "specialist" someone is, and how "polymathic" someone else is exists on a spectrum. Each person's background is unique. And their level of specialism versus polymathic generalist approaches may morph over time. But the basic idea here is, people tend to veer mostly toward one or the other—and we need both types in organizations, in order to be successful.

Two Basic Types of Organizational Roles

There is a better way. The alternative to the approach described earlier is to consciously identify which roles are best suited to narrow specialists, and which ones are appropriate for polymathic people. Just as there are two types of basic skill sets a person may have—the specialist skill set versus the polymathic generalist toolkit, there are two basic types of roles associated with those people, as well.

There is a simple way to make this determination:

1. **Specialist Roles:** The types of roles where narrow specialists thrive are those that are stable and routine—where innovations are not necessarily required, and if creativity is helpful in the role, it is by refining a process or concept within that discipline that does not cross over into another field. In other words, the innovations that might be appropriate in that role are not overly complex, and they remain within one organizational silo. Specialist roles tend to exist in "kind" learning environments where solutions are fairly easily identified, there are no VUCA problems with which to contend. The future is predictable in this kind of environment, and solutions are easily predicted. Examples include roles in human resources or finance, generally speaking. (Many of these kinds of routine roles may become automated with AI.)
2. **Polymathic Roles:** The types of roles where polymathic generalists do well are in positions where there may be a lack of clear structure, a lot of uncertainty, where creativity and innovation are therefore in demand. Polymaths do well in these "wicked" learning environments where solutions are more difficult to identify, where they will be asked to tackle VUCA problems. The future is unpredictable in this kind of environment. Examples may be roles in our political system, product development, and some IT roles.

Understanding this bifurcation—that modern organizations require both specialist roles and polymathic roles—is a central theme of this book.

Specialist Roles That Are Unlikely To Be Automated

In the age of AI, many specialized tasks are becoming automated. If it's predictable or routine, with clear rules to consistently enforce or enact, then it can be programmed into AI to do. As a general rule, specialized roles for humans are fading, while the demand for generalist talent is more and more in demand. The most employable humans, in the modern era now, will largely be polymathic generalists working with an AI stack.

However, some specialized roles may always demand humans for them. But overall, the role of more and more humans who work, is to be a polymathic generalist—good at asking questions, seeing the bigger picture, integrating ideas, synthesizing new insights into being, and co-learning with AI tools which are the new "specialists." But there may still be some roles where human specialists still make sense, even in the context of AI tools.

The age of specialization is fading, overall. Some specialist roles will remain human-centered, but the reason they remain human won't be specialization itself. It will be because the work sits at the intersection of judgment, responsibility, meaning, and lived presence in the world. AI automates tasks, not roles. Many specialized tasks will be automated, but roles that bundle specialization with irreducibly human capacities are likely to persist.

Although AI can advise, simulate, and predict, it cannot be *responsible*. For example, judges and juries, certain physicians making life-and-death calls, military and national security decision-makers, child welfare determinations, and high-level regulatory authorities may still be highly specialized and in demand, but not automated. These roles require a human who can answer for their decisions.

There are other roles that demand deep human to human trust, like therapists, trauma counselors, spiritual leaders, certain educators and mentors, or negotiators in sensitive diplomatic or labor contexts. AI is unlikely to take over these roles, which humans are likely to want fellow humans to do.

Some positions may require embodied, contextual judgment which only a human could do. Certain forms of expertise are inseparable from being physically present in a dynamic environment. For example, skilled tradespersons working in unpredictable settings are unlikely to become automated. Emergency responders, certain types of surgeons, and field-based scientists and investigators are likely to remain roles for humans to do, even in the age of AI. And even as AI becomes more and more embodied through robotics, these roles rely on improvisation more than programming, tacit knowledge, and real-time sensing that resists full automation.

Humans are likely to remain in-demand for roles that define meaning—roles that don't demand efficiency, but sensemaking and interpretation. For example, although AI can make art, humans may prefer human-made art, through cultural creators who understand the human experience since they belong to the human race. Philosophers and ethicists are likely to remain human. Certain types of writers and thinkers may always stay human. And narrative strategists and sensemakers may be more in demand than ever in the complex and fast-paced world of AI.

In response to AI becoming more and more embedded inside organizations, many teams may opt to create new kinds of roles, especially roles that integrate across domains. Examples include systems designers, translators between disciplines, leaders who synthesize across technical, human, and ethical domains, or polymathic strategists. These kinds of people are likely to become increasingly in demand within organizations not so much because they know everything, but because they are good at learning and connecting the dots.

The dominant narrative used to be that of specialization. We were told to pick a thing, get in swim lane, pick a silo, and stick to it for life. We believed that it was smart to put blinders on, professionally. We bought into the idea that this sort of exclusive dedication to a field would secure success, higher pay, job security, prestige—that by being an "expert" we could succeed professionally, through a narrow focus. But to a large extent now, that kind of narrowness has become a liability. There is power in diversification and multi-capabilities, especially as job markets are shifting quickly and specialized tasks are becoming increasingly automated. Nowadays, to have professional success, individuals need to have the capacity to keep learning broadly. AI will largely automate expertise, but it will not automate responsibility, meaning, or judgment in a human world. Machines will need human collaborators who do only what humans can do. AI can analyze, optimize, and scale, but the human edge is creativity, adaptability, and meaning. So roles that demand these uniquely human capabilities are likely to persist even as widespread automation takes root.

Kind Versus Wicked Learning Environments

In their 2015 article in *Current Directions in Psychological Science*, Robin M. Hogarth, Tomas Lejarraga, and Emre Soyer introduced the distinction between kind and wicked learning environments. Hogarth also elaborated on this in his book, *Educating Intuition*.[1] Hogarth and his coauthors state that in kind learning environments, information is acquired, or learned, whereas in wicked learning environments, one has to make choices or predictions. Accordingly, in kind learning environments, there is a close match between information that one has at their disposal, and the problem at hand, whereas in wicked learning environments, this match does not exist. In kind learning environments, feedback is accurate and plentiful. In wicked domains, information that one has might be poor, misleading, or entirely missing. However, it is not as if problems are entirely kind or wicked; they exist on a continuum. The implications of this model mean that if an environment is kind, a person can fairly accurately make inferences and predictions about how to best respond to the problem at hand. If someone makes an error in this context, it is likely human error. In contrast, if an environment is wicked, the solution is not so clear.

In his book, *Range: Why Generalists Triumph in a Specialized World*, David Epstein explains the difference between these two environments blatantly: "Facing uncertain environments and wicked problems, breadth of experience is invaluable. Facing kind problems, narrow specialization can be remarkably efficient."[2] This simple but powerful concept is a key takeaway from *Range*.

---

[1] Hogarth, R., T. Lejaragga, and E. Soyer. 2015. "The two settings of kind and wicked learning environments." *Current Directions in Psychological Science* 24, no. 5, pp. 379–385; Hogart, R. 2010. *Educating Intuition*. Chicago: University of Chicago Press.

[2] Epstein, D. 2019. *Range: Why Generalists Triumph in a Specialized World.* New York: Riverhead Books.

Hiring Polymaths

Any good organizational strategy should involve making sure you have the right people on the bus, so to speak, and then putting those people in the right seats on the bus. Talent acquisition and management is critical to a business's success—perhaps more important than any other factor. I encourage you to hire polymathic people to join your team, because of the great value they can bring, alongside the expert specialists. Organizations must stop discriminating against polymathic people—for their own benefit. In the following, I will address some of the ways you can strategically hire, and then appropriately support, this population.

Interviewing Job Candidates in an Age of Specialization: Distinguishing the Knowers From the Learners

There are ways to distinguish candidates who have a bent toward narrow specialization, and those who are more polymathic by nature. You should be able to figure this out during interviews by asking some poignant questions.

Questions for Specialist Roles: For example, when you are interviewing candidates for specialist roles, it makes sense to dig deep into their area of expertise to ensure they have a command over their field of mastery. You might ask questions like:

1. Please tell us about your prior experience doing the kind of work this job requires.
2. Tell us about your educational background as it pertains to this position.
3. Why do you enjoy doing the kind of very focused labor this position demands?

Questions for Polymathic Generalist Roles: When interviewing polymathic generalists, you may not be looking so much for a specific skill set or collection of talents—though that may be helpful—but rather, what you really want to uncover is a general way of thinking. You want to discover if they have a polymathic mindset. Further, polymathic people tend to be good *systems thinkers*, because of their broad exposure and variety of tools in their proverbial toolkits. They are continual, lifelong, self-directed learners. They can connect the dots to see bigger-picture solutions, to make linkages, synthesize, and therefore solve problems creatively. Another important takeaway of this book is that if you are seeking innovations to get ahead in the marketplace or to simply stay sustainable in an ever-evolving and competitive landscape, polymathic generalists may be a very strategic key to obtaining the innovative solutions you desire. While interviewing someone for this type of role, you may ask questions such as:

1. Please tell us about the different types of skills you have and how you think that variety might apply to or inform the work at hand.
2. Please share examples where you innovated using information from multiple perspectives or disciplines.
3. Do you think of yourself more of "in the weeds" or a "big-picture thinker?" (A good polymath can do both, but the focus will likely be more on remembering, always, the big picture.)

The point is, you'll want to understand the way they tend to think, more broadly, rather than honing in, necessarily, on specific skill sets or experiences, like you would want to with a narrow specialist. What you are looking to uncover is: is this person a strategic, big-picture thinker, who envisions solutions that may be "outside the box"? Or are they very focused on executing day-to-day tasks in a prescribed, reliable way?

The takeaway here is this: whereas a specialist focuses on *knowing*, the polymath focuses on *learning* and adapting. When considering individuals to fill certain types of roles in your business, you will want to distinguish if the person you might hire is a "knower" or a "learner." Knowers fit better in routine specialist roles, while learners thrive in more ambiguous positions requiring new and better, ever-evolving solutions informed by continual learning and adapting. Knowers strive to apply their existing knowledge, while learners strive to continually expand what they know so it can be applied in new and creative ways.

The Value of Learning Agility

Author Alvin Toffler in his book "*Future Shock*," said "The illiterate of the 21st century will not be those who cannot read and write, but those who cannot learn, unlearn, and relearn."[3] This is equivalent to the concept of learning agility. Learning agility is an important skill for your employees to have, particularly for roles in harsh, wicked, VUCA environments. Learning agility is the ability to be in a new situation without clear guidelines on the best path forward but figure out a good solution anyway. People with high learning agility can harness lessons from past experiences, identify pertinent information that they will need to obtain, collaborate with others who bring useful perspectives, and weave all that data together to help inform a strategic solution, even in response to a totally new problem at hand. People with high learning agility do well with uncertainty—and they are comfortable with ambiguity.

Organizational behavior expert and psychologist, Karl Weick, studied wilderness firefighters and found an interesting observation. Sometimes, firefighters need to drop their tools and flee an area where a fire is raging in order to survive. Weick said, "Dropping one's tools is a proxy for unlearning, for adaptation, for flexibility … It is the very unwillingness of people to drop their tools that turns some of these dramas into tragedies."[4] What he found was that very experienced groups become rigid under pressure and "regress to what they know best." That can be a very dangerous thing to do especially in the face of complex problems that demand complex solutions, rather than the answers from yesteryear.

Dr. W. Warner Burke studied learning agility and identified nine dimensions of it, as follows:[5]

1. Flexibility (being open to new ideas and solutions).
2. Speed (trying new things and quickly learning what worked and didn't).

---

[3] Toffler, A. 1970. *Future Shock*. New York: Bantam Books.

[4] Weick, K.E. 1996. "Drop Your Tools: An Allegory for Organizational Studies." *Administrative Science Quarterly* 41, no. 2, pp. 301–313. JSTOR, www.jstor.org/stable/2393722. Accessed 30 May 2021.

[5] Burke, D. See: https:// easiconsult.com/learning-agility-offerings/

3. Experimenting (exemplified by trying new behaviors).
4. Performance risk-taking (being willing to try new activities even if one fails or is challenged).
5. Interpersonal risk-taking (being willing to have discussions where the participants have different opinions).
6. Collaborating (being willing to work with others and learn throughout the process).
7. Information gathering (seeking out new information and learning to stay current).
8. Feedback seeking (asking for feedback on one's ideas as well as one's overall performance).
9. Reflecting (thinking about one's own performance—what went well, what didn't—to figure out how to improve for the future).

Learning agility is particularly important for organizations wanting to quickly resolve problems and stay on the cutting edge, and polymathic people may be a good way of harnessing the power of learning agility, since they exhibit many of these behaviors by virtue of their polymathy itself.

Organizational Agility

Just as learning agility has value at the individual level, organizational agility, at the meso level of analysis, is also noteworthy. McKinsey & Company define organizational agility as "the ability of an organization to renew itself, adapt, change quickly, and succeed in a rapidly changing, ambiguous, turbulent environment. Agility is not incompatible with stability—quite the contrary. Agility *requires* stability for most companies." They go on to argue that agility needs stability in order to be successful: "Agility needs two things. One is a dynamic capability, the ability to move fast—speed, nimbleness, responsiveness. And agility requires stability, a stable foundation—a platform, if you will—of things that don't change. It's this stable backbone that becomes a springboard for the company, an anchor point that doesn't change while a whole bunch of other things are changing constantly."[6] An alternative definition of organizational agility by Organizational Change Management experts at the MITRE Corporation is "the capacity to adapt quickly and effectively in response to, or in expectation of, changes in the organization's environment."[7] The key with organizational agility is the ability to adapt—and this is something that polymaths are very good at, at the individual level—and so naturally they would be a helpful element in ensuring that an organization stays agile.

Knowledge Creation

Scholar C. J. Spender has argued that the two primary goals of any business are the (1) generation and (2) application of knowledge.[8] "Knowledge creation" is important so that organizations can compete in the marketplace—which requires that they evolve and adapt over time, to the market conditions and customer needs. How can you position your organization to create new insights and innovations—to create new knowledge? I believe by having polymathic people on your team, you are better positioned to be able to create new knowledge, since these types of people naturally tend to be creative, think outside the box, and innovate. Given their disparate, varied backgrounds, polymaths are well suited to see issues from new perspectives, and in the process, create new knowledge that can benefit your business.

Polymaths and Critical Thinking

Anybody can learn to be a critical thinker. However, someone who has a broader array of experiences and knowledge is particularly well suited to

---

[6] McKinsey & Company interview, retrieved from https:// www.mckinsey.com/business-functions/organization/our-insights/the-keys-to-organizational-agility#.

[7] Kirkpatrick, S., S. Miller, A. Terragnoli, and A. Sprenger. 2020. A white paper entitled "Development of an Organizational Agility Assessment for Government and Nonprofit Organizations."

[8] Spender, J. 1996. "Making Knowledge the Basis of a Dynamic Theory of the Firm." *Strategic Management Journal* 17, special issue (winter), pp. 45–63.

ask questions, push back, and think critically. In other words, the more a person learns, the better positioned they are to ask the right questions, which help uncover truth. Of course, a narrow specialist can also be a great critical thinker—within their chosen field. However, it may be difficult for them to apply the same reasoning to areas with which they are not familiar. In this way, polymaths are particularly well suited to think critically more holistically—which can be of great use especially as organizations develop their strategies to excel or develop responses to deal with unexpected difficulties that arise.

Systems of Collective Intelligence

This book has argued that a polymath has both breadth and depth professionally, which can allow them to uniquely integrate concepts from multiple domains and therefore, innovate, at the individual level. However, the same logic applies to our collective: we need breadth, depth, and integration as a group, as well. If all we have are narrow specialists to solve the problems of our time, then those solutions may be delayed, short sighted, not preemptively anticipated when they could have been, and may lack a more holistic "systems thinking" approach.

The siloed, assembly line approach to thinking is an outdated model for humanity that needs to be updated. The alternative is to—in addition to specialists—also have more polymathic people who can do important work, which can bolster the rest of your organization. We can all benefit from having more polymaths on our teams because of the diversity of perspectives that they bring, and because of their unique position to help create new and useful innovations that benefit your business.

As long as your organization continues to employ narrow specialists, polymaths can also play an important role synthesizing the knowledge from those specialists. Polymaths can serve as great bridge builders between specialists; they can frequently speak multiple professional languages, and bring together ideas from different domains, working in collaboration with deep, narrow specialists to cocreate more systems thinking approaches to solve difficult problems collectively.

In fact, polymaths can often see big-picture solutions where narrow specialists cannot; instead of focusing on only one area, like specialists do, polymaths focus on multiple fields and have the bricolage knowledge associated with multidisciplinary expertise. On the other hand, if your business consists only of narrow specialists, and no polymathic bridge builders, your organization will be in jeopardy of missing out on potential logical leaps forward as those specialists exist within their disciplinary silos and cannot necessarily see beyond them. As the saying goes, "Don't lose sight of the forest for the trees."

When the world was simpler, the specialist-only approaches worked fine; however, the world is becoming more complex, and therefore we need to become more complex as well, to meet that complexity. Complexity is not a bad thing; in fact, the increasing complexity we see in modern times is an opportunity for businesses and society more largely to refine themselves—to get better, to evolve. In this context, on the business front, a more robust approach to solve problems is by having a *variety* of types of professionals on your team—both specialists and polymathic generalists—rather than only narrow specialists. Doing so makes your business more robust, and more likely to be agile in an ever-changing landscape. Rather than simply responding to crises, your organization will be better positioned to be prepared for challenges, anticipating what may be coming your way beforehand—because of the more holistic and integrated viewpoints, which are a part of your team, allow for this more proactive way of possibly anticipating future conditions.

And if you believe that polymaths are important at the individual level, and also at the organizational level because of the great strengths and benefits they can add to the larger whole, then it makes sense as well that perhaps our entire society—at the macro level—could also benefit from having more polymaths. What if planet earth is one big neural network, just waiting for more polymaths to emerge as hubs of connectivity among different nodes?

Interlinked Yet Fragmented Systems

In her book, *The Silo Effect: The Perils of Expertise and the Promise of Breaking Down Barriers,* Gillian Tett observes that we currently experience a striking paradox: that in the modern age, the globe is more interconnected than ever before, yet our lives within that interlinked world are still fragmented. "Many large organizations are divided, and then subdivided into numerous different departments, which often fail to talk to each other—let alone collaborate. People often live in separate mental and social 'ghettos,' talking and coexisting only with people like us. In many countries, politics is polarized. Professions seem increasingly specialized, partly because technology keeps becoming more complex and sophisticated, and is only understood by a tiny pool of experts."[9] Tett argues that silos are not all bad—in fact, we need specialist departments and teams; this helps us deal with complexity, in some ways. But according to Tett, "Silos can also sometimes cause damage. People who are organized into specialist teams can end up fighting with each other, wasting resources. Isolated departments, or teams of experts, may fail to communicate, and thus overlook dangerous and costly risks. Fragmentation can create information bottlenecks and stifle innovation. Above all else, silos can create tunnel vision, or mental blindness, which causes people to do stupid things." Thankfully, polymaths can help build bridges between these silos, and help alleviate these problems.

Complex People for Complex Times

Polymaths are multifaceted people who defy convention; they break "out of the box" of society's expectations. In short, they are complicated individuals. In fact, many polymathic people have combinations of skills, experiences, and knowledge that may, on the surface, appear to not go together. Polymaths are often highly distinctive—no two ever exactly alike, with their unique combinations. Essentially, they are more complex humans—well suited to complex times and problems we now must contend with in the 21st century.

Polymaths in Leadership Positions

Polymaths can be very strategic to put in leadership positions, particularly if that individual desires that kind of a role. That said, not all polymaths

[9] Tett, G. 2015. *The Silo Effect: The Peril of Expertise and the Promise of Breaking Down Barriers*. New York: Simon & Schuster Paperbacks.

should be in formal leadership positions. Some polymaths are much more interested in solo work without having to interact with other people to the extent that someone in a leadership position must. However, there are a number of facets of polymathy that can position someone to be a really excellent leader, if that's a path that appeals to them.

For example, if someone has had experience across multiple functions in a business—and then it is put in charge of a team made up of professionals from those very functions—then that leader is especially well suited to manage that diverse group of people. The reason is because that leader understands the different concepts and ideas those people are grappling with on a daily basis.

Polymathic leaders can be particularly effective in these areas:

- Network connectors—they can become hubs of connectivity.
- Environmental scanning.
- Speaking multiple professional "languages."
- Being able to zoom in and out between the details and big-picture observations.

Given part of what HR does is working with leaders to recruit, retain, and develop their employees, it is important in a chapter about HR to mention polymaths and leadership. Further, those HR professionals may also need to recruit employees into leadership positions, and then also help retain and develop them. So, it is important to consider polymaths in official positions of leadership, in a chapter on Human Resources. However, Chapter 6 of this book covers polymathy and leadership in more detail.

Diversifying the Concept of Diversity

Organizations frequently cite diversity as a core value, with HR departments often leading efforts to promote inclusive practices. Yet in many cases, what is meant by "diversity" remains narrowly defined, typically limited to demographic characteristics such as race, sex, gender identity, religion, disability status, and sexual orientation. While these dimensions are critically important, they do not capture the full range of differences that shape how individuals think, learn, and contribute. In other words, diversity is not only demographic, but also cognitive; diversity also exists in how minds work. While these categories are critically important, it's worth noting that not all aspects of identity are fixed at birth. Some evolve over time, shaped by personal experiences, individual choices, or societal frameworks. Religion and disability, for example, may be inherited, chosen, or acquired, and are often subject to social labeling and interpretation.

True inclusivity requires a broader and more dynamic understanding of diversity—one that reflects both the complexity of identity and the fluidity of human experience. A representative team should mirror not just the static demographics of society, but the richness of how people live, think, and grow. And diversity must go hand-in-hand with inclusion: it's not enough to simply invite people to the table—they must be heard, respected, and empowered. When organizations fail to address bias in hiring, promotion, or daily operations, they not only limit innovation and foster resentment but risk falling into groupthink and stagnation. Diversity is not just a social imperative; it's a strategic one. Leaders must keep it at the forefront—not just as a checkbox, but as a commitment to building organizations that are more creative, humane, and resilient.

The concept of diversity itself needs to become more diversified, though. Too often, diversity is viewed primarily through group-level identity categories—such as race, gender, religion, disability status, or sexual orientation. While these categories are essential to recognize and respect, they don't tell the whole story of human difference. Some aspects of identity are inherited or visible at birth, while others emerge through lived experience, personal choices, or shifting social norms.

If we truly believe that diversity matters, we must also recognize that it exists within individuals—not just between them. A single person can embody multiple ways of thinking, being, and knowing. This is known as **intrapersonal diversity**: the internal range of interests, identities, abilities, and perspectives that one person holds. When we expand our understanding of diversity to include this inner complexity, we not only create space for polymaths—we also create more inclusive, innovative, and human-centered cultures.

A person who is highly intrapersonally diverse is essentially a polymath. Teams have *inter*personal diversity whereas an individual may have *intra*personal diversity—diversity within themselves. This diversity shows up by having multifunctional capabilities. This diversity may have been developed over time—it is not necessary that a person develop their intrapersonal diversity all at once. Usually, it is a process that may last for an entire lifetime. That diversity can show up in the forms of professional experiences or personal ones including hobbies.

Develop Those With Polymathic Potential

If you agree that organizations will fare better to have a strategic mix of specialists alongside polymathic generalists, working collaboratively, then this begs the question: how can we support people to really step into their polymathy? The answer is to support and develop those who are already polymathic, as well as those who could (and who want to) become more diversified in their skill sets. It takes a certain amount of conscious choice to make this happen. In fact, most people who are themselves polymathic, did not consciously decide one day, "I want to be a polymath." They simply followed their curiosity, continued learning, and remained committed to being as authentic as possible within their own personhood (rather than trying to fit into a standard mold of what a professional "should" look like). This helped create individuation within that person. But what would our world look like if people actually did decide to be polymaths, and consciously curated their learning to craft their own polymathic development?

Developing people who are already quite polymathic to further bolster their multifaceted skill sets is important; but businesses should also consider how they can support narrow specialists to become more polymathic as well. If there is a narrow specialist who wants to expand their skill set and knowledge base, support that (but do not force it). How will you know if this appeals to a specialist? Ask them. Annual performance appraisal discussions are a particularly appropriate time to reflect on the work and contributions an employee has made, and to also consider what types of growth would be most useful in the future for that person. It is important to support specialists continuing to be specialized if that is what they desire; but it is also critical to let them know you are open to expanding their horizons, as well, to learn about other functions in your company. Also consider what tasks in their role could be automated by AI tools, creating more mental bandwidth for the employee to expand their learning and capacities into new areas to enhance their work along with AI support. Make a point of bringing up this issue, and seeing what response you get; from there, you can make developmental plans accordingly.

Retaining Polymaths

Of course, it is not enough to simply hire polymaths; it is important to retain them as well. Otherwise, you may invest countless resources into obtaining a particular, well-qualified, powerful person onto your team, only to lose them because you were not able to keep them satisfied on the job. If you care about reaping a return on the investment you put into getting that person into your organization, it is important to figure out how to keep them, as well.

There are several ways that you can keep polymathic people happy at work. Here are a few pointers:

1. **Appreciate their unique skill set.** Verbalize your appreciation, in private and in public. Create a culture where both specialists and polymathic generalists feel appreciated, and part of a larger collective bigger than any one person—but where each individual makes a difference and matters.
2. Give them as much **freedom** and **flexibility** as possible; let them determine their own roles and ways of adding value into the system.
3. Encourage them to **own their polymath identity**—to really step into it and leverage it to the utmost.
4. Create **systems** and **opportunities** that support their polymathic contributions. The next few sections will provide some ideas for the types of scaffolding organizational leaders can put into place to provide this kind of support.

Community of Practice for Polymaths

Being a polymath is not easy; it is frequently fraught with challenges such as being misunderstood, underappreciated, underleveraged, and labeled as being "distracted" and "uncommitted." Living life as a polymath in the age of specialization also makes career decisions and explorations particularly difficult and even risky. These are just a few of the unique challenges that polymaths have faced in the 21st century.

As an organizational leader, one way of combating these difficulties would be to help provide a "place" for polymathic people where they can talk about their polymathy with others like them. Creating an environment where they can collaborate, commiserate, compare notes, share stories, and create a sense of shared polymathic identity could be immensely helpful in ensuring that your employees step fully into their polymathy—which in turn can lead to better performance on the job.

So, one idea is to set up a community of practice just for the polymathic generalists on your team. In addition to the support that the members of this group would feel from such a collective, it may also lead to powerful collaborations among the already diversified individuals who would be brought together as a group of diverse individuals. Creating this sort of context for polymaths to support one another and potentially collaborate could reap very rich rewards for an organization. It is a low-risk, low-cost way that could have a big payoff in terms of employee morale, engagement, and creating cross-functional collaborations. The whole can end up being greater than the sum of the parts. And employees may also feel happier because they feel seen, valued, and free to be themselves—which can in turn make them more likely to collaborate and even "go above and beyond" at work.

Idea Parties

It has been said that creativity is intelligence at play; so, in a way, brainstorming can be very fun, particularly for polymathic people who tend to be very adept at ideation. One creative way to solicit new ideas is to have an "idea party." Since many offices frequently have social gatherings anyway—why not make it a productive one? Bring specialists and polymaths together to brainstorm around a certain idea or area of organizational strategy, and see what happens. At a minimum, it could really energize the participants. And at best, this ideation might lead to a very creative innovation that would not have occurred otherwise.

Innovation Competitions

If your organization would benefit from innovations, why not create a structure to encourage the development of innovative ideas? Create a competition, set a rubric for evaluating the submissions, and offer prizes to the winners. Perhaps part of the prize might be the support to implement the winning ideas—which in and of itself might be rewarding enough, on its own. Polymathic people tend to really value creativity, and if given the opportunity to think outside the box and receive recognition for their good ideas, it could be very rewarding—and productive—for an organization to create these sorts of opportunities.

Expansion Awards

If having a broad array of tools in one's professional toolkit does indeed help someone solve problems while also increasing their capacity to create novel and useful solutions (in addition to the personal enrichment that comes from that kind of exposure), then it would behoove organizations to then reward broad exploration they see exemplified among their employees. There is a simple way to do this: provide incentives for employee learning and experiences even into new areas the employee may not have explored before. For example, if an employee works in HR but wants to learn more about Information Technology (IT), encourage them to shadow an IT professional for a day, or interview someone in that department, to learn more about that field. You could even award points for the employee reading a book, or even something new and adventurous they did in their personal capacity outside of work. The point is to purposefully and clearly encourage broad learning and experiences—inside and perhaps even outside of work. Keep track with a points system, and periodically acknowledge employees with "Expansion Awards" for their efforts to learn widely. You could also reward those who go out of their way to help others from different departments learn as well—so both the learner and the teacher could be acknowledged for their efforts in this regard.

Other Awards Programs

To go along with the idea of competitions for innovative ideas, also consider simply rewarding excellent, innovative work that gets done outside of the confines of a competition. Perhaps a self-starter envisioned a new idea and made it happen; or perhaps a team of individuals collectively thought outside the box to launch a new product or service. Reward that behavior! By rewarding good behavior, it encourages more positive contributions. It is both the right thing to do, and the strategic thing for management to do as well.

Hold Employees Responsible for Results, Not Hours Worked

Today, the "when" and "where" of how work gets done is becoming increasingly irrelevant. The Internet makes this possible. And something that more and more people appreciate is having flexibility and work–life balance. Of course, polymaths tend to be people who may have various hobbies or even side hustles, in addition to their main full-time job. And so, if an organization wants to appeal to polymathic types, who have a lot of interests and pursuits, it can be a good strategy to be flexible in terms of when and how work gets done—especially given the fact that the Internet makes this so easy nowadays especially for knowledge workers.

Further, it just makes good sense to focus on the work, or outputs, rather than when and where the labor took place. The old model of "butt in seat" for 40 hours a week was and frankly, still is, so arbitrary. If a highly talented, capable, intelligent, efficient polymath can do a job in 20 hours a week, and for someone else that same level of work takes 60 hours a week (perhaps with even subpar results), then we are actually incentivizing people to be inefficient—especially if they are paid by the hour. In other words, if we live in a world that says we will pay you for your time, then we reward people for belaboring tasks and to some extent, being inefficient—because then if they work longer, they will make more money. The better way to measure someone's work is to hold people responsible for their contributions and for making a positive impact; reward people by how much good they do for the business, rather than the amount of time spent doing the work.

Plus, if we have the opportunity to cocreate a world we all want to live in, why not create a system of which we would want to be a part? If you personally could choose to have your contributions measured by how long it took you, versus the work itself, what would you choose? My guess is you'd choose to have your work judged by the actual work itself, not how long it took you. And if that is the case, that opens the door for your work to take you less than 40 hours a week, freeing up more time for other pursuits. So, why don't we all just agree that it makes sense to support a system where we measure contributions on their effectiveness and value? And then perhaps we could all even enjoy more free time, too.

Be a Macromanager

If a micromanager is someone who tries to control every part of the work that a subordinate does—no matter if that part of the work is big or small—then a macromanager is someone who does the opposite: who does not direct the person in the weeds, but who does focus on if the work itself is valuable, at a high level. In fact, polymaths have reported that there is nothing that will douse the flame of a polymath more than being micromanaged. Polymaths are highly intelligent, capable people—and a boss directing how every little piece of their work should get done is quite demeaning—if not annoying. Steve Jobs once said, "It doesn't make sense to hire smart people and tell them what to do; we hire smart people so they can tell us what to do." If a manager feels the need to micromanage a member of the staff, then there are a couple of possible root causes creating this problem: (1) the employee is not a good fit for the job—perhaps he or she lacks the skills or experience to be able to work independently or is not trustworthy, or (2) the manager operates from a place of fear, rather than empowering his or her colleague to do the job in the way he or she believes is best. Either situation is problematic and should be addressed head on. The best situation is for a manager to treat her employees with respect by being a macromanager, and focusing on the big picture, rather than directing in great detail on how the day-to-day tasks should get done.

The best way for an employer to leverage a polymath's talent is to identify a goal you want them to accomplish, obtain their agreement they will take on the project, and provide flexibility and autonomy so they can use their talents to reach the goal. This allows for the individual to use their creativity to the greatest extent possible—otherwise, if you direct too much how the work should be done, the energy and enthusiasm the polymath will bring to the work may be limited. To realize their fullest contributions, they require some level of autonomy to design how they do the work—and in the end, if the final product or service is what you are hoping for—does it really matter the day-to-day specifics of how they got there?

Sure, you may provide guardrails and boundaries—give them high-level guidance. Sure, you will want to check in on a regular basis to see how the work is going, and find out if there is anything you can do to support their efforts. When needed, provide support, input, observations, or help overcome roadblocks, too. But one of the great strengths polymathic people have is the ability to self-teach, to continue learning—so even if they may not know exactly how to get from here to there, they are likely to figure it out without you having to hold their hand every second. The best thing you can do is support them by encouraging their own creativity and leveraging their immense capacity to learn their way through problems, and see the magic that will happen once you provide a supportive environment for them to make the best contributions possible. If they run into roadblocks, offer to help with that, if you can. But the bottom line here is this: trust the polymaths on your team—and trust this process.

Development of Polymaths

How do you keep an employee engaged who might not even know the word polymath, but is one? Or how do you help polymathic generalists who own that identity, and want to step into it further? Perhaps most importantly, what systems or opportunities can you put into place to truly unleash the full capacities of a polymath at work? Here are some ideas to consider:

1. **Formal Training or Self-Study:** First, polymathic people value continual, self-directed learning. Accordingly, create an environment where they can have some level of agency in deciding what they

learn, knowing how important continual, self-directed learning is to them. Provide time and funding for them to explore what they are curious about—even if what they want to focus on does not seem directly applicable to the job they are in right now. This learning may come in the form of formal training—taking short classes or even pursuing entire degrees—or it may be something as simple as doing some research on the Internet. Learning comes in many forms. But it takes time, and sometimes it takes money—so if needed, provide those resources so that your employee can expand their knowledge more and more, over time.

2. **Job Rotations and Career Mobility:** If you want to keep a polymath engaged, then you must understand how important continual learning is for a polymath—that defines their core nature—as someone who wants to continue to learn, grow, and improve. Polymaths do not want to become stagnant especially in terms of their learning. This may mean that organizations should create paths of upward or perhaps even lateral mobility, through a career lattice rather than a ladder approach, so employees can switch roles over time, learning, growing, and contributing in different ways and continuing to expand their intellectual "toolkits" along the way. You might even allow for short detail assignments or job rotations, even if only for a few months, or perhaps part-time as they continue with their primary role part-time as well. Plus, the fact is that polymathic people do not want to feel constrained; they value freedom very much—especially intellectual and professional freedom. If you want to keep a powerhouse like a polymath on your team, support them having a sense of freedom by creating pathways for career mobility, since with each new job or assignment, they learn more—and that's something they value very much; that intellectual stimulation is very important to them. Set the specialists on a specialist track, whereby they advance by becoming more and more expert in their chosen field; likewise, polymaths should be rewarded or promoted by gaining breadth (in addition to depth). Unfortunately, further specialization is typically seen as the only way to grow in one's career, but smart organizations need to realize that that's only half of the story—for people who are narrow specialists. For those who are polymathic,

they should be rewarded and promoted because of the breadth of expertise they develop. Let's stop telling the story that the only way to advance professionally is to become further specialized—that may be true for specialists, and quite counterproductive for the powerful polymaths on your team.

3. **Self-Directed Work Time:** Another idea is to allow perhaps 80 percent of their time to be spent on the core duties in their job and allow the remaining 20 percent of their time to be spent as they wish. (Of course, these percentages can be adjusted as appropriate.) The point is, give them some freedom, and see what happens! You might end up with a really great idea or product emerging by allowing them the flexibility to define how they spend a portion of their time and granting some level of autonomy for them to self-identify what kinds of solutions they create. In organizations dealing with VUCA problems, this can be a particularly effective strategy not only to keep a talented polymath engaged but also to harness the power of their multicreative capacities to fashion new solutions in a difficult environment. This appeals to a polymath because it allows them to add unique value in the organization by leveraging their curiosity and creativity. And most polymaths find great pleasure in contributing and adding value—because it makes them feel competent and useful. This is a way to encourage internal intrapreneurship, which is when an employee can act like an entrepreneur without leaving your business—but by harnessing their creative capacities to launch new projects or products, while remaining on your team.
4. **Special Projects:** Of course, encouraging a polymathic person to take on a special project is another way to both keep them engaged and reap the rewards of their labor to help move your organization forward. A special project that is new to them—not the "same old" work they typically do—is particularly appealing as it provides an opportunity to learn and gain some new skills.
5. **Shadowing:** Because shadowing other professionals (whether within the same organization or outside of it) represents an opportunity to learn, this is another option you could encourage a polymath to engage in, that would likely appeal to their sense of curiosity. Alternatively, your organization could create formal shadowing

opportunities for people to partake in. The point is: shadowing can be useful as a tool for learning, to see how other people work, think, communicate, and learn about different types of work being done in and outside of your company.

6. **Interviews:** Another way that individuals can learn from other people is by having discussions with them—and an interview is one way to facilitate these kinds of discussions. An interview could be done over lunch in a friendly, social way, over the telephone or video conferencing, or in person. It can be casual or more formal using interview questions that have been developed ahead of time. To solidify the learning that took place during the interview, employers can ask employees to share what they learned either in writing or verbally. The bottom line here is that it is worthwhile to learn from other people's experiences—not just our own. Interviews are a great way to hear other people's stories, get advice, and even learn from their mistakes. Polymaths can learn from both specialists and other polymathic people. Also keep in mind, interviews do not necessarily need to be private—you could have a special guest being interviewed, a host conducting the interview, and an audience watching it. You could even record this for viewing at a later date. There are multiple ways to conduct and capture information from interviews where listeners can learn from the experience of someone else. Plus, if you want to create a culture where people are aware of the dichotomy between specialist and polymathic roles and people, consider highlighting this as part of an interview series where you explicitly discuss these kinds of issues openly.
7. **Mentoring and Coaching:** Another idea is to encourage or provide a polymathic person with a mentor or a coach, as this provides additional opportunities for learning. Of course, a mentor and a coach are different: a mentor typically shares his or her experiences and makes recommendations or gives advice, whereas a coach is focused on asking a lot of strategic questions to help the coachee reach his or her goals. In either case, however, there is an opportunity for learning—which again, is something that a polymathic person values, at their core. Therefore, providing opportunities for mentoring or coaching is something that organizations can do to keep employees

satisfied and engaged, and to also help those individuals strive toward reaching their fullest potential.

8. **Networking and Collaborations:** Since one way that people learn is through social experiences, networking, and collaborations with others are great opportunities for a polymath to expand their intellectual and professional horizons. This can be accomplished through formal networking events, informal introductions, or by putting together cross-functional teams to work on projects together. The idea here is that people can learn from others, so providing opportunities for social exchanges is one way a polymath can learn—which of course, is a big way to keep them happy and engaged.
9. **Reading:** One primary way that polymathic people tend to learn is through reading. Too often, companies may hope that their employees read books that enrich that person's knowledge and perspective, but do not provide the books, nor any time to go through them. So, another simple idea is to create a library of resources (whether digital books or ones in hard copy) and encourage employees to spend a certain amount of work time studying those texts. Relying on people to do this in their free time might work—but it also might not. So, if you believe in the power of good ideas, often found between the pages of a book, then encourage reading, even on company time.
10. **Organizational Debates:** It is important to encourage critical thinking and dialogue. Polymaths typically are great critical thinkers; they love to question convention, and how things have been done in the past, to decide for themselves if they think the status quo is good, or if there is a better way of operating. Encourage discourse. Create an organizational culture where it is okay to disagree—and perhaps not just "okay," but respected and encouraged. Otherwise, you put your organization at risk of groupthink, which can be quite risky. You may even organize formal meetings that are structured entirely to have debate. See which winning ideas rise to the surface. It may be very intellectually stimulating and energizing to do some old fashioned, friendly, intellectual sparring between colleagues. The important part is, everyone needs to understand that disagreement does not mean there must be animosity; there is a way to disagree in a respectful way, to ensure that there are no hurt feelings in the process.

11. **Skill Parties:** Since polymaths enjoy learning so much, one idea is to encourage people—the specialists in your organization, too—to share about a special skill or talent. Share information. Explain a process. Exhibit an example. In this way, people can learn from one another—and it is interesting. Plus, the person sharing their knowledge has an opportunity to feel elevated and special—and who doesn't like that? So, have a party—and make it about sharing and learning about different people's talents. You could even have fun with this one by creating certain themes, using decorations, bringing in food and beverage, and so on. What a fun way to create a culture of continual learning and employee appreciation.
12. **Task Variety:** Polymaths find the idea of doing the same tasks every day to be drudgery. To the extent you are able, try to give polymaths the opportunity to switch between the types of tasks they do on a day-to-day basis. Just as doing the same type of job over the entire course of a career would be very unappealing to a polymathic person, the same logic applies at the day-to-day level: they like variety. So, if you can, give it to them.
13. **Learning Stipends:** Polymathic individuals are deeply motivated by learning, and one way to support this is by providing learning stipends—dedicated funds that employees can use for their intellectual development. These stipends can be used to attend conferences, purchase books, enroll in courses, or even access coaching or personal development tools. Importantly, the learning supported by stipends doesn't need to be directly tied to their current job description. In fact, allowing polymaths to pursue wide-ranging topics of interest often yields unexpected benefits to the organization, as they cross-pollinate ideas across domains. These stipends signal trust, investment, and a culture that values learning as a core part of professional life.
14. **Sabbaticals:** While sabbaticals are more often associated with academia, organizations that employ polymaths may find great value in offering them even on a smaller scale. Polymathic minds benefit from time to reflect, explore, create, or engage in immersive study. A sabbatical—whether it's a few weeks, a few months, or part-time over a longer period—gives polymaths a chance to recharge and return

with renewed insights, innovations, and energy. These breaks often lead to high-leverage breakthroughs and allow polymathic individuals to reengage with their work from a broader, deeper perspective. Companies looking to retain polymathic talent long-term should strongly consider integrating sabbaticals into their talent strategy.

By having a menu of developmental options for polymathic people, this is a strategic way to keep them engaged, and make sure they understand that you want to retain them as valuable employees in your organization.

It is worth noting here, though, that the way you keep a specialist engaged is very different from how you would keep a polymath happy at work. Rather than the focus being on a breadth of new learning opportunities, you should focus on helping a specialist gain deeper expertise in their chosen field. While many of the previous ideas could and perhaps should also be applied to support the narrow specialists on your team, make sure to modify them accordingly so the focus is on helping them gain mastery *within* their discipline rather than focusing on new learning across domains. While we can and perhaps should teach specialists, so they can continue to gain mastery in their field—even if in a prescribed, linear way—polymaths, on the other hand, should be encouraged to focus on their continual, self-directed learning with a focus on cross-disciplinary skill and broad knowledge acquisition.

Creating an Internal Opportunity Exchange

One of the challenges HR leaders face when supporting polymathic talent is visibility. Organizations often know employees by their job titles rather than by the full range of their capabilities. A marketing analyst may also be an experienced coder. An engineer may be a skilled facilitator. A finance manager may have experience in product design or public speaking. When those additional capacities remain hidden, the organization underutilizes valuable talent.

An internal opportunity exchange is one way to address this gap. Rather than relying solely on formal promotions or occasional job rotations, organizations can create structured mechanisms that make skills, interests, and short-term project needs visible across the enterprise.

Employees can indicate not only their current roles, but also secondary skills, areas of curiosity, and developmental goals. At the same time, teams can post project-based needs, innovation challenges, task forces, or stretch assignments.

This approach allows HR to move beyond static job descriptions and toward dynamic talent deployment. For polymaths in particular, such systems offer several advantages. They create opportunities to contribute outside narrow role boundaries. They allow employees to test interests before making permanent career moves. They increase cross-functional collaboration and reduce silo effects. Most importantly, they signal that breadth is not a liability but an asset. For specialists, the benefits are different but equally meaningful. A specialist may contribute deep expertise to a cross-functional initiative while gaining exposure to adjacent domains. In this way, an opportunity exchange does not privilege polymaths over specialists; it creates a structured environment in which both forms of talent can be strategically integrated.

HR leaders implementing such systems should ensure clarity around accountability and workload expectations. Participation should be purposeful rather than chaotic. When designed thoughtfully, however, an internal opportunity exchange can become a powerful engine for innovation, engagement, and retention — particularly for high-capacity, versatile employees who thrive when given room to explore.

Team of Teams

Real organizational progress becomes more likely if you can figure out a way to harness the talents of deep, narrow specialists alongside broad, polymathic generalists—together, in tandem. This allows for deep expertise to be combined with broad ideas and cross-disciplinary creativity. So, this begs the question: How can organizational leaders best support collaboration between specialists and polymaths? How can you facilitate a sort of organizational *noosphere*, where constituent parts work together as a single, collaborative whole, much like how a brain works? This section will share some ideas for how you can support a culture and create some organizational scaffolding, which will help these two types of employees work symbiotically, in concert.

General Stanley McChrystal, in his book, *Team of Teams*, makes an argument for why organizations, particularly those in fast-paced, complex environments, should function as a team made up of teams, as the title implies.[10] Whereas many organizations are made up of position-based or functional teams, McChrystal makes an argument for why project-based, matrixed teams, made up of a mix of different types of professionals with various talents, backgrounds, and perspectives, can be particularly suitable and even more powerful than the traditional approach.

There are a variety of reasons why this model makes sense. For example, each team can be stood up as needed, rather than having fixed teams that stay the same no matter what. Adaptability trumps efficiency in this model, where fixed solutions are less important than emergent ones; this is ideal for complex environments. He says that this allows for more flexibility to cope with changes, helps the organization be more adaptable and resilient, and therefore positions businesses in complex environments to ultimately be more successful. Whereas the traditional organizational model is built upon a kind of hubris, which implies that we know what to expect and so we will have a fixed organizational structure to respond to what we "know" is coming our way, this other model is based on a willingness to admit that we do not always know what the future holds, and we should expect the unexpected. Adaptability is the goal. So rather than one big, fixed team, the idea is to have a team of teams that can ebb and flow in and out of existence as the needs demand.

And on those teams of teams, I believe that it makes sense to carefully select a mix of cross-functional specialists and generalist polymaths to collaborate strategically. In this case, the whole becomes greater than the sum of the parts. There is a synergy that can emerge from collaborative, agile teams made up of diverse members, especially when those members not only have different professional backgrounds but also when they tend to see problems differently at a fundamental level. You need a mix of "knowers" and "learners." The question then is, how to form those teams in a way that makes the most sense.

---

[10] McChrystal, S., T. Collins, D. Silverman, et al. 2015. *Team of Teams*. Portfolio Penguin.

Coordination of Specialists With Polymaths

Polymaths, by nature, tend to see the bigger picture, whereas specialists tend to focus more on the details. Of course, many polymaths are adept at being both detail-oriented and big-picture thinkers—able to logically zoom in and out as needed—but their real advantage is the ability to see the bigger picture where specialists might not be able to. Because of this, I suggest putting polymaths in positions akin to project managers, especially if the project team at hand is one made up of a variety of different stakeholders from different functional backgrounds. It would not make sense to put a narrow specialist as a project lead unless that specialist was expert precisely in project or team management, as their professional focus. The better approach is to put the generalist polymaths in charge of the large project, coordinating with specialists on the team who do a lot of the fine-grained work. That team should include polymaths on the team as well—not just the project manager as the only polymath. The specialists would focus on specific elements of the project, whereas the polymaths would focus on making linkages, filling in gaps, learning new knowledge as needed to bolster up the project more largely, adding value through their multidisciplinary expertise, and helping create bigger picture strategies.

Another thing to consider is that polymaths may be much more likely to identify ideas or solutions that would inform what the project team looks like to begin with; they tend to be good at ideation. Plus, they are usually good at seeing the big picture—and the specialists can help realize that large, strategic vision by working on the various subelements of the project, in coordination with polymathic colleagues helping put it all together. The idea here is to strategically build a team of teams where the strengths and approaches of these two types of roles is something you think about, explicitly, rather than putting together a team of people, more haphazardly, and hoping it will work out. Instead, build teams made up of polymaths and specialists in ways that make sense given each of their unique strengths. Those strengths should inform the roles they play in the organization and on the teams of which they are a part.

Both types can and should complement one another. The specialist delves into his or her forte while the polymath builds cohesion among the various elements of the project or team. One has a fine-grained view, focused on the details, while the other has a more coarse-grained, bigger picture perspective. Polymaths are also good at tying things together, or synthesizing ideas that might come up on the team. They can see the linkages and tell stories in ways that make sense given the larger picture. Both the narrow and the broad approaches have value on their own, but together, they create a real positive, powerful force. Specialists zoom in; polymaths zoom out. You need both vantage points to be successful to the maximum extent possible.

A few quick pieces of advice on this front, though:

1. Allow for members of the team to find the work best suited to their talents, depending on the project at hand.
2. Make sure that the team sets norms and agrees to respect one another's differences. It is critical that the polymaths appreciate the specialists, and the specialists appreciate the polymaths, for the value each brings. Make this understanding and appreciation a part of your organizational culture. Otherwise, people may reject this approach, because it is not necessarily easy to deal with a group of diverse people who see the work from different perspectives.

Typical Work Preferences of Specialists Versus Polymaths

Overall, polymaths tend to deal with uncertainty and ambiguity better than specialists—so make sure that when you assign work to those different types of employees, you keep this in mind. Specialists prefer routine—they like to know the plan, whereas polymaths prefer variety, whether in the form of day-to-day tasks or longer-term work projects. At any given time, if you are unsure if someone prefers routine and stability, versus variety and change—then just ask. You may or may not be able to adjust their workload to suit their preferences, but at least if you know what they like, and an opportunity arises to provide routine versus more ambiguous work, you'll know their preferences and can act accordingly. To the extent possible, allow them some individual agency and discretion when choosing their roles in a project or even with their workloads more generally; this will lead to better engagement and enthusiasm for the work they do, whether it is a generalist or a specialist, which should lead to a better (and perhaps quicker) product or resolution at the end of the day.

You may find that specialists need more structure and guidance, whereas polymaths prefer more freedom to explore how they might contribute (which may morph over time). Another thing to note is that depending on the team at hand, someone may be an expert specialist on one team, and be a polymathic generalist on another team. Of course, if someone is a multidisciplinary expert, then they can wear both the specialist and the generalist hat, depending on the demands of the work. Roles may shift; perspectives may change. That is okay.

In sum, give the polymaths flexibility and freedom, and offer the specialists more constraints and specific guidance on what you need from them exactly. And in general, allow for flexibility in the roles people play—perhaps on one project, an employee is a polymathic generalist, and in another setting, that person functions as a specialist. It depends on the team composition and the project at hand—and what type of enthusiasm, energy, and bandwidth the employee can bring to bear at any given time.

The Bottom Line of This Chapter

This chapter emphasized the importance of integrating both specialists and polymaths in organizations to optimize innovation, adaptability, and performance. HR professionals and leaders play a critical role in creating environments that recognize, support, and retain polymathic talent.

- **Two Types Framework:** Organizations thrive when they intentionally balance the contributions of specialists and polymathic generalists. Recognizing that different roles require different skill sets, the chapter advocates for the right mix of specialist and polymathic roles to enhance organizational performance.
- **Polymathic Strengths:** Polymaths excel in learning agility, knowledge creation, systems thinking, and creativity. These traits position polymaths as valuable assets in navigating

complex and ambiguous environments, where innovative solutions are required.

- **Strategic Role of HR:** HR professionals serve as cultural architects, shaping inclusive environments where polymathic individuals are empowered to thrive. The chapter provides practical strategies for hiring, retaining, and developing polymaths, emphasizing the need for a supportive organizational culture that values diverse perspectives and encourages continuous learning.
- **Adapting Roles to People:** Rather than forcing polymaths into rigid roles, organizations should evolve positions around high-potential individuals. Polymaths are particularly well suited to roles that require dealing with uncertainty and innovation, while specialists thrive in stable, routine environments. By recognizing these differences, leaders can better assign roles and responsibilities that align with individual strengths, thereby enhancing overall team performance.
- **Reframing Career Paths:** Nonlinear resumes and diverse experiences should be seen as assets, not red flags, especially when evaluating polymathic candidates.
- **Organizational Health as a Foundation:** A psychologically safe, human-centered culture supports both specialist and polymathic contributions and precedes sustainable performance.
- **Empowerment over Control:** Polymathic employees need scope, autonomy, and meaningful challenges to remain engaged and contribute at their best.
- **Intrapersonal Diversity:** Diversity exists within individuals as well as across groups. HR should acknowledge the value of internal variation in identity, experience, and skill.
- **Expanding Diversity, Equity, and Inclusion (DEI):** DEI initiatives should include cognitive and experiential diversity, moving beyond traditional demographic categories to recognize diverse ways of thinking and contributing.

- **Leadership as Talent Development:** Great leaders recognize and cultivate talent, helping people grow beyond rigid job descriptions while fostering both individual growth and organizational success. Effective leaders are those who can unleash human potential, support a networked collective, strategize, share a vision, navigate complexity, and influence organizational culture positively. This foundational approach ensures that both specialists and polymaths can contribute to their fullest potential.

In conclusion, this chapter advocates for a balanced approach to human resources, where the integration of specialist and polymathic talents leads to a more dynamic, innovative, and resilient organization. By fostering a culture that values both depth and breadth of knowledge, organizations can better navigate the complexities of the modern business landscape and drive sustained success.

Chapter 7 Reflection Questions and Discussion Prompts

Human Resources and the Polymath

Attracting and Hiring Polymathic Talent

1. How might traditional hiring processes unintentionally filter out polymathic candidates?
2. What signals in a résumé or interview might indicate polymathic breadth rather than lack of focus?
3. How could your organization redesign job descriptions or interview criteria to value both depth and range?

Strategic Placement and Role Design

1. In what roles or functions would polymathic employees create the greatest leverage in your organization?
2. How can HR ensure polymaths are not "boxed in" to overly narrow job scopes?
3. What would it look like to design hybrid or boundary-spanning roles intentionally?

Developing Polymathic Potential

1. Which current development programs (rotations, mentoring, stipends, sabbaticals) genuinely encourage breadth rather than specialization?
2. How can HR balance formal training with self-directed exploration?
3. What safeguards can prevent polymathic employees from being overextended or unfocused?

Career Mobility and Internal Pathways

1. How transparent and accessible are cross-functional mobility pathways in your organization?
2. What barriers discourage employees from exploring roles outside their original discipline?
3. How could internal marketplaces for skills or projects unlock polymathic potential?

Retaining High-Value Polymaths

1. What frustrations might cause polymathic employees to disengage or leave?
2. How can HR detect when a polymath feels underutilized?
3. What retention strategies go beyond compensation and speak to autonomy, challenge, and growth?

Coordinating Specialists and Polymaths

1. How should teams be structured to ensure specialists and polymaths complement rather than compete with one another?
2. What role does HR play in clarifying expectations and reducing friction between deep experts and broad integrators?
3. How can performance systems recognize different forms of contribution?

Communities of Practice and Innovation Structures

1. What mechanisms (innovation competitions, idea parties, expansion awards, communities of practice) could institutionalize polymathic collaboration?
2. How can HR measure the real impact of these initiatives beyond participation rates?
3. What risks exist if such programs are symbolic rather than structurally supported?

Performance Management and Accountability

1. How might shifting from "hours worked" to "results delivered" better support polymathic contributors?
2. What does macro-management look like in practice?
3. How can accountability systems encourage autonomy without sacrificing clarity?

HR as Strategic Architect

1. How can HR leaders position polymathy as a competitive advantage rather than a personality trait?
2. What data would you need to demonstrate the ROI of polymathic development?
3. If you were redesigning your talent strategy from scratch, where would polymathy fit?

Preparing for the Future of Work

1. As automation increases, which uniquely human polymathic capabilities become more valuable?
2. How can HR anticipate future skill intersections rather than hiring for yesterday's needs?
3. What long-term structural changes would make your organization a magnet for versatile talent?

CHAPTER 8

New Technologies and the Polymath

"Do what you can, with what you have, where you are."

—Theodore Roosevelt

The purpose of this chapter is to look at the relationship between new technologies and polymathy in humans. Given that polymathy is about learning, and technology is a tool that enables us to learn but that also changes the nature of learning itself, these two topics go hand in hand. Also—the most notable technology of the modern era, AI—is inherently polymathic. So when we think of intelligence—whether human or AI—polymathic expression showcases what is capable when thinking is expressed in its broadest, deepest forms. These two concepts—technology and polymathic learning—are important to think about together, especially when trying to understand polymathic employees who will engage with technology to do their work.

Why Polymathy Is So Relevant in the Computer Age

One reason polymathy is particularly relevant now—more than at any time in history—is the role of technology. New technologies have freed us to become more polymathic. They serve as extensions of our brains and capacities, offering relief from many routine or time-consuming tasks. For instance, we no longer need to memorize vast quantities of information or store knowledge in bulky paper-based formats; digital systems allow us to retrieve information instantly from almost anywhere in the world. In effect, information now lives at our fingertips—or in our pockets—thanks to smartphones. Of course, this digital reliance introduces new vulnerabilities: systems can be fragile, susceptible to cyberattacks, or compromised by misinformation. Yet despite these risks, the benefits of this cognitive outsourcing are profound. By offloading routine functions to machines, we are free to use our time and talents in more creative, integrative, and polymathic ways.

Technology literally makes it easier for us to do work, too. We no longer live in the time of punch cards. We do not have to rely on cumbersome, slow processes like the professionals of decades past. We can pull up a spreadsheet and do vast calculations at the click of a mouse button, rather than manually calculating our numeric analysis. We can have AI tools put together documents, summaries, images, and so much more. We no longer must write snail-mail letters to communicate—we can send e-mail, make a phone call, or hop on a video chat for instant, live communication. Because new technology makes work more efficient than in decades or centuries past, it therefore changes the nature of the very work we do and therefore, polymathy is particularly relevant today because it frees us up to explore our multiple capacities more than ever before.

AI as an Enabler of Polymathy

In only a matter of a couple of years, the rapid rise of AI has extended our cognitive capabilities on a much larger scale than prior technologies did. AI-driven tools and applications can automate routine tasks, allowing individuals to focus on higher-order thinking and creative problem-solving. This shift enables polymaths to leverage their diverse skills more effectively, as they are freed from the burden of mundane tasks. For instance, AI can assist in data analysis, pattern recognition, and even in generating insights across multiple domains. This capability aligns perfectly with the polymathic approach of integrating knowledge from various fields to solve complex problems.

Automation of Simple Tasks

David Autor has said that the more easily and clearly we can describe any given task, the more likely it is to be automatable.[1] Conversely,

[1] Autor, D. "Polanyi's Paradox and the Shape of Employment Growth." NBER Working Paper no. 20485, September 24, doi: 10.3386/w20485.

skills that are difficult to articulate, describe, or summarize have traditionally been less susceptible to automation. However, with the rapid advancements in AI, even complex tasks involving synthesis, creativity, and strategic thinking are increasingly being tackled by AI systems. This shift underscores the need for humans to focus on tasks that leverage our uniquely human traits, such as emotional intelligence, empathy, and ethical judgment. While AI can handle many aspects of strategic thinking and creativity, the nuanced understanding and contextual awareness that polymaths possess remain invaluable. Thus, polymaths, who are well-educated, well-read, and well-informed, can still thrive by combining their broad skill sets with these uniquely human qualities, navigating a world where technology continuously evolves.

Technology by and From Polymathic Thinkers

Over the years, many polymaths have contributed greatly to society—including some of the most influential figures in modern technology. Consider Steve Jobs, who combined his passion for calligraphy and aesthetic simplicity with technological innovation to create Apple's iconic products. Or Elon Musk, a tech entrepreneur whose ventures span a remarkable range of fields: SpaceX (aerospace), Tesla (automotive and clean energy), Neuralink (neurotechnology), and OpenAI, which he cofounded to advance AI safely for humanity—though he is no longer affiliated with it. Musk's wide-ranging impact and ability to operate across multiple disciplines highlight a deeply polymathic mind, although he has been somewhat controversial in recent years. When thinking about technology and polymathy, it becomes clear that many of the visionaries shaping our future do so by drawing from diverse domains of knowledge, creativity, and innovation.

Technology Fosters Connectivity

The entire world is connected via the worldwide web; the Internet creates more connections between people across the globe. It is as if the world is a brain, and individual humans are neurons; technology allows for more synaptic connections between individual neurons, making the larger whole more able to work together collectively toward common goals. The Internet connects us to other people in ways that were not possible before the digital era. And through that connectivity, we can learn, collaborate, and work together in ways that were not possible in the past. Technology fosters connectivity not only between people but also between ideas—which is very polymathic in nature.

Technology Supports Self-Directed Learning

One of the hallmarks of polymathy is that it involves self-directed learning. Today, the way that many people pursue self-directed learning is through some kind of computer, and particularly via the Internet. In yesteryear, it was much more cumbersome to obtain information to learn. For example, you had to go to a school, depend on a teacher, or visit your local library; learning frequently involved physically going somewhere to obtain information. Now, technology makes learning easy, relatively speaking. It also makes it readily accessible to the masses. Many polymaths, in fact, now feel like it is difficult to turn off the learning; it is hard to stop. Because polymathic people tend to be highly curious, and given it is so easy to go down rabbit holes of learning on myriad topics, the Internet strengthens their polymathy even further. In this age of computerization, self-directed learning is easy, attainable, and even hard to turn away from.

Technology Can Support Polymathic Development

New technology also supports polymathic development. The Internet makes it easier than ever to explore almost any topic with relative ease. This democratization of knowledge makes becoming polymathic more achievable for more people. And for those already inclined toward polymathy, it accelerates their ability to expand knowledge across multiple domains. Many polymaths today view the Internet as both a vast learning resource—and, at times, a tempting distraction—because of how effortlessly one can access information from myriad fields.

While the Internet has made learning dramatically more accessible—literally at the touch of a few keys—it has done so in ways that traditional education systems often cannot. Even many people living in poverty around the globe now have access to smartphones or Internet cafés, opening doors to self-education. In this way, technology holds the potential to be a great equalizer. However, it is important to acknowledge the ongoing digital divide: access to reliable Internet, modern devices, and digital literacy remains unequal across regions and socioeconomic groups. Still, for those who can connect, technology offers a historically unprecedented opportunity to explore and express their polymathy.

The Rise of AI and its Transformative Impact on Various Sectors

In the early 2020s, large language models (LLMs) emerged as a transformative force across a wide range of industries, from health care and finance to transportation and education. Widely accessible—often for free or at low cost—these AI systems have already begun reshaping the way we work, learn, and make decisions. Their ability to process vast amounts of data, identify patterns, synthesize information, and generate predictions has driven significant advancements and efficiencies. For example, AI-powered diagnostic tools are revolutionizing health care with faster and more accurate results, while algorithms in finance optimize trading strategies and risk management.

In this rapidly evolving landscape, integrating polymathic intelligence is essential. Polymaths—who think across disciplines and connect diverse knowledge domains—help bridge gaps between technical innovation and human-centered concerns. Their holistic perspective ensures that AI is not only technically robust but also ethically grounded and socially responsible. In an increasingly interconnected world, drawing insights from multiple fields is critical for guiding AI development toward inclusive and sustainable progress.

The Evolution of Technology and AI

Technology has evolved at an unprecedented pace over the past few decades, with AI at the forefront of this revolution. From early computing machines to advanced neural networks, technological advancements have paved the way for AI systems capable of performing tasks that were once the exclusive domain of humans. New industries are increasingly relying on AI for automation, data analysis, and the decision-making processes. This shift is revolutionizing the labor force, creating new opportunities while also posing significant challenges. One key challenge is ensuring that the workforce adapts to these changes, developing the necessary skills to work alongside AI. Opportunities abound in the form of increased productivity, innovation, and the potential to solve complex global issues. However, the ethical implications of AI, such as privacy concerns and bias in decision making, require careful consideration. Polymaths, with their diverse skill sets and ability to understand complex systems, are well positioned to navigate these challenges and harness the opportunities presented by AI. Their broad learning and ability to learn, unlearn, and relearn, is critical in the journey to learning our way to using AI tools effectively and ethically.

Synergy Between Polymathic Professionals and AI

The development and implementation of AI inherently require an interdisciplinary approach. AI projects benefit immensely from the integration of knowledge from various fields, such as computer science, psychology, ethics, and design. Polymathic intelligence enhances AI innovation by bringing together diverse perspectives and skills. For example, Leonardo da Vinci's interdisciplinary approach—combining art, science, and engineering—can be applied to new AI projects to foster creativity and holistic problem-solving. Diverse knowledge and skills are crucial in addressing the multifaceted challenges posed by AI, from technical hurdles to ethical dilemmas. Polymathic thinkers can synthesize information across disciplines, creating more robust and innovative AI solutions that are both effective and socially responsible.

Critical Observations on Polymathy and AI

As AI continues to advance, the importance of embedding ethical considerations and human values in its development cannot be overstated. Polymathic thinkers play a crucial role in this process by integrating insights from multiple domains, ensuring that AI systems are created with a deep and holistic understanding of their potential impacts.

Historically, narrow specialization within siloed disciplines has led to unintended—and sometimes harmful—consequences. For example, economic incentives in industries like coal or automotive manufacturing have often discouraged innovation in renewable energy, thereby contributing to long-term ecological harm. These types of cascading effects demonstrate how decisions made within one domain can ripple outward, impacting systems on a global scale.

This is precisely why polymathic perspectives are so vital—especially as the stakes around AI and other emerging technologies grow ever higher. Polymaths are particularly adept at anticipating unintended consequences, drawing from their wide-ranging knowledge to identify risks and propose integrative solutions. By fostering interdisciplinary collaboration, polymathic thinkers can help steer AI development in ways that align with human values, social justice, and the long-term common good.

Polymaths as Guides for Sustainable and Inclusive Technological Progress

Polymathic individuals play a vital role in guiding sustainable and inclusive technological progress. Their holistic systems thinking enables them to see the bigger picture and understand how different elements of a system interact. This perspective is crucial for developing AI technologies that are not only innovative but also equitable and sustainable. Human–AI collaboration, where human polymathic intelligence synergizes with AI's capabilities, can lead to creative and beneficial outcomes. The perspective of deep specialists is also still relevant and helpful depending on the matter at hand, but the days when the default that everyone should be a specialist no longer works in the age of AI.

Polymathic People and Adaptability in a Quickly Changing Landscape

Polymaths, with their ability to pivot and adapt to new challenges, are more resilient to the disruptions caused by automation and AI. They can seamlessly transition between different roles and industries, leveraging their diverse skill sets to remain relevant and impactful. In this way, polymathic individuals help ensure that technological advancements benefit society as a whole, fostering an environment where human potential is amplified by AI rather than overshadowed by it.

A Cautionary Note

In his book, *Think for Yourself*, Vikram Mansharamani argues that critical thinking is more essential than ever in today's age of expert authority and advanced technology.[2] He writes:

> Experts and technologies are useful—indeed essential—but it is the mindless and blind outsourcing to them that must be guarded against, that generates unnecessary risks to our well-being, and that limits opportunities to realize our true potential. This happens, in part, because of the narrow specialization that often accompanies expertise. A tight focus and siloed thinking are increasingly problematic (for both us and the experts we rely on) as we face complex problems.

Mansharamani makes a compelling case for integrated thinking as a necessary antidote to the overly specialized approaches that dominate many fields today. He warns against the uncritical deference to experts and algorithms, emphasizing the need for conscious, mindful engagement. As he wisely notes: "There are times when it makes sense to outsource our thinking, but this must be a conscious choice, one proactively and mindfully selected."

Rather than defaulting to blind obedience or passive acceptance, he urges us to reclaim control over areas of our lives where we may have unknowingly outsourced our agency. Even as technology supports us in powerful ways, we must remember: it does not think for itself—and we should not stop thinking for ourselves.

---

[2] Mansharamani, V. 2020. *Think for Yourself: Restoring Common Sense in an Age of Experts and Artificial Intelligence.* Boston: Harvard Business Review Press.

Consider the example of GPS navigation: if your GPS advised a route that you knew to be wrong or unsafe, would you still follow it without question? This simple scenario highlights a broader truth: while tools can guide us, only human judgment can steer us.

The Digital Gig Economy

For people who have polymathic talents, modern technology has made it easy to sell their services across the globe. Freelancers, who are often polymathic, can land gigs to do work for people from across the world; this gig economy is made possible, in large part, to the platforms that support those services—they depend on technology. For people with polymathic talents searching for "side gigs" to earn extra income, technology makes it much easier to land customers and clients, regardless of their physical location.

In fact, according to McKinsey, approximately a quarter of people working in the United States and Europe are considered these kinds of "independent workers."[3] Short term, contract work without promise of longer-term prospects is very common nowadays. And as digital marketplaces become more widespread, this trend is only expected to grow.

The gig economy would be much more difficult if it were not for modern technology; and of course, many people with side gigs and hustles are juggling multiple types of work—which is polymathic by nature. In other words, many polymathic professionals—especially freelancers—are enabled by technology to pursue their multiple talents, even for customers from different parts of the world. In fact, a relatively new website called Polywork—a sort of competitor to LinkedIn—aims to highlight the multiple capacities of professional workers—because the time when people were mostly just one type of professional is fading while polyprofessionalism is on the rise.

In the digital gig economy, "work" is no longer synonymous with "job." Work is something people do for money (generally speaking), whereas a job implies more permanence—a position with wages,

[3] "Independent Work: Choice, Necessity, and the Gig Economy." McKinsey Global Institute, October 2016.

benefits, advancement opportunities within a firm, and so on. But many people no longer have jobs—they have work. In fact, they might have multiple types of work. They are contractors, gig workers, or people who have found multiple ways to earn money through professional endeavors. Many of those people end up blending their interests together in very polymathic ways.

Rather than being narrowly defined by a single job, people are increasingly defining themselves based on their ability to do many kinds of work. The gig economy accentuates this rising trend. Plus, many people do not feel fulfilled by a single type of contribution; it can be rewarding to contribute, instead, in multiple ways. The gig economy provides a kind of financial safety net since people are not so dependent necessarily on one client, one source of income, one single skillset, or a single "job." The gig economy has downsides, of course. Making deliveries or driving for Uber are not particularly high-skill or necessarily rewarding types of work. Many of those gigs do not provide health care or retirement benefits. But the gig economy—for good or bad—is here and is unlikely to go away anytime soon.

The Role of Human Beings in the Digital Age

This all begs the question: now that technology frees us to change how and what we work on, what should the role of a human being be in modern society? The best answer, I would argue, is for humans to focus on uniquely human tasks. We should not squander our intelligence, time, or capabilities on work that machines or AI can do for us. If a task can be automated, why devote our energy to it?

And we shouldn't just look at what technology can do today—we must also anticipate what it will be capable of in the coming decades. Preparing a future-ready workforce means cultivating human talent for roles that technology cannot easily replace.

Polymathic talent, when combined with modern technology, has the power to do extraordinary things. Polymaths who leverage their intellectual capacities alone can achieve remarkable feats. But when they also tap into the amplifying power of technology, their potential multiplies. Technology acts as a force multiplier—it extends our reach, sharpens our tools, and accelerates our progress.

Crucially, as AI becomes more adept at specialized tasks, it enables us to move away from rigid roles defined by narrow expertise. While AI has made strides in creativity, innovation, and even strategic thinking, it still lacks the emotional intelligence, ethical depth, and nuanced understanding required for human connection and complex judgment. These are precisely the areas where polymaths, with their broad and integrative skill sets, shine.

Automation, rather than dehumanizing the workforce, gives us an opportunity to lean into our humanity. By offloading routine and specialized work, technology invites us to focus on higher-order functions—empathy, ethical reasoning, imagination, and holistic problem-solving. In doing so, we are not diminished by machines—we are elevated.

It remains unlikely that machines will truly master compassion, empathy, or the subtlety of interpersonal communication anytime soon. And even if they do one day, that future is likely many decades—or even centuries—away. In the meantime, the work of the future will increasingly demand those very human qualities. Technology asks us to rise—to bring our fullest humanity to our work and our world.

Rather than compete with machines, we can collaborate with them. Let us stop being cogs in the machine and start becoming more of who we truly are. When we embrace our human potential—and let technology complement it—we open the door to extraordinary possibilities.

Leveraging Tech Tools

One of the ways to enhance one's polymathy is by using the tools available to you. So, a piece of advice for anyone wanting to enhance their own polymathic potential, or to support the polymathic expression of others, is to ensure that they are leveraging the tools at their disposal. These tools are constantly being expanded and improved upon, as well—so continue to research what technology can help you reach your goals, whether personally or at the organizational level.

We humans create our tools, and then our tools shape us, in return; it is a symbiotic relationship that way. Father John Culkin explained this concept succinctly: "We become what we behold. We shape our tools then our tools shape us."[4] Polymaths who leverage tools can enhance their capacities notably; polymaths who do not leverage their resources, including technology, to the fullest, may find that they run into limitations on what they can accomplish, more and more. Embrace technology, and see how your polymathy, or your employees' polymathic talents, can flourish even more.

The Age of Automation

For the foreseeable future, much of what we've traditionally called "work" will increasingly be automated. Technology is accelerating this shift. As a result, many jobs of the past will disappear—while others will evolve. Either way, one truth is clear: people will need to adapt in order to continue earning a living. If you're rooted in a single field and that work becomes automated, what then?

Polymathy offers a powerful response to this uncertainty. It serves as a personal safety net—an adaptive mindset that creates options. While specialists may struggle when their niche is disrupted, polymathic generalists are more agile. They pivot. They learn—because learning is what they do—and they evolve with the times. With a diverse set of tools at their disposal, polymaths are better prepared to weather change and navigate new opportunities.

The COVID-19 crisis offered a stark reminder of this reality. As the pandemic disrupted industries like retail and hospitality, millions were forced to reinvent how they worked. Those with broader skill sets and learning agility were better positioned to pivot. In a world shaped by technological upheaval—and unpredictable global events—polymathy is not just a luxury. It's a smart strategy.

Developing polymathic intelligence equips individuals to stay relevant, adaptable, and employable. It ensures that when one path becomes obsolete, others remain open. In an age defined by automation and rapid change, polymathy is one of the most effective ways to future-proof your livelihood.

---

[4] Kirsch, M. 2019. *The Wicked Company*. Virginia Beach: Koehlerbooks.

Life Extension Technology and the Impact on Learning

Another way that modern technology impacts the importance of continual, polymathic learning is because as our knowledge, tools, and technology improve, so do our lifespans. Medical technology is becoming so advanced that people can simply replace body parts (literally) as they break down, as you might switch a part on a car. Plus, advances in diagnostic testing allow diseases to be identified at much earlier stages—sometimes even before symptoms appear. Technological advances allow us to undergo procedures that our ancestors would have never dreamed possible. And treatments for diseases are becoming more robust and sophisticated—all of which means that people are living longer than ever before.

However, in living longer, we may very well have to work longer, too. We can no longer assume that a college degree we obtained at 22 will somehow serve as a solid basis for the professional knowledge we will need forever after. (It could be argued that college is not really that great at preparing people for the real working world anyway.) The point is, in the past, careers might have spanned 30 years; in the world of the future, that number may be closer to 40, 50, or even more.

In that context, being committed to continual learning—as polymaths are—becomes ever more critical. We cannot work for decades on end and become stagnant in what we know, especially as times change. Therefore, the *future of work is tied to the future of learning*. In this new world, where human beings live longer than ever before because of the advanced technologies available to us, we must continue to learn. Plus, as we live longer, becoming polymathic professionals across disciplines, over time, becomes more possible than ever before since we will simply have more time to explore those different career avenues. In the *age of automation* also comes the *age of longevity*—thus underscoring the point again that advanced technology and human lifespan are intertwined, and both impact our capacity for learning, especially polymathic learning.

In their book, *The Adaptation Advantage*, Heather McGowan and Chris Shipley put it aptly:[5]

> The old model that parsed life into sequential steps of education, career, and retirement is blurring. Once we were "educated" early in our lives enough to get us on a 40-year career ladder that we climbed until we retired and then, by design, soon after died. Today, considerable leaps in human longevity have stretched that career phase out a decade or longer. A single dose of "education"—a process that infers an end state of being "educated"—isn't sufficient for a career arc that looks more like a spiral. Instead, we need to swap education for learning, a continuous state of discovery and reinvention. Work, then, leverages that learning and the work itself becomes another form of learning.

Polymaths are people who live this way—who view life itself as a classroom, an opportunity for continual learning. They don't just learn by happenstance; they hunger for continual learning. As a result, they are particularly well suited to adjust to the new model, where—beyond just being educated—the ability to learn continually is critical.

Technology, Abundance, Freedom, and Human Potential

Technology has drastically improved the human condition particularly over the past 100 years or so. With those improvements has come more abundance. Across large swaths of the globe, people have their basic physiological needs met such as food, access to clean water, warmth, and rest—as well as their safety needs. In other words, many (though certainly not all) human beings on the planet are no longer focused on just getting by day to day in ways that people had to focus on in centuries past. We have mostly moved beyond mere survival. We have advanced and evolved to a better place as a species, in many ways. Technology and human advancements, more generally, have lifted many of us out of subsistence mode. Now we are freer to consider what else to do with our

[5] McGowan, H., and C. Shipley. 2020. *The Adaptation Advantage*. Wiley.

capacities and talents, since survival is no longer something we must focus much energy on anymore.

Abraham Maslow's well-known *Hierarchy of Needs* posits that the goal of any human being is to self-actualize. In 1954, he defined self-actualization as the desire to "become more and more of what one is, to become everything that one is capable of becoming."[6] Technology plays an important role in freeing us up to focus on our highest potential—it helps us reach toward self-actualization. We do not have to spend a lot of time doing monotonous or routine tasks—for example, laundry or doing the dishes. We have laundry machines that make this work much easier for us, and at some point in the not-so-distant future, humanoid robots will be commercially available to make this household chore "and others" even easier on us. Our economy allows us to easily outsource tasks, often using technology as a means to make those arrangements. We can call up transportation quickly and easily from our smartphones, for example, or have food delivered to us if we are short on time or do not feel like cooking. Even basic technology like the abovementioned washing machine example, as well as more recent advancements like modern smartphones, enhance our lives and frequently save us time—precious time that can be used to focus elsewhere. The bottom line here is that technology allows us to focus our energy in different ways than we did in the past, when humans were more focused on survival. We are more abundant than ever, more freed from mundane tasks more than ever; technology gives us more freedom than before, allowing us to become our best selves—including in all the multifaceted, polymathic variety that may entail.

Working With Technology

As technology continues to advance, the nature of the work we do will also shift; and the line between what tech does for us, and what we actually do in the workplace may become blurred. In his book, *The Inevitable*, Kevin Kelly says, "This is not a race against the machines. If we race against them, we lose. This is a race *with* machines. You will be paid in the future based on how well you work with the robots. Ninety percent of your coworkers will be unseen machines. Most of what you do will not

[6] Maslow, A. 1970. *Motivation and Personality*. New York: Harper and Row.

be possible without them. And there will be a blurry line between what you do and what they do."[7] Even the ability to learn the technology that we work with, will be an important skill in the world of the future. Going back to the theme of this book: continual, multiple learnings; this continues to be important, especially in the context of modern technologies that can accelerate learning. As technology disrupts our world, we have to learn our way into the future.

Human as a Type of Technology

Here's a thought experiment to consider: what if human beings are a kind of technology? And what if the universe—or even the multiverse—is, in its own way, technological too? While we may never know for sure, there are intriguing signs that suggest this might be true.

For instance, just as computers rely on code, humans rely on DNA—a form of biological "programming" that shapes who we are. We have hardware (our bodies) and software (our minds), which we continuously upgrade through learning. In this analogy, polymaths are like hardware with multiple software systems installed—they're versatile, adaptive, and capable of running many different programs at once.

So, if you were to think of yourself as a type of technology, what kind would you be? Would you rather be a first-generation cell phone—reliable, but built for one function—or a 2020s-era smartphone with countless evolving apps? The smartphone, like the polymath, is flexible and updatable. It's built to handle complexity.

Polymathic people are also modular—more like a Swiss Army knife than a single-use tool. A standalone screwdriver is valuable, of course. But if you're heading into unfamiliar territory and don't know what you'll face, wouldn't you rather have the multitool?

Would you prefer to be really good at one thing, or ready for a wider range of challenges? Perhaps the answer depends on the journey you're on. But one thing is certain: if you see yourself as a form of evolving technology, then learning is the upgrade mechanism. Polymathy becomes a way to future-proof yourself—an ongoing system update for the modern world.

---

[7] Kelly, K. 2016. *The Inevitable: Understanding the 12 Technological Forces That Will Shape Our Future*. New York: Viking Press.

The Risk of Specialization in Technological Revolutions

In turbulent times—especially during rapid technological revolutions—we must anticipate and develop the kinds of skills that will be most valuable on the frontier of society. Otherwise, we risk becoming outdated or unnecessary. In such a world, continual, lifelong, lifewide learning—a core trait of polymathic individuals—should become a norm for everyone, not just specialists.

In the future of work, specialists will need not only to upskill within their domains but also to cross-skill—expanding their capabilities across disciplines. This kind of skill diversification is a key element of polymathic resilience. Over the course of long careers, adaptability may come not from digging deeper into one narrow trench, but from building a broader toolkit that allows people to pivot, connect, and create in new contexts. This is the superpower of the polymath—they are not only capable of learning continuously; they crave it, across a wide range of disciplines.

As AI and automation take over many narrowly defined tasks, we may see a rising demand for polymathic talent—individuals who can connect the dots, adapt quickly, and synthesize across fields. Even beyond self-identified polymaths, there will be growing opportunities for people who are agile learners—those who can pivot in the face of change.

The risk of deep specialization in this shifting landscape is clear: if your job becomes automated, where is your safety net? After years—or decades—of investing in one narrow path, what happens when that path is overtaken by machines? This is where polymathy offers a distinct advantage. It provides resilience. It acts as a form of personal insurance—diversifying your intellectual and professional capital in a way that allows you to stay relevant, useful, and creatively engaged, even as the world changes around you.

Supercharging Polymathic Talent With Technology

A strong polymath who knows how to leverage the tools and technology at their disposal, in strategic ways, is well positioned to add tremendous value wherever they work, and to be very successful professionally. They essentially extend their own capability out further, by using tools and technology that supercharge their own capacities. Rather than depending on their own knowledge, they tap into something beyond themselves—through technology. For any person who is wanting to strengthen their capabilities, mastering tech tools in strategic ways is a great way to supercharge your polymathic talent. Is there an app, software, or hardware that would help you reach your personal or professional goals? Is there some learning you could do around a form of technology where you feel weak—which, if you mastered, would help you take your work to the next level? Think about how you can use technology yourself to upgrade your learning; also consider how you can leverage technology to improve the skills and work of the people in your organization, more largely, as well.

Technology as a Game Changer in the Course of Human History

Modern technology has been a game changer in the course of human history. It makes possible what would have seemed impossible to our ancestors just a few hundred years ago. For example, we do not have to memorize information like we did in the past, because we can simply pull it up on a handheld device. We do not have to know it all, because we can tap into information as needed—using our devices such as smartphones and computers, essentially as amplifiers of our own minds. We can have the idea, and AI tools can expand and enhance the vision we imagine with our creations. These tools have become extensions of our personhood, allowing us to leverage knowledge even if it exists and is stored outside of our own brains. In other words, nowadays, we can quickly and easily find and retrieve information we do not internally store in our minds; we can simply pull it into our minds if and when needed.

The proliferation of modern technology is pivoting the human race in a new direction, however. And it is doing so exponentially fast, too. In fact, "Moore's Law" states that computer capabilities roughly double each two years, though the cost is halved. What the 2030s will look like may be drastically different from even what the 2020s look like now—in terms of the technology widely available to humans, and what that technology means for us in terms of how we live and work. Next, here is a glimpse of what that not-so-distant future might look like, and how it pertains to polymaths and human learning, more generally.

Technology Impacts How We Learn and Work

Futurist, Director of Engineering at Google, and Cofounder of Singularity University, Ray Kurzweil, makes predictions, based on technology.[8] He has been doing this with quite good accuracy for several decades. His predictions are not woo-woo, based on intuition or wild guesses; they are based on his knowledge and command over what technology is capable of doing.

Kurzweil has predicted—among many other things—that in the relatively near future, most learning will be accomplished through intelligent, adaptive courseware that is presented by nonhuman teachers. In that model, what is the role for humans—besides doing the learning? Do we need human teachers anymore? Kurzweil argues that in that world, human adults will play the role of counselor or mentor, rather than being "instructors," per se. This sort of technological approach to learning also means that these virtual teachers can be available to help with a student's learning, regardless of time or place—which is not the case when depending on a human instructor in a traditional classroom environment. Learning can be done whenever it is convenient for the learner—even formal education. So even learning itself—how and when and from whom we receive it—is changing, because of technological advancements. And of course, as I have said multiple times by this point, polymaths are learners—and technology is sure to impact how we learn now and into the future.

Furthermore, as a general rule, polymaths tend to be readers; reading is a primary avenue to learning. A kind of "reading" can also be done through listening to audio files or watching videos, since these methods of information sharing also lead to learning, in similar ways that reading does. Indeed, reading physical books is becoming increasingly rare, as we listen to digital audiobooks that exist in the cloud, or as we read digital

---

[8] Kurzweil's predictions, retrieved from https:// en.wikipedia.org/wiki/Predictions_made_by_Ray_Kurzweil

books (or other forms of information) on a screen, such as a tablet or laptop. Many people turn to YouTube for their self-directed learning. Plus, virtual reality (VR) 3D headsets already exist, are fairly widespread, and are becoming more commonplace, coupled with auditory input such as headphones or speakers built into the headsets. And special glasses or contact lenses—even smartphone apps—can deliver augmented reality (AR) or VR; that is already here. Holographic technology is coming to the masses soon, too. And soon, implantable computer chips on the neocortex of the human brain will be available, merging human intelligence with AI. All of these tools can and likely will impact the way that human learning and working occurs.

In fact, Kurzweil predicts that by 2029, eyeglasses and headphones that deliver VR or AR will become obsolete, as implants (either permanent or removable ones) that go into the eyes and ears take their place. Such implants will allow for more direct interface with technology to help us, whether through learning or navigating our world more generally. Kurzweil also predicts that computer implants that go directly into the brain will become available in the not-so-distant future, too, making it possible to enhance our human capacities, for example, by improving memory, speed of learning, or our overall intelligence.

The point here is that technology has already changed our world drastically, and it will likely continue to do so—perhaps even at exponential rates as we move into the future. Many of these examples sound as if they come from science fiction novels; then again, some of the current technology we already have and take for granted also would have sounded like science fiction just a few decades ago. If in the 1980s, you were told that we would each have a magical tool we could fit in our pockets, that would allow us to access nearly any person or any piece of information across the globe, and within seconds—it would have sounded impossible. Yet, that is what a smart phone does for us, and that technology has been around for over a decade already. Arthur C. Clarke aptly said, "any sufficiently advanced technology is indistinguishable from magic." But it is not magic, it is just technology. And more of this kind of unbelievable, sci-fi capability is headed our way, ready or not.

The Nature of Knowledge May Change Based on Technological Advances

Kurzweil also predicts that approximately by 2029, computers will become so adept at learning, that they will be able to create new knowledge without human help. Plus, technology will be able to scan through existing information that is stored on the Internet (whether a website, e-book, movie, video, etc.), and make sense of it; this means that regardless of when or where information was generated by human beings and stored on the Internet, new technology will be able to grapple with it and literally know all of that information at once—in ways that human beings could never do due to the sheer amount of it all. This may allow for integrations of information or synthesis of information that was not possible with a human mind, because those interconnections would have been impossible, because we humans cannot store or access the same, vast amount of information when compared to what computers will be capable of—and in fairly short order.

The Augmented Mind: Will AI Make Us All Polymaths?

As brain–computer interface technologies advance and artificial intelligence becomes increasingly embedded in daily life, we may be approaching a new chapter in human cognitive evolution. With developments such as neural interfaces, wearable AI copilots, and real-time access to the vast knowledge repositories of the World Wide Web, the boundary between internal memory and external intelligence is beginning to blur.

Imagine a future in which knowledge need not be memorized but accessed instantly and contextually. Rather than storing vast amounts of information in our biological memory, individuals could retrieve, synthesize, and apply knowledge on demand. In such a world, does everyone become a polymath?

On the surface, it may seem so. If technical expertise, historical knowledge, medical insight, or linguistic fluency can be accessed in real time, the barriers between disciplines appear to dissolve. The bottleneck shifts from possession of knowledge to navigation of it. The ability to query, filter, interpret, and integrate information becomes more valuable than recall alone.

Yet polymathy has never been merely about storage capacity. It is about synthesis, judgment, creativity, ethical reasoning, and the ability to connect ideas across domains in meaningful ways. Even if AI systems can supply information, humans must still determine what questions to ask, which connections matter, what trade-offs are acceptable, and what vision should guide action.

Cognitive augmentation may democratize access to knowledge, but it does not automatically create wisdom. If anything, it raises the bar. The polymath of the future may be less defined by what they know internally and more by how skillfully they orchestrate human and machine intelligence together.

The more pressing question may not be whether AI will make us all polymaths, but whether we will cultivate the integrative thinking, ethical grounding, and creative imagination necessary to use augmented intelligence responsibly. Technology may expand the reach of the human mind, but it does not determine its direction.

In this sense, the future of polymathy may not lie in replacing human breadth with artificial memory, but in merging computational power with distinctly human capacities: curiosity, empathy, judgment, and the drive to connect disparate ideas into coherent possibility.

Technology and Automation Will Change the World of Work

This may be an obvious point, but of course, as technology advances by leaps and bounds, many sectors will become almost entirely automated. Kurzweil predicts that this will be the case especially for manufacturing, agriculture, and transportation industries. Though this may sound threatening—because of what this means for human jobs—he also predicts (possibly idealistically) that because of our advances in technology, that poverty, war, and disease will be very nearly eradicated across the globe. This underscores the point even more that the more agile we can be, whether as individuals or more largely as organizations, the better we will fare as technology continues to change our world drastically—and relatively quickly, too. Polymaths are well suited to be agile, because of their ability to quickly learn, to use different tools in their toolkits, and because they are able to pivot their focus because of their multiple capacities.

More recent analyses suggest that job disruption due to automation and artificial intelligence is not only continuing but accelerating. The OECD Employment Outlook 2023 estimates that approximately 27 percent of jobs are highly exposed to automation technologies, with many more roles likely to experience significant task redesign rather than outright elimination.[9] Similarly, the World Economic Forum's Future of Jobs Report 2025 projects that by 2030, tens of millions of jobs may be displaced even as new roles emerge, reshaping the nature of work across sectors.[10] The International Monetary Fund has also noted that up to 40 percent of jobs worldwide could be affected by AI-driven work redesign.[11]

In other words, the transition ahead could be rough for the unprepared. But it is coming. Yes, some jobs will change dramatically — and some may disappear — but that does not mean that humans become irrelevant. We will have to shift what we do at work. And to be successful, we have to learn; we need to get really good at learning — like polymaths are.

Of course, human beings will always be needed to translate and augment what technology does for us. After all, we created the technology, and it exists to make our lives easier. We do not necessarily need to fear a dystopian future where machines rule over us. Instead, with thoughtful planning and purposeful policy agendas, we can create a world where humans are freed to do more meaningful and creative work than ever before. What is certain is that we will have to be agile, more and more, given the fast-paced, changing reality that automation and digitization bring to our lives.

---

[9] Retrieved from https://www.oecd.org/en/publications/oecd-employment-outlook-2023_08785bba-en.html

[10] World Economic Forum. 2025. The Future of Jobs Report 2025. Retrieved from https://www.weforum.org/publications/the-future-of-jobs-report-2025/

[11] International Monetary Fund. 2024. World Economic Outlook Update. Retrieved from https://www.imf.org/en/Publications/WEO

Flexibility Versus Adaptability

Authors Heather McGowan and Chris Shipley explain in *The Adaptation Advantage*, that there are two concepts that are sometimes conflated but which are distinctly different ideas: flexibility and adaptability.[12] Flexibility involves the ability to pivot from one tool in your toolbox, to shift from one approach to another. In contrast, adaptability requires adding something to that toolbox—or perhaps even removing a tool from the toolbox altogether if it is no longer relevant or useful. They argue in their book that "the future of work, for both individuals and organizations, relies on rapid learning, unlearning, and adaptation." Further, they contend that to successfully learn and adapt, two things are necessary: first, we have to be willing to let go of the way we have worked in the past, and second, we have to let go of who we think we are to some extent—we have to allow our identities to shift in order to make that adaptability possible. They also explain that in a world where rapid learning, unlearning, and adaptation are critical, we must become more comfortable with ambiguity and vulnerability, which allows us to lean into learning as our main coping mechanism to deal with uncertainty, which in turn helps us become champions of our own human potential. In a world where technology is changing rapidly, we must become masters of adaptability—not just flexibility.

What's clear is that technological forces require rapid learning. This is the new normal. This is not going away. Change will only get faster and faster, too. The key to adaptation is through learning, so we can work effectively. Polymathic people are especially adept at learning and adaptation, and so our need for polymathic thinkers will become even more important as technology advances.

Polymaths in the Modern Age

Waqas Ahmed, in his book, *The Polymath: Unlocking the Power of Human Versatility*, argues that there is an important link between technology and polymathy: "With machine intelligence and the so-called technological

---

[12] McGowan, H., and C. Shipley. 2020. *The Adaptation Advantage*. Wiley.

singularity looming (not to mention nuclear, environmental, and economic catastrophes that are more imminent), the world has little choice but to see a *revival of the polymath*, as it is only this species of multifaceted, complex, creative, versatile and inimitable human that will have any value or relevance in a highly complex, automated, super-intelligent future."[13] Mr. Ahmed believes that polymathic approaches are needed, more and more, in our modern, technologically advanced world; that a return to polymathy is the logical adaptation we humans make as we head into the future as he describes it. Polymathy as a way of being, thinking, working, and living, must be revived now; it is time.

The Bottom Line of This Chapter

Chapter 8 explores the intricate relationship between modern technology and polymathy, emphasizing how the digital age has amplified the relevance and impact of polymathic thinking. In today's world, technology acts as an extension of our brains, allowing us to automate routine tasks and focus on more complex, human-centric activities. This shift frees us to explore our multiple capacities, making polymathy particularly relevant and valuable.

- **Relevance of Polymathy in the Digital Age:** Technology has automated many simple tasks, enabling humans to engage in more sophisticated, creative, and strategic work. Polymaths, with their broad skill sets and ability to synthesize information across domains, are less likely to be replaced by automation, reinforcing their importance in the modern workforce.
- **Influence of Polymathic Thinkers on Technology:** Many technological advancements have been driven by polymathic individuals—people who integrate diverse knowledge and skillsets in original ways. Some, like Steve Jobs, exemplify field polymathy: he fused design, user experience, business acumen,

[13] Ahmed, W. 2018. *The Polymath: Unlocking the Power of Human Versatility.* Wiley.

and computer science within the tech sector to transform how we interact with technology. Others, like Elon Musk, span multiple domains within technology—from electric vehicles and space exploration to AI and neurotechnology—demonstrating a broader form of polymathic integration. Then there are those like Richard Branson, whose ventures extend across entirely different industries—music, aviation, media, space tourism—showcasing multifield polymathy at a systemic level. What unites these figures is their ability to synthesize ideas across boundaries—whether within a single domain or across many—to spark innovation, challenge norms, and shape the future. In this way, polymathy is not just an individual trait but a driving force in technological and societal transformation.

- **Connectivity and Self-Directed Learning:** Technology fosters global connectivity, allowing for unprecedented collaboration and access to information. This enhances self-directed learning, a hallmark of polymathy, making it easier for individuals to pursue diverse interests and expand their knowledge.
- **Development and Accessibility:** The Internet and modern technology democratize learning, making education accessible to more people than ever before. This accessibility supports the development of polymathic skills across a broader segment of society.
- **Cautionary Note on Critical Thinking:** While technology provides immense benefits, it is crucial to maintain critical thinking and not blindly outsource decision making to experts and machines. Polymaths, with their integrated thinking, are well suited to navigate and question the complexities of the modern world.
- **Impact on the Gig Economy**: Technology enables the gig economy, allowing polymaths to leverage their diverse skills for various clients globally. This trend reflects a shift from traditional job structures to more flexible, project-based work.

- **Future of Human Work**: As technology continues to evolve, humans should focus on uniquely human tasks such as creativity, emotional intelligence, and strategic thinking. Polymaths, with their versatile capabilities, are well positioned to thrive in this new landscape.
- **Lifelong Learning and Adaptability**: Longer lifespans and rapid technological advancements necessitate continuous learning. Polymaths, who inherently pursue lifelong learning, are better prepared to adapt to changing professional landscapes.
- **Technological Enhancements**: Future technologies, such as implants and advanced AI, will further enhance our capabilities. Polymaths can leverage these tools to extend their reach and impact even more.
- **Risks of Specialization**: In a world where automation is increasing, specialization may pose risks. Polymathy offers a safety net, allowing individuals to pivot and adapt to new roles and challenges.
- **Supercharging Polymathic Talent**: Using modern technology, polymaths can amplify their talents and achieve greater success. Leveraging the right tools can significantly enhance their productivity and innovation.
- **Exponential Technological Growth**: Technology is advancing at an exponential rate, transforming how we learn and work. Understanding and adapting to these changes is crucial for success in the future.

In conclusion, this chapter underscores the synergy between modern technology and polymathy. As the world becomes more complex and technology-driven, the need for versatile, adaptive thinkers—polymaths—will continue to grow. Embracing polymathic approaches in tandem with technological advancements can lead to unprecedented innovations and a more resilient, adaptable workforce.

Chapter 8 Reflection Questions and Discussion Prompts

Polymathy in the Age of Technology

1. How has technology enabled or amplified your own polymathic tendencies?
2. In what ways has automation freed you—or your team—from routine tasks to focus on higher-order thinking?
3. Can you recall a time when leveraging technology allowed you to integrate knowledge across fields?

AI and Human–AI Collaboration

1. How do you personally feel about working alongside AI tools? Do you view them as partners, threats, or something else?
2. What are some ways AI has expanded or challenged your capacity for creativity or problem-solving?
3. How might you or your organization ensure ethical and inclusive use of AI through interdisciplinary thinking?

Self-Directed Learning and Information Access

1. What has changed in the way you pursue learning since the rise of the Internet and digital platforms?
2. How do you manage the tension between information abundance and focus as a polymathic learner?
3. What tools or strategies help you stay curious and organized in your lifelong learning journey?

Polymaths in Tech History and the Workforce

1. What traits do Steve Jobs, Elon Musk, or Richard Branson demonstrate that align with polymathic thinking?
2. How do you think polymathy has shaped the direction of major technological innovations?
3. Do you see yourself—or someone you admire—as a polymath influencing or working within tech spaces?

Critical Thinking in a High-Tech World

1. Have you ever caught yourself blindly trusting technology or an expert without questioning the judgment behind it?
2. What strategies can help ensure that critical thinking remains central in an age of algorithms and automation?
3. How do you decide when to delegate decisions to technology versus when to assert human judgment?

The Gig Economy and Poly-Professional Identity

1. Do you engage in multiple income streams or professional identities? How has technology made this easier (or harder)?
2. What do you find fulfilling or frustrating about project-based or freelance work enabled by technology?
3. How does your online professional identity reflect your polymathic range of skills or interests?

Longevity, Learning, and the Future of Work

1. As lifespans extend, how do you think your learning and career path will need to evolve?
2. What do you find most exciting—or most daunting—about the idea of working and learning over a 50+ year workspan.
3. How might your organization support polymathic development across long careers?

Technology as a Tool for Empowerment

1. Are there any technological tools you haven't yet mastered that could help you grow or amplify your impact?
2. How do you ensure that you are using technology as a force multiplier rather than a source of distraction?
3. What's one way you could better support your team or colleagues in leveraging technology for polymathic growth?

Flexibility, Adaptability, and Identity

1. How comfortable are you with letting go of past work identities or habits to adapt to change?
2. What's an example of a time you had to unlearn something in order to grow professionally or personally?
3. How do ambiguity and change affect your motivation to learn or reinvent yourself?

The Future of Learning and Knowledge Creation

1. What do you think the role of human teachers should be as AI-driven learning tools become more prevalent?
2. How might immersive technologies (like VR, AR, or implants) change the way you engage with learning?
3. How does your understanding of knowledge change when machines can synthesize more than any human ever could?

CHAPTER 9

A Call to Action

"You cannot discover new oceans unless you have the courage to lose sight of the shore."

—Andre Gide

The purpose of this final chapter is to synthesize and condense much of what this book has addressed so far—to discuss next steps, and why it is important to think about polymathy as a strategy that can be used to help organizations succeed. This chapter will also address why polymathic expression is important on the individual level, as well, in addition to the benefits it can bring organizations. This chapter is a sort of call to action for HR professionals and business leaders, to take steps to help empower polymathic expression within organizations, and some additional, final reasons why doing so is important.

The Myth of Specialization

We have been fed a myth that the only way to become our best selves and to contribute to society is to be narrow, focused, and specialized in one area—and one area alone. We're told to pick a lane and stay in it, professionally and even personally, as though depth must come at the expense of breadth. For some people, this kind of deep specialization may indeed bring joy. But for many others, it feels stifling, even dehumanizing. How can a person be their fullest, truest, most authentic self if they're instructed to stay in a single silo forever—especially if that goes against their very nature?

Today, this myth is being challenged like never before. As the world becomes more interconnected, information more accessible, and our horizons more vast, naturally curious people are seeing all the world has to offer—and they want in. They want more of the action. They don't just want to watch history unfold; they want to help shape it from multiple angles. The rise of the polymath is, in part, a response to the complexity of the world we live in, and to the richness now available to us.

Given that our work takes up most of our waking hours for decades of our lives, being able to experience freedom and fullness in our work isn't just nice—it's necessary. That sense of fulfillment at work spills over into our lives as a whole. And well, that's kind of important, isn't it?

Society conditions us to become little cogs in big machines—hyperspecialized, predictable, and interchangeable. But must we blindly follow this script? Or will we begin to question the ideology behind it? One of the hopes I had in writing this book was to help you see through the dominant cultural lie: that specialization is the only—or even the best—path to individual success. Increasingly, people are waking up to this deception. And it's not just Gen Z—it's happening across generations. As lifespans extend and the world becomes more accessible, more and more individuals are rejecting narrow definitions of identity and success. They're seeking lives of depth *and* breadth, integration, synthesis, *and* creativity—no longer content to contort themselves into single-dimensional roles.

People often want to go "all in" at life itself—and one way of doing this is by showing up in polymathic ways. By learning, expanding, trying—even if those elements that are selected do not seem on the surface to go together. And that's part of what makes being a polymath so interesting is that it further enables us to explore our onlyness—our unique individuation. Want to make the world a better place? Make yourself the best version you can be. And for many, the way to do that is to be multifaceted in the way that polymathic people are—to be a real original.

So, at the individual level, having more multifaceted experiences is worthwhile and appealing for many people—but it is also strategic at the organizational level, too, and even on the societal scale. Polymaths can be a tremendous strategic resource in a business setting. They are multitalented individuals who have a zest for continual learning; when you hire a polymath, you are hiring someone dedicated to continually improving themselves, through lifelong, lifewide, self-directed learning. It is as if you have a resource that is constantly refreshing, refining, and upgrading itself. Plus, overall, polymaths tend to be great contributors; because of the large swath of tools in their intellectual and skill-based toolkits, they have a lot to offer in a professional setting.

The trouble is, historically, most organizations have mostly ignored them, or pressured them to pretend to be specialists, to fit in with the dominant ideology. Imagine if instead of sidelining polymaths, we acknowledged, appreciated, and empowered them to make the maximum contributions possible. What if we elicited their full talents instead of tamping them down? I believe that organizations that figure out how to do this will reap rich rewards for those efforts.

Self-Curation

At the end of the day, being a polymath is about self-curation; it is about granting oneself the freedom to live authentically—from a place of curiosity and self-expression, rather than conformity. Society more largely may pressure individuals to follow a certain kind of path or live according to a certain kind of narrative—but polymaths instead choose to break the mold and forge their own, singular identities through finding unique combinations, rooted in curiosity and self-expansion.

Of course, who we are as people impacts how we show up as professionals at work. What if instead of becoming who we are professionally, based on pressures and expectations, we each allowed ourselves to flourish through an exploration of the multiple parts of ourselves? In this way, our professional identities could be something we purposefully design, or at least intentionally allow to emerge—on purpose—rather than preplanning the single professional identity we will fit into for our whole careers. One's professional identity may be fluid in this context. May we all become the masters of our own lives; let us free ourselves from the expectations of society and opt instead to cocreate a better world, where we all get to pursue the full depth and breadth of our potential, and our identities can shift as they naturally will, over time. Even if you are not polymathic yourself, what a wonderful thing to be able to support others being authentically who they are, with all the rich striations and variations that exist within their personhood—and for them to be able to bring their full selves to work, to help benefit your organization.

Polymathy as Personal Empowerment

When you think of your life, what question or pursuit is more important than figuring out how to live well—living fully and authentically? Polymathy is a way of being "all in" at life itself. Rather than restriction, polymaths opt for expansion, rooted in curiosity and a desire for self-actualization. We are each born into this world from our parents; we did not get to pick our race, sex, citizenship, time of our birth, where we grew up, or level of physical and mental health. There are many aspects of our reality, individually, that we had no say over. But perhaps life should really be about giving birth to *ourselves*, in a way—about choosing who we become, or at least allowing who we really are to shine through.

That is what polymathy allows for: freedom and self-curation. Rather than ignoring our capacities so that we can fit into society's expectations, polymathy reminds us that we can allow all the parts of our multifaceted, ever-evolving selves to emerge, on purpose. Instead of letting society's expectations master us, we should all strive to become the *masters of ourselves*. And we all should look beyond the shells of the people we know and work with to see deeper into who they really are, too—in their minds. Let's stop squishing people into boxes and seeing them unidimensionally; recognize that humans are complex, multifaceted beings, who want to be authentic. And organizations who can see and appreciate this truth will fare better than those who don't or won't recognize this reality. Plus, once we all bring our full capacities to the fore, I believe that beautiful things will happen in organic, unpredictable ways.

Organizations Must Adapt to Modern Times

There was a time when specialization, and a sort of intellectual assembly line, or division of labor approach, for human progress, made a lot of sense; but we have outgrown that stage at this point. At the individual level, knowing more and more about less and less worked for us, for a time. But a shift is occurring, and we need now more than ever a mix of people who think and see the world differently to collaborate in new ways, like never before, if we are to maximize our human potential, and meet the complexity of modern times. Specialists must work in collaboration with polymaths to holistically solve the problems of our time, while also inventing new and wonderful ways of enhancing our human experiences. We should both combat the problems we face, and invent ways of adding value and joy to enrich our lives, both; focus on the challenges, and also on the good. Polymaths are well suited to contribute in both ways, alongside specialist experts. To do this, organizational leadership needs to facilitate a cultural shift, whereby this sort of strategic collaboration takes place.

The old models for how we should hire, develop, and retain employees have remained stuck in the past, even though our world has changed drastically over the past couple of decades—especially with the advent of modern technologies and the rise of digital culture in our world. We need to think about how we can leverage the power of a diverse collective in tactical, holistic ways to help us advance what we know and what we can do. We live in an age of great complexity—we should not apply the same business tactics from the last century in the face of the challenges we face in the modern world; in the future, this is even more the case. We must adapt with the times.

This may mean going against the traditional rules we have set in place for our organizations. It may feel uncomfortable to do so. It may feel risky. I encourage you to do it anyway, for all the reasons explained in this book. I hope that you have come to appreciate the capabilities and value in polymathic thinking and approaches, and have some ideas in mind for how you can be strategic about attracting, placing, developing, and retaining polymathic talent more in the future.

Polymathic Entrepreneurship

Polymaths often gravitate toward entrepreneurship. Many who try to work within traditional organizations eventually grow frustrated—especially in businesses that attempt to "squish" them into narrow specialist roles. These environments typically fail to harness the polymath's full range of capabilities. As a result, many highly talented polymaths end up walking away from the safety and security of employment, joining the growing ranks of self-employed entrepreneurs.

Entrepreneurship, of course, comes with its own challenges and risks. But for polymaths—especially those who are highly intelligent and capable—few things are more demoralizing than feeling that their talents are being wasted. The decision to leave is often not just about freedom; it's about using one's mind to its fullest.

And now, with the rise of AI, this trend may accelerate. As AI takes over more specialized tasks, traditional jobs will become fewer and more fragmented. Employment by others may no longer be the default. People who want to continue working meaningfully may need to become self-employed, whether by choice or necessity. In this new world, polymaths—those who are curious, adaptable, and capable across domains—may be uniquely positioned to thrive.

Workload Unhappiness

On the other hand—though not as common as polymaths feeling underutilized—some polymaths are so capable that their employers overtask them relentlessly. This can also be difficult, especially since many polymaths love the freedom and flexibility to identify their own "special projects" that harness their capabilities and add value to their environment, colleagues, or customers.

What is clear in either case, whether a polymath is being underutilized or overtaxed, is that most organizations do not leverage polymathic talent very well—either they do not utilize a talented employee's full capabilities very well, or they overdo it. And in either case, the polymathic employee is left with a negative experience. Like Goldilocks and her porridge—too hot, too cold, or just right—it is important for managers to figure out the right balance between giving polymaths a challenge at work—with breadth and variety—while also not overburdening the polymath so much that they have no freedom to enjoy their job because they are stretched so thin that they have no bandwidth for passion projects they self-identify and launch.

The Need for Knowledge Creation Outside of Academia

Part of what helps humanity, at a high level, advance, is the fact that we can find, create, and harness *new* information to help us reach certain goals; this could be summarized with the phrase, "knowledge creation." Knowledge creation is critical for us so that we may advance and evolve—and make better lives for ourselves over time, as a result. Put simply, new knowledge is helpful and valuable. For the most part, one of the main producers of new knowledge—of research, study, examination, and validation—has been in academia.

However, academia is *highly* siloed and departmentalized. University departments are typically very poorly integrated. Obviously, based on the way most universities are set up, the vast majority of college students themselves are expected to pick a major (usually just one) to study, and focus narrowly on that topic area alone—literally to put blinders on so that they may direct their attention on their chosen subject. In fact, in academia, professors and researchers are rewarded for becoming hyper-specialized; the tenure and promotion process shows that this is the case. For this reason, we—as a species—cannot depend on academia entirely for knowledge creation. If we do, it is likely to be fragmented. Sadly, there are many questions that are not asked and research topics that are not looked into, precisely because of the way that universities are structured. Information at the intersection of disciplines is easy to go unnoticed. Innovative research topics combining fields is understudied. The scholarly literature is overwhelmingly dominated by single-disciplinary expert scholars. This has negative implications for the types of research being conducted (or not), unfortunately.

Founder of the Khan Academy, Salman Khan, has criticized the "ghettoizing" of learning in academia, in his book, *The One World Schoolhouse*:

> Genetics is taught in biology while probability is taught in math, even though one is really an application of the other. Physics is a separate class from algebra and calculus despite its being a direct application of them. Chemistry is partitioned off from physics even though they study many of the same phenomena at different levels. All of these divisions limit understanding and suggest a false picture of how the universe actually works.

Furthermore, in academia in particular, there is often a bifurcation of arts versus sciences, and even that is somewhat arbitrary. To the polymath, everything can connect to everything else—as it should. The quintessential

Renaissance man, Leonardo Da Vinci, said it well: "Study the science of art. Study the art of science. Develop your senses—especially learn how to see. Realize that everything connects to everything else."

Therefore, it is ever more important for private businesses and institutions to lean into, more and more, creating new knowledge in more integrated, holistic ways than our academic counterparts would—because we cannot depend on academia to help in this regard. They are likely to continue to add new and valuable information in very specialized ways, for the most part. This means that if we want to have more holistic information being added to the archive of what we humans know, in integrative ways, using systems thinking approaches, then private businesses may have to take the lead on that front.

Anybody Can Be More Polymathic

Not everyone will be "a polymath," that is—someone of eminence, sophisticated erudition, and creative genius; however, everybody can be more polymathic. Everyone can choose to continue to learn, experience, and expand what they know and what they have been exposed to in work and in life more generally. Polymathy is not only for the elite. Polymathy is for anybody who chooses to have both breadth and depth in their professional capabilities and avocational pursuits. It is for people who strive to be multiexperts rather than singular experts. This is a choice we all must make—and perhaps remake—for ourselves throughout the course of our lives: will we choose breadth, depth, or both?

The Workplace of the Future

People are not just their jobs; workplaces must recognize that human beings are complex, multifaceted creatures. Even if it is more efficient, most people do not want to put themselves into professional boxes—even if just eight hours a day; this is unnatural for many people, and simply uncomfortable. People want to be able to be themselves, authentically—their whole selves. They want to be able to use their talent for good—and fully. They want to be able to continue to learn. They want to be able to change over time. We should cocreate a society where this is not only possible but encouraged—a world where people can express their inner polymathy and thrive individually while also helping their employers reach their organizational goals.

In this context, degrees, while still perhaps helpful, mean less and less—and the ability to learn, adjust, and adapt means more and more. Polymaths *are* learners—they learn many things. And so, in a world where the ability to learn becomes ever more critical, polymathic people are especially well suited to that world. Candidates for jobs in the future may have to prove that they are learners to get hired, and then they will also continue to have to learn to perform well in those positions. The ability to learn, unlearn, and relearn is the most critical skill employees need in the future of work.

If the COVID-19 global pandemic showed us anything, more than ever, it is that people's mental wellness affects their performance at work; people are not machines who blindly produce widgets no matter what is happening around them. Subjective well-being matters for performance. And so, if we know that polymathic exploration and expression is very important—even healthy—for many people, then why not accept and support that, knowing that happy employees will contribute better on the job? An employee's happiness is not something that management should simply ignore as not their business; leaders should figure out how to keep employees happy, knowing that a support system—a scaffolding for happiness—will help produce better results at work. Keep your employees happy and it will reap rewards for the organization through better performance. After all, negative, disgruntled, unhappy employees are likely to be difficult to manage and hard to keep engaged in their work. The workplace of the future should encourage individuals to be mentally well—and one way of doing that is through allowing them to truly be who they are, fully.

The workplace of the future will demand employees who express their unique human capacities, alongside technology, more and more. That workplace will demand that polymathic generalists coordinate in strategic ways with narrow, specialist experts. Employers will seek out candidates who are skilled in systems thinking, who show initiative, demonstrate mental dexterity, and emotional intelligence. Employers will seek out candidates who can communicate well, and who are creative and innovative—that is, through engaging in analogical thinking, to find new solutions or approaches from one domain and apply them in a new way or context. Employers will seek out adaptive, "multitool" type employees more and more, to solve problems through pivoting in new directions as needed.

Polymathy as a Route to Self-Care

For many people, who have demanding and sometimes stressful jobs, polymathy can also be a route to self-care. Polymathic pursuits, especially through hobbies, can be a means of balancing the stressors at work with more pleasurable, avocational experiences. This is yet another reason why polymathy should become part of our discourse in modern society—not only because it is strategic for businesses to be aware of and to leverage smartly but also because at the individual level, it can be an effective coping mechanism for dealing with stress. Polymathic exploration and expression can be healing for people; the alternative is to have, for example, a stressful job, with no outlets to relieve the stress. Plus, for many people, the variety and freedom that comes with polymathic exploration—especially outside of work—is simply fun. And having fun is a great way to relieve stress and do self-care.

The Age of the Poly Sapien

"*Homo sapiens*" literally means "*wise man*" in Latin. The term was introduced in 1758 by Carl Linnaeus to distinguish modern humans from *Homo erectus*—"*upright man*"—a prior species within the same genus. In essence, we evolved from being "upright" to being "wise." [1]

Interestingly, *homo* in Greek means "*same*," so *homo sapiens* could also be interpreted, through a Greek lens, as "*same wisdoms*" or "*identical minds.*" Of course, in Latin, *homo* is simply a root meaning "*man*" or "*human.*" In this way, the phrase carries double meanings, depending on linguistic origin.

---

[1] Retrieved from https:// www.britannica.com/topic/Homo-sapiens.

But perhaps it's time to evolve the name again. Wouldn't it be more accurate—or even visionary—to describe ourselves as *poly sapiens*? In this new era, we are beings with many forms of intelligence, many ways of knowing, and access to tools that amplify our cognitive reach far beyond anything our ancestors could have imagined. *Poly*—meaning *many*—could better reflect the multiplicity of wisdoms we now possess.

So, in the grand story of our evolution, do we still fit within the *Homo* genus and *sapiens* species? Or has a new kind of being emerged on Earth—something post-*Homo*, something fundamentally new? *Poly sapiens* might be a more fitting name for this next stage of our development: a species defined not by singular wisdom, but by a convergence of many.

Poly-Professionals

The definition of the word "professional" is "relating to or connected with a profession." The implication here is that if you are professional, it is in "a" single area. We need to expand our thinking beyond this limited understanding of what a professional is and should be. I propose that we begin using the term "poly-professional" to indicate that someone can be professional in multiple fields or functions. In fact, being this way is a great strength and advantage—and that we need a mix of regular professionals and poly-professionals if our organizations are to thrive in the most strategic ways. Although the word "polymath" indicates "many learnings," the term "poly-professional" shows that this person has experience in multiple domains, in a professional setting specifically. Having this sort of verbiage in our lexicon can be helpful, especially as this way of being becomes increasingly more prominent in our ever-demanding, evermore complex world where multiexpertise is often needed.

The Pipeline Problem

We need polymathic, multiexperts, but the school system does not (yet) create them. Is there discourse around polymathy—a general ethos in our society supporting this? Not really. Said differently, we have a pipeline problem. We don't talk about it, and we don't develop it in our youth. There is reason to believe that the workplace of the future will demand more polymathic knowledge and skills from us—but we do not yet have an infrastructure in place to foster this. There is no societal scaffolding ready to go, at scale, to begin developing polymathic talent in large measure. We may run into a problem where the talent and skills we need lag behind the actual development of workplace talent that is available. This is a problem.

Humanizing Our Work

For some time, we have existed in a society that has prioritized productivity and efficiency over individual actualization or happiness. We have become little cogs in big wheels, to some extent, in our attempt to make the larger societal machinery work. In a way, this has dehumanized us. Now it is time to bestow a new kind of freedom upon ourselves and others—and we can do this, in part, by adjusting our expectations at work. Given what we do for our jobs is so much of our experience of being alive, work is a good place to start to make this change.

Let us see the humanity in each of us, and unleash our capacities in freer ways, rather than in restricted ways—for the benefit of organizations and our collective, unfolding advancement. Let's try something new and see how it goes; let's try humanizing our work so that people can bring their talent to their jobs. With this approach, organizations figure out how to benefit from those individual talents, rather than dictating what the person must do and making the person limit their contributions in such narrow, constricted ways. Let's put people first and let them express their capacities while connected to their jobs, rather than putting jobs first, and forcing people to limit their contributions based on a fixed and finite job description. It is up to business leaders and HR professionals to help make this shift happen; if they do not humanize our work in this way, it may never get done. They are the gatekeepers to help make this shift.

Diversity, Equity, and Inclusion

We frequently hear about the importance of DEI—and rightly so. It matters deeply. But we also need to expand our understanding of what diversity means. Neurodiversity and experiential diversity should become a part of this discourse. This isn't to minimize traditional forms of diversity such as race, sex, gender, or sexual orientation. Rather, if we believe that everyone deserves fair representation and that our diversity makes us stronger, we must begin thinking about diversity itself more diversely—including polymathic and neurodiverse (particularly intellectually gifted) individuals in that conversation.

In traditional workplace environments, polymathic professionals have often been discriminated against. They struggle to land interviews because their multifaceted experiences can appear "unfocused" or "uncommitted." Their résumés don't tell a neat story of singular specialization, and for many employers, that's a deal breaker. But hopefully, by now, this book has helped show how polymathic people add immense value to teams. They deserve more recognition, support, and opportunities to thrive in organizational settings.

One of the reasons polymathic individuals are so valuable is their capacity to connect across difference. Because they belong to many different "in-groups" across domains, they can find common ground with more people—and more kinds of people. This isn't just an intellectual skill—it reflects a kind of adaptive empathy. Many polymaths develop strong emotional intelligence precisely because they've had to adapt themselves to different environments, cultures, and groups. They've learned how to read the room, understand diverse perspectives, and navigate complex social dynamics with nuance.

In this way, polymathy supports DEI efforts not only through broader representation but by actively facilitating connection. It builds bridges. It shifts the focus from mere difference to deeper commonality. And because people tend to bond through shared experiences or understandings, polymathic individuals—who have experienced more and explored widely—are often able to be those connectors and healers across lines of identity.

Polymathy could even serve as a route to healing historical wounds—through curiosity, empathy, and exposure to many ways of being. If more of us become polymathic in what we know, what we experience, and who we interact with, we may naturally foster better relations across race, gender, sexuality, class, and beyond.

As mentioned earlier, polymathy is a type of diversity—an individual-level diversity. Instead of limiting diversity to what exists between groups, let's recognize intrapersonal diversity too: diversity of thought, experience, exposure, and emotional insight. These are crucial in business and in life—and they deserve our attention.

The Importance of Questions: Introducing the Polymaths Laboratory

One of the core hallmarks of polymathy is a deep curiosity—a relentless drive to learn, explore, and connect ideas across disciplines. At the heart of this curiosity lies a deceptively simple tool: the question. Questions are powerful. They open doors in the mind. They challenge assumptions, unlock insight, and allow us to see familiar problems in radically new ways. Whether asked inwardly or in conversation, questions are often the key to clarity, direction, and innovation.

To harness this power, I created *The Polymaths Laboratory*—a dynamic, multidisciplinary problem-solving method designed to help individuals and teams navigate complexity with greater creativity and clarity.[2] The Polymaths Laboratory is not a traditional workshop. It's an innovation lab. A strategic, collaborative space where small groups come together to rethink problems from multidisciplinary perspectives using a blend of powerful questioning, problem identification, systems thinking, and polymathic insight through the power of co-learning.

Participants are guided through carefully designed exercises that challenge them to:

- Ask better, deeper, more strategic questions.
- Frame problems more precisely—often discovering that what seemed like "the problem" wasn't the real problem at all.
- Tap into knowledge from multiple disciplines to generate unconventional solutions.
- Develop actionable strategies they can take forward into their lives and work.

---

[2] The Polymaths Laboratory is part of the Polymathic Method created by Dr. Angela C. Meyers. See https://www.drangelameyers.com/polymathic-method for details.

These sessions are energizing, collaborative, and often transformative. They help break people out of their habitual thinking and equip them with tools to navigate uncertainty and complexity with greater ease. For polymathic thinkers—people who thrive at the intersection of ideas—the Polymaths Laboratory offers a space to fully engage their gifts. But it's not only for polymaths. Anyone willing to approach a challenge with curiosity and openness can benefit from this process.

In a world that's changing fast, we need new approaches to problem-solving—ones that are human-centered, multidimensional, and imagination-rich. The Polymaths Laboratory is one such approach. It honors the power of the question, the value of many ways of knowing, and the deep intelligence that emerges when we think together. It is a practical approach designed to elicit polymathic solutions to complex challenges faced by individuals or organizations.

Investing in Existing Talent

Unfortunately, most businesses "don't yet perceive mid-skilled workers as strategic assets," according to Harvard Business School professor, Joseph Fuller and colleagues.[3] In fact, 44 percent, almost half, of employers provide no upskilling or reskilling opportunities to their employees. In other words, businesses consistently undervalue developing the talent they already have onboard, especially in terms of growing that talent. Instead of looking to "buy" talent from outside the organization, consider ways that you can develop the talent you already have on hand into the talent you need for the future. By investing in your people and (hopefully) creating long-term partnerships with them, you communicate that you value your employees; this is a way to create loyalty from them. In the talent wars of the future, where organizations will have to compete for the top talent, investing into the talent you already have is one strategy

[3] Fuller, J., J. Wallenstein, M. Raman, and A. de Chalendar. 2019. Future Positive: How Companies Can Tap into Employee Optimism to Navigate Tomorrow's Workplace, BCG Henderson Institute and the Harvard Business School. https://www.hbs.edu/managing-the-future-of-work/Documents/Future%20Positive%20Report%205.20.pdf.

to position your business well to remain competitive. Both attract and develop top talent and keep them loyal by treating them well so you do not lose them.

Talent Development as a Business Imperative

The fact is that any business is only as good as the talent that makes up the organization. You may have the best product or service on the market, but if your internal staff cannot effectively run the business, it may fail altogether. As such, it is critical that your staff do not become stagnant; everyone on your team should be committed to continual self-improvement through learning. This is critical.

Of course, traditional classroom training is helpful, but learning must go beyond that. Training, even if it is in bite-sized bits, should be relevant and integrated into people's day-to-day work lives. Any development plan should include experiential learning. It might even look like project-based learning, stretch assignments, or include incentives that encourage employees to learn on their personal time. Get creative in designing what "learning" looks like in your organization. Embed learning wherever possible. Use the tools, technology, and other resources available to ensure that learning takes place, intentionally, across your organization.

It is in any business's self-interest to create ecosystems that promote lifelong learning of its employees. Consider creating employer–employee learning contracts that reflect a shared agreement to continuous learning and upskilling or reskilling. These sorts of arrangements exemplify a partnership between the business and the employee—a real commitment on both sides to continual learning and improvement, which helps ensure that employees' skills do not grow stagnant and irrelevant over time. Such a reciprocal arrangement encourages employers to make investments into their employees' development, while also inspiring and incentivizing employees to put purposeful effort into their own learning, knowing this is something that is important to their employer.

Generating Strategic Foresight

In a world with exponential changes, we need strategies to help us constantly adapt; however, if those adaptations are simply reactions, it puts us at a disadvantage. It is better to be prepared, to generate foresight and to do so rigorously and strategically. Much of this book argued for why having polymathic talent on your teams is exactly that—a way of preparing for the future, rather than being in a position to have to react to it later. Polymathic people are good at learning; they enjoy change, variety, newness, and challenges. They could even be considered rapid learners. Because they can learn, they can also unlearn. They tend to be good at problem-solving, pulling from myriad experiences and learnings from the past to help them face challenges. They are typically committed to continual learning and improvement. In a world where we may all have to reimagine how we work, as our environment shifts, polymathic employees are particularly adept at retooling themselves to become what your organization needs, rather than simply continually working like they did in the past years.

We are well prepared for the past but are ill prepared for a future of work that is yet to be known, exactly, yet. That is why polymathic talent is so critical—because it gives individuals more options, more paths to readiness, and opens them up to continual learning to be ready on an ongoing basis. Given the likely cross-functional nature of work in the future and with the complexity of it all, generating foresight—being prepared wherever possible, helps position people to be successful by putting them in a position of readiness. What's more, polymathic employees can be particularly useful to help develop that strategic foresight and can help position your business to be ready, rather than reactive, to the challenges ahead.

Unlearning, Adaptation, and Changing Identities

This book has emphasized the importance of continual learning in a business context, and rightly so—polymathic people are, by definition, lifelong learners. But alongside the ability to learn, there is another essential capability we must cultivate: the ability to unlearn.

As information evolves and the world changes, we are sometimes called to release ideas or ways of working that once served us but no longer do. Growth doesn't just mean adding new skills; it also means letting go of outdated assumptions, practices, and even aspects of our identity.

To truly adapt, we must be willing to periodically let go of who we think we are—and instead, reinvent ourselves. Our professional identities shouldn't be rigid. Unless we're identifying broadly as polymathic professionals—a flexible identity in itself—our more specific roles and skill sets must remain fluid. We are living in an age of acceleration, and in this environment, clinging to fixed identities may offer temporary comfort but ultimately hinders our growth. Paradoxically, the very moments when we crave stability are often the times we must lean into vulnerability and openness instead.

"Adapt or die," as the saying goes. Polymathic individuals are often well prepared for this. They are accustomed to shifting roles, wearing multiple hats, and holding various identities under one cohesive sense of self. This makes them especially equipped to thrive in a world where unlearning and reinvention are vital forms of resilience.

In times of uncertainty, many people default to what they know. They seek solid ground, often clinging to it for a sense of control. But in doing so, they may miss the opportunity to evolve. It's often through challenge—not comfort—that true growth occurs. Let's not fear challenge. Let's embrace it. These moments are not interruptions to our path—they are the path. Each challenge offers an opportunity to adapt, to expand, and to become better versions of ourselves—at work and beyond.

Where we once focused on IQ as the primary predictor of success—and later came to value EQ (emotional intelligence)—the future may well belong to those with high AQ: adaptability quotient. In a fast-paced, ever-changing world, rigidity is a liability. Adaptability is a superpower.[4]

A Note for Polymathic Employees

Although the primary audience for this book is for people in formal positions of leadership and HR professionals within organizations, if there is someone reading this who is in neither of those roles, they may be wondering what to do with the information presented in this book. If you feel like you are a polymathic person and are wondering what to do, here is some brief advice: if you are an employee in an organization, and you

[4] McGowan, H. and C. Shipley. 2020. *The Adaptation Advantage*. Wiley.

believe you have polymathic talent, it is your responsibility to use it; do not let your talent go to waste. Make your polymathy part of your brand; make sure people understand you are a continual learner with multiexpertise across functions—that you're a go-getter, whipper-snapper, self-starter. Let that be your selling point, and your greatest strength at work. Figure out how to convey this messaging in a way that you are comfortable with. If you are naturally polymathic, do not change yourself just to fit in a mold. And realize that it is not always easy being a polymath in the age of in the age of specialization, though it seems to be winding down. We still need polymathic talent in organizations, very much—and so there is an important and valuable place for you. Businesses need your contributions, and it is up to you to help them tap into your full talent.

And if you are an HR professional or business leader—the same guidance applies to you, except with an added level of responsibility: do not let your talent go to waste, nor the talent of your employees. It is twofold. Make sure to figure out who among your staff is polymathic; figure out ways to leverage their skill sets. Find out what skills are underutilized and adjust accordingly.

Polymathy: Life as Artistic Expression

Living life as a polymath is an opportunity to become a true original—to express your onlyness. For polymaths, life itself becomes artistic expression, an opportunity for creativity. Life becomes an adventure. You can achieve originality through the unique combination of experiences, knowledge, and skills that you foster in yourself. Don't be a duplicate or a copy of someone else's design; be you. This can be done through a mix of either purposeful design or happenstance—going with the flow of life and seeing what comes along.

If you were asked to paint a picture, would you rather have varying shades of one color, or would you rather paint with the full rainbow? Narrow specialists paint with one color—their favorite, whereas polymaths paint in full color—in fact, they live in full color. And just as I am sure you would like your life to be the most beautiful expression of your inner self, as an HR professional or business leader, you can make a positive impact by encouraging others to do the same—by creating conditions where their flourishing can come to fruition, in living color.

Awareness, Discourse, and Appreciation for Polymathy

One of the big challenges with polymathy getting the credit it deserves is the fact that it is rarely discussed; in fact, most people do not know the word "polymath." Even for people who do not have that word in their lexicon, often this concept goes undiscussed—even using other neighboring words. Without conscious awareness of this important way of living, being, and working, we run the risk of not really leveraging something that could be very powerful to help propel humanity forward. Plus, I believe that exploring life in a polymathic sort of way is just the natural way humans are meant to be—that it is actually unnatural that we have been made to be otherwise. For the sake of efficiency, we have organized ourselves into specialists with narrow expertise—but I posit that we need to shift away from an efficiency model now and move to a more strategic one—leveraging the strengths of specialists and polymaths, combined, is a much better path forward.

I hope that this book helped you gain a deeper appreciation for the importance and power that polymathy can have at the individual, organizational, and even societal levels. I also hope that it has inspired you to talk about polymathy more explicitly—to make plans for how you can leverage it in your business, and perhaps even your personal life more, moving forward.

The Bottom Line of This Chapter

Chapter 9 synthesized the key themes and insights of this book, calling HR professionals and business leaders to action. It emphasized the transformative potential of polymathy at both the individual and organizational levels, especially in today's complex, technology-driven world.

- **Challenging the Myth of Specialization**: This chapter dismantled the prevailing notion that specialization is the only path to success. It highlighted the limitations of a narrowly focused approach and advocates for the broader, multifaceted exploration that polymathy offers. Encouraging polymathic expression allows individuals to bring their full, authentic selves to their work, fostering creativity, innovation, and fulfillment.

- **Polymathy as a Strategic Resource**: Polymaths are invaluable assets in the workplace due to their diverse skill sets and continuous learning mindset. Organizations that recognize and harness the potential of polymaths will benefit from their ability to adapt, innovate, and contribute in multifaceted ways. Instead of sidelining polymaths, businesses should empower them to maximize their contributions.
- **Self-Curation and Personal Empowerment**: Polymathy is about self-curation, granting individuals the freedom to live authentically and pursue diverse interests. This chapter emphasized the importance of allowing professional identities to be fluid and self-designed, rather than rigidly defined by societal expectations. Polymathy enables individuals to explore their full potential and contribute uniquely to their organizations.
- **Adapting to Modern Times**: The old models of specialization and division of labor are no longer sufficient in the face of modern challenges. Organizations must facilitate strategic collaboration between specialists and polymaths to solve complex problems and create new value. Business leaders need to embrace new approaches to hiring, developing, and retaining polymathic talent.
- **Polymathic Entrepreneurship and Workload Balance**: Polymaths often become entrepreneurs due to frustration with organizations that fail to leverage their full capabilities. This chapter discussed the need for a balanced approach, ensuring that polymaths are neither underutilized nor overburdened. Managers must find the right balance to keep polymaths engaged and productive.
- **Expanding Knowledge Creation Beyond Academia**: The chapter critiqued the siloed nature of academia and emphasized the need for businesses to lead in creating integrated, holistic knowledge. Polymaths, with their

cross-disciplinary expertise, are well suited to drive innovative research and knowledge creation in ways that academia may not.

- **Polymathy for Everyone**: While not everyone will achieve the level of a renowned polymath, everyone can adopt a more polymathic approach to learning and professional development. This chapter encouraged individuals to seek both breadth and depth in their pursuits, enhancing their adaptability and value in the workplace.
- **The Workplace of the Future**: The future workplace demands employees who can adapt, learn continuously, and leverage their unique human capacities alongside technology. Polymaths are particularly well suited to thrive in this environment, where the ability to learn and adapt is paramount.
- **Polymathy as Self-Care**: Polymathy can also serve as a form of self-care, providing individuals with diverse, enjoyable activities that balance work-related stress. Engaging in polymathic pursuits can enhance overall well-being and job satisfaction.
- **Evolving Human Identity and Work**: The chapter explored the concept of humans as "poly sapiens," with many wisdoms and capacities. Advocating for redefining professionalism to include polyprofessionals, who bring multiple areas of expertise to their work. This approach aligns with the need for adaptability in a rapidly changing world.
- **Humanizing Work and Embracing Diversity**: The chapter called for a shift in how we view and support employees, recognizing their multifaceted identities and promoting a more human-centered approach to work. It also highlighted the importance of expanding the discourse around diversity to include neurodiversity and experiential diversity.
- **The Power of Questions and the Polymaths Laboratory:** Emphasizing the importance of curiosity and continuous learning, the chapter introduced The Polymaths Laboratory as a powerful approach to problem-solving and professional

development. It encouraged the use of multidisciplinary questions to unlock new insights and foster growth.

- **Investing in Existing Talent**: Businesses must prioritize developing their current employees, creating opportunities for upskilling and reskilling. This chapter underscored the importance of viewing employees as strategic assets and fostering a culture of continuous improvement.
- **Generating Strategic Foresight**: Polymaths are well-equipped to help organizations anticipate and prepare for future challenges. Their ability to learn, unlearn, and adapt positions them as valuable contributors to strategic foresight and organizational readiness.
- **Unlearning and Adaptation**: The chapter discussed the importance of unlearning outdated knowledge and embracing new identities in response to changing environments. Polymaths, with their adaptability and willingness to evolve, are well suited to navigate this dynamic landscape.
- **Polymathy as Artistic Expression**: Living as a polymath allows individuals to express their unique combination of experiences, knowledge, and skills. This chapter encouraged embracing life's full spectrum of possibilities, fostering creativity and originality.
- **Awareness and Appreciation of Polymathy**: The chapter called for increased discourse and appreciation of polymathy, urging business leaders to recognize and leverage the power of polymathic thinking. It advocated for a strategic shift toward integrating polymathic talent into organizational frameworks.

In conclusion, this final chapter is a call to action, urging business leaders and HR professionals to embrace and support individuals to express their polymathic intelligence and capacities. By doing so, organizations can harness the diverse talents and innovative potential of polymathic employees, positioning themselves for success in an increasingly complex and uncertain world.

Understanding Polymathic Talent

1. How would you define "intrapersonal diversity" in your own words, and how does it show up in your life or team?
2. What assumptions do most organizations make about what a valuable employee looks like—and how might polymaths challenge that?
3. Have you ever dismissed a candidate or colleague for appearing "unfocused?" Could that have been unrecognized polymathy?
4. In what ways could someone's multiple career shifts be reframed as strengths rather than liabilities?
5. What talents or interests have you hidden or downplayed in past work environments, and why?

Polymaths in the Age of AI

1. Why is human versatility especially valuable in a world increasingly shaped by AI?
2. What tasks or roles in your organization are already being impacted by AI, and how might polymaths be uniquely positioned to adapt?
3. Do you feel that your current role is safe from automation? Why or why not?
4. How can generalists and polymaths become "superusers" of AI tools?
5. What mindsets are essential to thrive alongside AI?

Organizational Gaps and Opportunities

1. Have you witnessed a talented generalist being underutilized or misunderstood in your workplace?
2. What policies or cultural norms might unintentionally disadvantage polymathic thinkers in hiring or promotion?
3. How might your organization shift its evaluation criteria to better recognize polymathic talent?
4. What are the risks of overlooking polymathic employees in a rapidly changing business landscape?
5. Where do you see the greatest opportunity to harness polymathic potential in your organization?

HR and Leadership Applications

1. As an HR professional or leader, how do you currently identify high-potential employees? What might you be missing?
2. What kind of roles or project environments might be ideal for a polymath?
3. Have you created space for employee-led innovation or intrapreneurship? How might polymaths contribute?
4. How does your team handle ambiguity, novelty, or disruption—and what role could a polymath play in navigating those?
5. What would change if you started treating intellectual range as an organizational asset?

Polymaths Themselves

1. If you identify as polymathic, how has your experience in the workplace reflected or contradicted what's discussed in this chapter?
2. Do you feel that your multidimensionality is embraced or misunderstood in your professional life?
3. Have you ever been told to "focus" or "pick a lane?" How did you feel or respond?
4. What environments have allowed you to be the fullest version of yourself?
5. What professional goals do you have that draw on multiple skill sets?

Future-Focused Thinking

1. How might future leaders differ from past ones in terms of cognitive flexibility and range?
2. What would it look like to build a team where diversity of thought and capability is intentionally nurtured?
3. How might we measure success differently in polymath-friendly workplaces?
4. What does "career progression" look like for someone with a polymathic trajectory?
5. What could your organization do today to better prepare for the future of talent?

About the Author

Dr. Angela C. Meyers is a pioneering voice in the study of modern polymathy—part scholar, part storyteller, part systems reformer. With a career that has spanned the White House, academia, nonprofit leadership, and community activism, she brings a rare breadth of experience to her work, and a lifelong devotion to human potential.

Angela authored the first doctoral dissertation focused on polymathy, and has since been recognized as one of the world's foremost experts on the subject. Through her writing, teaching, and public speaking, she has helped legitimize polymathy as a vital framework for understanding talent, leadership, and learning in a time of accelerating change.

She is the founder of Polymaths Place, a global community of curious, multifaceted thinkers, and the creator of The Polymathic Method, a framework designed to help individuals and organizations harness the power of range, adaptability, and synthesis in the age of AI.

Angela spent nearly 15 years as a civil servant in the federal government of the United States, including roles at the Executive Office of the President under Presidents Bush and Obama, and later as a leadership development strategist for the U.S. government. Her earlier work in shelters for survivors of domestic violence and in higher education taught her just how essential both systems and stories are to human thriving. Since leaving government, she has become an advocate for criminal justice reform and prison transparency, often working at the intersection of policy, ethics, and human dignity.

Her academic background includes a doctorate in Human and Organizational Learning from George Washington University, a master's in Communication Management from the University of Southern California (USC), and dual undergraduate degrees in Psychology and Communication, earned as a Presidential Scholar, also from USC.

A polymath herself, Angela moves between roles with both fluidity and depth—researcher and activist, coach and consultant, mother and futurist. She lives near Washington, D.C. with her daughter, Lily, and is committed to using her voice and intellect in service of a more humane, intelligent, and versatile future.

For more information on Dr. Meyers' consulting work, training programs, polymath laboratory innovation sessions, coaching, and assessment offerings, visit www.drangelameyers.com.

Index

www.ingramcontent.com/pod-product-compliance
Lightning Source LLC
LaVergne TN
LVHW050613100826
845148LV00011B/1570